Capricious Borders

CAPRICIOUS BORDERS

Minority, Population, and Counter-Conduct Between Greece and Turkey

Olga Demetriou

berghahn
NEW YORK · OXFORD
www.berghahnbooks.com

Published in 2013 by
Berghahn Books
www.berghahnbooks.com

Library of Congress Cataloging-in-Publication Data
Demetriou, Olga.
    Capricious borders : minority, population, and counter-conduct between
Greece and Turkey / Olga Demetriou.
        pages cm
    ISBN 978-0-85745-898-8 (hardback : alk. paper) -- ISBN 978-0-85745-
899-5 (ebook)
    1. Minorities--Greece. 2. Minorities--Turkey. 3. Greece--Boundaries. 4.
Turkey--Boundaries. I. Title.
    DF747.T8D46 2013
    305.80094961--dc23

                                                                    2012032942

British Library Cataloguing in Publication Data
A catalogue record for this book is available from the British Library
Printed in the United States on acid-free paper

ISBN 978-0-85745-898-8 (hardback)
ISBN 978-0-85745-899-5 (ebook)

To Livia, for prompting questions on authority

CONTENTS

List of Illustrations

Tables

Figures

Maps

ACKNOWLEDGEMENTS

This book is the result of many debts accrued over many years in many places. Most of all to the people of Komotini, who took me in not only during the first year of my fieldwork, but during the many return visits that followed, opening their houses when I needed a place to stay, rescheduling their holidays when I stopped for short visits; people who had earlier opened drawers, photo albums, chests, to share their worries, laughter, hope, bitterness, or boredom; people who worked with me through the intricacies and presumptions of identity, as we tried to figure each other out. I hope they will find acceptable what I have chosen to share in this book and the things that I did not.

As an anthropological endeavour, this book owes its existence primarily to the late Peter Loizos, who has reviewed and advised on countless 'drafts' for two decades, from undergraduate essays to journal articles and policy reports – including an early version of this manuscript. All of his comments have shaped my writing and his insistence on a 'classic ethnography' largely accounts for the data that I present and scrutinize. Yael Navaro-Yashin encouraged me to continue pursuing difficult questions and her friendship has been invaluable through the years. She also provided comments on much of my work, helping it to articulate what I tended to obscure. Effie Voutira offered incisive comments on this manuscript that have helped me to hone my arguments – a separate debt to her remains for her hospitality in Thessaloniki, and for having yet to refuse a request. Hastings Donnan and Elizabeth Davis also provided thoughtful comments on the manuscript. In thinking about borders and subjectivity during the drafting of the book, I have returned time and again to discussions within the COST-funded 'Remaking Eastern Borders in Europe' network. I am thankful to Sarah Green for being the driving force behind this, and to Rozita Dimova, Lenio Myrivili, Stef Jansen, Venetia Kantsa, Tuija Pulkkinen, Sissie Theodosiou, and Jane Cowan for many discussions. For teaching me a different perspective on human rights and the power of working within its limitations, I thank Halya Gowan, whose friendship has been invaluable.

I am grateful to numerous colleagues at the LSE, Oxford and Cyprus for helping to shape my thinking over the years: Louiza Odysseos, Marios Sarris, Umut Özkırımlı, Lucia Nixon, Renée Hirschon, Kerem Öktem, Maria Hadjipavlou, Anna Agathangelou, Myria Vassiliadou, and Gregory Ioannou. At the PRIO Cyprus Centre, where the writing up of the manuscript took place, I have learnt much from Costas Constantinou, Arne Strand, and Greg Reichberg. For invitations to present work on which the arguments here draw, I thank Charles Stewart (UCL Anthropology Seminars), Rita Astuti (LSE seminars), Yiannis Papadakis and Hülya Demirdirek (EASA conference panels), George Papanikolaou (Oxford Modern Greek Studies seminars), the late Fred Halliday (LSE Middle East Studies seminar), and Hakan Seçkinelgin (LSE European Institute seminar). Financial support during various stages of research and writing was secured from the Royal Anthropological Institute (Emslie Horniman fund), the British School at Athens (Hector and Elizabeth Catling fund) and the Wenner Gren Foundation (post-doctoral grant). As a result of these presentations, an earlier version of chapter four was published as 'Streets not Named: Discursive Dead Ends and the Politics of Orientation in Intercommunal Spatial Relations in Northern Greece', *Cultural Anthropology* 21(2): 295–321, 2006. Part of chapter five was published as 'Prioritizing Ethnicities: The Uncertainty of Pomak-ness in the Greek Rhodoppe Mountains', *Ethnic and Racial Studies* 27(1): 95–119, 2004.

I have been particularly fortunate to work with the people at Berghahn Books through the publication process. Ann Przyzycki de Vita has made our collaboration superb, as did Lauren Weiss, Charlotte Mosedale, and my editors, Julia Goddard and Nigel Smith. My thanks to all of them who ensured the book remained on track and says what I intended it to say.

None of this would of course have been possible without Vania and Themos Demetriou's support of my insistence in pursuing an obscure field of study – and their unwavering engagement with it and my writings. Much of the domestic labour of recent years has been borne by them, allowing me to prioritize writing. For questioning things that I did not think needed argumentation, I am grateful for Tania Demetriou's unforgiving eye.

Murat Erdal Ilıcan has followed me on this journey and has shared the ups and downs of fieldwork and writing. His patience, honesty and passion, especially at those moments when 'the project' seemed to be taking over our lives, have been precious. His careful scrutiny of my analyses has guided the book throughout, and his insights on property rights have been especially helpful in shaping chapter six. Livia, who was born into this project and has been refusing to succumb to its timing dictates, has probably taught me the most. Her evaluation will be the harshest.

NOTE ON TRANSLITERATION

The spelling of Turkish words in the Latinized alphabet has been maintained, along with the diacritics used in the following letters: 'ç' pronounced as 'ch' in 'chapter', 'ğ' unpronounced but elongating the preceding vowel, 'ı' pronounced as 'u' in 'Turkey', 'ö' pronounced as 'eur' in entrepreneur, 'ü' pronounced as 'ue' in 'cue', and 'ş' pronounced as the 'ci' in 'capricious'.

In the transliteration of words from the Greek alphabet, I have taken a cue from Turkish practice – when Greek words are transliterated in the print media, for example, which I have found is particularly effective in approximating the pronunciation – and have phoneticized them as far as possible. Thus, for example, 'y' and 'g' will appear in the word 'loyigí' (pronounced as in 'year' and 'delegate' respectively), even though under more mainstream transliteration schemes the same word might have appeared as 'loghiki'. Occasionally, 'g', 'b' and 'd' will be found in transliterations of sounds that are often represented by 'k', 'p', and 't' respectively. I have always found the diphthong transliteration difficult, and in the case of the Greek letter 'γ' this is complicated by its differential pronunciation as 'y' in 'year' and 'r' in the French 'rue'. To signify the latter, I have enlisted the transliteration of the Turkish 'ğ' into Greek, which slightly erroneously, but nevertheless also effectively in terms of pronunciation, often transforms 'ğ' into the 'γ' (always of its 'rue' version): thus, for example, 'anağnórisi'. Diphthongs that remain are 'dh', pronounced as 'th' in 'then', 'th', pronounced as 'th' in 'theme', and 'ou', pronounced as 'u' in 'question'.

The distinction between Greek and Turkish words is signified by the accents ' ' that mark intonation stresses in Greek.

CHAPTER 1

COTTON, TOBACCO, SUNFLOWERS

Analogic Borders

At the point where the Evros river becomes the Meriç, halfway across a bridge that connects Greece to Turkey, a mobile phone will switch networks. In an increasingly digitalized age, where signal roaming is constant, the liminality of the river border contracts to an instant on the screen, often an instant of 'no reception'. The physical roaming of herders, migrants, fighters, and refugees that rendered the area of Thrace a border is now largely illegal, as migration is heavily controlled. In this digital border of the 0-1 binary, the either/or question is constant: a kind of aporetic roaming that destabilizes the precept of fluidity that theory assumes. The binary logic here permeates all senses of 'belonging'. Is this Greece or Turkey? Is the language Greek or Turkish? Are the people Greeks or Turks? Are the fields Greek-owned or Turkish-owned?

The analogic presence of people who straddle the border, who may be registered in both countries, speak both languages, socialize and engage in market exchanges in both locations, seems a remnant of the past, but at the same time must be constantly re-evaluated: what makes them so? What are they, really? Barthes saw in such digitalization 'a vast, "digital", not "analogical", translation of the world [from nature to society]' (Barthes 1973 [1964]: 82). The binarism represented by the digital code is for him merely 'a metalanguage, a particular taxonomy meant to be swept away by history, after having been true to it for a moment' (ibid.). In these terms, the coevalness of the globalized 'post-national era' with the 'digital age' poses an unnerving question about the duration of this 'moment', especially in the face of a nationalistic backlash post-War-on-Terror – a backlash in which the 'integrated' are as suspect as 'radicals' and targeted by similar security apparatuses. The analogic difference, vilified in the period of the nation-state, is being re-digitalized most effectively in the field of technology (when reception signals coexist and vie for their appearance on the screen, or when thermographic security cameras surveilling illegal migration reconstitute incremental differences of temperature into the gradations of red-blue coloration). On the plane of culture this re-digitalization often renders analogic difference a heritage asset in the celebration of diversity. Cultures that 'lived together' in the past are celebrated only after the 'wholeness' of each one has been ascertained and coded (as dress habits, cuisine, religious monuments, etc.) on the basis of difference from other 'wholes' read into that 'togetherness'. At the same time, living together in the present is constrained by the detention facilities that are now a staple feature of border control. Differences of the past can thus be pluralized in celebrations of past multiculturalism, while difference in the present is digitalized according to the binary legal/illegal. Such difference is what Thrace represents.

During the decade in which I have been working on this book, the progress of the global neoliberal order has seen the Thracian border develop into an entrepreneurial region in various legitimate and illegitimate ways (private business and human trafficking come to mind). When I arrived in Thrace (1998–1999), Greco-Turkish relations hit rock bottom after Greece was shown to have harboured Turkey's most wanted Kurdish separatist, Abdullah Öcalan, and then bounced back to unprecedented intimacy when the respective foreign ministers inaugurated an era of 'Greco-Turkish friendship' (*Ellino-Tourkiki filía/Türk-Yunan dostluk*). Those two places, the Thrace of fieldwork and the Thrace of writing, are 'borders' primarily because they are about difference. But they are connected by the conceptual underpinnings that determine their differences – the distinctions between 'here' and 'there' that in their very shifts maintain the operation of distinction. As Sarah Green puts it, this operation determines what counts as difference and what does not (2005). And in the Balkans, she reminds us, power cascades down such differences and their shifts:

> multiculturalism [as it] is currently used, in practice, as a means to creatively garner recognition, resources, and rights, or even to challenge current orthodoxies, is inevitably the currently hegemonic form, since the resources come only from powerful institutions with investments in the hegemonic form ... the contemporary Balkans, within this hegemonic context, are generating a particular kind of proliferation: of peoples who are unable to reconstitute themselves appropriately, being located in the midst of a scalar, hybrid (interrelational) clash between modernisms and postmodernisms, and who therefore either remain unnamed (and hence 'invisible') or have a name that cannot, on moral grounds, be given resources – unless they are reconstituted as people who are the victims of Balkan essentialisms [who] ... often also generate victims of their own at other times (2005: 157)

This book is an attempt to re-trace the production of 'facts' that produce such peoples as 'different' – in this case, as 'minority'. It examines, in other words, how such discourses of culture and difference are produced and become hegemonic, as well as the questionings that puncture them. Within the Foucauldian conception (Burchell et al. 1991; Foucault 2000; 2001; 2004; 2007), people are made to 'belong' and are excluded in ways that frame the thinking about particular populations. This may include their ordering into categories (Greek/Turk, majority/minority), their placing within the landscape ('people of the mountain'), the solidification of characteristics that 'describe' them (religiosity, linguistic competence), or the equivalence of value-laden terms with that description (backward, ignorant). Starting with demographic counting (Cohn 1984; 1996), a process of ethnicization unfolds, which decides who is in majority and who is not, without questioning what is meant by that 'who'. Mapping puts into motion a similar process of securitization through binarism and scaling (Green 2005; 2009), declaring some binary differences immaterial (e.g. regional cultures) and others crucial (inside/outside, neighbours/enemies). These processes that co-emerge with the state constitute prime examples of techniques through which places and people are invented alongside the traditions that prop up the nation-state. As Mitchell emphasizes, the multiple methods of collecting, compiling, and disseminating knowledge about specific subject groups eventually allow them to become governed into specific (colonial) subject positions (Mitchell 1991; 2002). In these conditions, subjectivity (Das and Kleinman 2000; Biehl et al. 2007) is of both normative and experiential import. It works on a grid where 'legislation and transgression are joined' (Das 2007: 78). Often, that grid is founded on the originary violence of what Das calls 'critical events' (Das, 1995); a moment that sets up the border between the law of binarism and the transgression of the analogue. The ethnography of such subjectivity then, must look to that originary violence in explaining how its repercussions are experienced and carried forth into the everyday (Das and Poole 2004).

The Minority as Population

From that originary violence stems a process of 'minoritization' whereby knowledges of what is henceforth 'minor' and what 'major' are naturalized and institutionalized, framing modes of oppression and resistance (Saldívar 2006: 153–157). Minoritization is therefore both a national and a colonial project. In the Balkan region, minoritization has legal and historical roots that stretch back to the originary violence of the Great War and the establishment of the League of Nations (Cowan 2001; 2007;

2009). And in conceptual terms, it stretches into the formation of 'the Balkans' as a problematic region (Todorova 1997) because it lacked the 'homogeneity' on the basis of which political order was established in the modern era.

In the area under study, the 'critical event' for this process occurred in 1923, when the border between Greece and Turkey was fixed half-way across the Evros–Meriç river. At this time western Thrace acquired the status of 'new land' (*néa hóra*) alongside other territories ceded to Greece at the end of the Balkan wars (1912–1913), charting the 'expansion' of the Kingdom of Greece. Thousands of refugees sought refuge in the area after the Lausanne Treaty stipulated that Orthodox Christians living in the Ottoman Empire would be forcibly moved to Greece in exchange for Muslims living in Greece moving to the newly established Turkish Republic. Nearly 120,000 Muslims (Oran 2003: 101) found themselves categorized as '*établis*', i.e. 'established in the region to the east of the frontier line *laid down in 1913 by the Treaty of Bucharest*' (Article 2, Convention concerning the Exchange of Greek and Turkish Populations, 1923 [attached to the Lausanne Peace Treaty, item VI], emphasis added; see also map 2.2).[1] Thus, 'Moslem inhabitants of Western Thrace' as this population and the region were referred to in subsequent articles (ibid.), were made an exception, and were able to remain in their homes, as Greek citizens. This exclusion from the exchange, and thus from the normalization of ethnic purity, established the *établis* and their region as 'exceptional' and thus problematic, putting into motion a number of attempts to solve this problem of 'heterogeneity'.

A first step, it could be said, was the discursive framing of this event as the 'incorporation of western Thrace into the national trunk' (*i ensomátosi tis dhitikís Thrákis ston ethnikó kormó*). This incorporation became a celebrated moment in the national history being written within the frame of a nation reaching *ethnikí ololírosi* ('ethnic completion', here understood largely in territorial terms). The geographic space that symbolized this territorial completion was then symbolically nationalized (e.g. through naming) and the local population was educated into this new history and geography, rendering the community inhabiting the 'new land' a national one. These affirmative measures were accompanied by confrontational ones which were focused on the purification of otherness, inherent in the ethnic, linguistic, and religious heterogeneity of the minority population. Such measures included the nationalization of land, both physically through expropriation and other policies, and symbolically through re-naming. Another measure, education, followed the double path of consolidating otherness as an ethnic feature (and separating out the 'Turks' in the process), and accommodating other 'others' (e.g. Pomaks) as quasi-Greeks on the basis of their non-Turkishness. In both sets of measures, these gradations of otherness remained a salient factor of inequality. The decisive questions were how to name that otherness, how far to incorporate it, and how to manage it. Naming, genealogy, and state care became the modalities in the process of minoritization.

Within this governmentality, where otherness defied incorporation and domestication, this otherness was pathologized: a prime example of this persists in the hegemonic views of a highly problematic gender order within the minority, whereby minority women are presented as psychologically diseased, and as such, bearers of the most pressing problems of 'the minority condition'. Psychological disease, it is worth recalling, not only provided Foucault with an invaluable entry point into the examination of subjectivity (Foucault 2001 [1961]) but has also been used in recent evaluations of neoliberal governmentalities (Corin 2007; Biehl 2007). Thrace, with a state-of-the-art psychiatric hospital in Alexandroupolis, has provided the location for just such an interrogation in one of the most penetrating ethnographies of Greek neoliberalism (Davis 2012). As a technology of government that categorizes particular populations on the basis of particular forms of life they are expected to lead, the condition of 'disease' problematizes those lives and specifies particular cures for them (e.g. the modernization of the minority). This medicalization of the 'minority problem' is thus exemplary of the biopolitical mode in which the governance of the minority operates.

But if the stereotypes of minority women fall squarely within the medicalized reading of biopolitics that has come to dominate recent work on subjectivity that draws on Foucault's lectures (Foucault 2003; 2006; 2007; 2008), my approach to biopolitics is slightly different. My aim in this book is to show how 'the minority condition' is produced by a biopolitical governmentality that goes beyond the strict bounds of medical and somatic discourse (of which the psychiatric is a prime example).[2] I therefore read 'biopolitics' on the basis of a specific governmentality that develops out of a notion of 'population' as 'a multiplicity of individuals who are and fundamentally and essentially only exist biologically bound to the materiality within which they live' (Foucault 2007: 21). It is this notion of 'population' that frames 'the minority condition' as a biopolitical experience. And in these terms I find it curious that Foucault chose to postpone his investigation of 'biopolitics' only after that of 'political economy' in the analysis of the government of population (a decision that I would argue also gave it less primacy). We must remember that his 'birth of biopolitics' lectures are by way of an introduction, by his own admission, to the examination of 'the attempt . . . to rationalize the problems posed to governmental practice by phenomena characteristic to a set of living beings forming a population: health, hygiene, birthrate, life expectancy, race' (Foucault 2008: 317).

What such 'political economy' introduces, in my reading, is an examination of the life of a population posed as a problem of government and indeed largely from the perspective of government, articulated by 'people who were . . . [close] to political practice', such as Machiavelli and Richelieu (Foucault 2007: 289). This perspective is precisely what makes political economy the cornerstone of political science – not anthropology. If instead political economy is posed as a problem of the anthropological everyday, or otherwise one of being governed, then the technologies of governmentality – from statistics and law to policing – become biopolitical technologies that determine one's life in its daily and ordinary aspects: spatial location, occupation, property, family relations, religious and political performance, etc. These aspects of life may perhaps precede pathologization. But they enunciate the somatization of experience of one's 'minority' position (in work, residence, leisure, and the home) as a condition of the everyday. The experience of this condition (living in specific locations, in specific kinds of homes, doing specific kinds of work, and having a specific life course charted out on the basis of one's name, ethnicity, or location) enables the political categorization of populations as 'problematic'. This categorization, however, only comes once their otherness as 'minority' has been naturalized. These are the 'politics of life' that I want to study in this book, in their emergence as symptomatic of 'the minority condition'. For 'minority' is not only the result of 'minoritization' on the institutional plane, but also a subjectivity that people inhabit in the everyday. As lived experience it becomes a 'condition' that one 'descends' into, as Das would have it (2007). Not an experience of a sublime 'everyday' that can be celebrated as the lifeworld people on the ground create (the 'stuff' of a people's 'culture') but an 'ordinary' of subjugation that one learns to cope with.

This is also why theorists have long argued that 'minority' does not have a numerical definition but rather a power-based one (Young 1990; Ramaga 1992; Kymlicka 1996; Gilbert 1996; May, Modood and Squires 2004). Between the agency and subjection that form minority subjectivity lie the conceptual dyads of tradition–modernity, progress–backwardness, savviness–ignorance, to which many minority members subscribe precisely in order to differentiate themselves from 'the minority'. These divisions create a community that is constantly unmade and remade but whose power-ridden conceptual foundation persists. At this point between resistance and complicity (Aretxaga 1997), individuals question grand narratives, reconfigure space into daily communication, think and re-think 'community'. These are attempts, not quite at resistance, but certainly at countering the attempt to conduct the 'minority' as a particular form of 'population' within Greece and to order it within a political economy of difference and homogeneity. The 'conduct' that is countered here is the Foucauldian double of 'conduction . . . [i.e.] the activity of conducting' and of its effect as 'the way in which one conducts oneself' (Foucault 2007: 193). But this is not the whole story. It is not only the 'conduct of others' as the management of 'a' population turning from Christian pastorate to state subjects (Foucault 2007: 191–195) that is at stake here. It is also the conduct of specific Others who, in being conducted and in conducting themselves in the frame of that post-pastoral statehood, question its assumptions (are they/should they be Others? do they belong to this Otherness?) and in that critique also induct (with emphasis now on the positionality of 'within') a crisis that is itself always uncertain and in question. This book places this counter-conduct at the centre of its analysis in an attempt to rethink the frictional relations within which 'population' emerges and which, as recent research has argued, are ultimately constitutive of governmentality (Cadman 2010; Odysseos 2011).

In the following pages readers will find a pastiche of initial observations and later reflections, as well as a set of stories portraying the experiences of young people a decade ago who were living on the geographic, social, political, and economic periphery of Greece and Turkey while also being at the centre of their nationalist discourses. These observations have been shaped to a large extent by my national and political positioning which in many ways reflected theirs. As a Cypriot, I had experienced a similar dissonance between the grandiose celebrations of Hellenic heritage produced by shared school texts in Greece and Cyprus (also used in minority schools) and the implied knowledge that one's position in that national imaginary is questionable (whenever one speaks in an idiom or with an accent, whenever one learns to recognize alternative histories of Cyprus or Turkey as private, and whenever one's life-path is shaped by their membership in a 'special' population, say through policies of university entrance quotas or designated positions in the military structure).[3] Having grown up in a house where a leftist understanding of politics often produced critiques of the state, I often felt 'at home' listening to informants diverge from the scripted nationalist narrative (Greek or Turkish) in their descriptions of events and situations. Still, I was the anthropologist and they often the 'informants'. In the politics of knowledge production a border was always under negotiation. All this of course points to the long discussion about 'native anthropology', of which the most relevant recent analyses to me are Panourgiá (1995) and Navaro-Yashin (2002). In addition to the much-debated limits in the definition of 'native' that this discussion produced (Narayan 1993), I would also like to appropriate a point that another Cypriot anthropologist working in Greece once made to me about the specific application of those limits in the context of Greece and Cyprus. It is the proposition that in view of the 'crypto-colonial' (Herzfeld 2002) relations of Greece to Cyprus, studying Greece ethnographically involves an attempt to de-colonize Cyprus. I offer this as an aporia, not only methodologically speaking, but also theoretically, in speaking about the location where counter-conduct and reflexivity merge.

Caprice, Statehood, and the Bordered Subject

Bilge, preparing for her wedding in 1999, explained that she would like to have had cotton and sunflowers in her bouquet. She lamented that the date fixed for the wedding was not the season for cotton, which is culti-vated in the plains of western Thrace outside Komotini. In late summer, vast expanses of cotton fields are watered by large pipes programmed to spout out water circularly over large areas throughout the hot afternoons. The water rinses the small cotton bushes which grow the hard-shelled buds in which cotton is encased. Once these pop, they are collected by hand and kept in large cage boxes until the harvest is finished. For the rest of the year the plains of the Rhodoppe prefecture (one of the three that make up western Thrace) are dominated by green or dry cotton fields where the emptied metal boxes sit, left-over lumps of cotton stuck in their mesh. Rhodoppeans have little use for these flowers beyond passing them on to the wholesalers' and industrial markets. Bilge's choice was thus an original way of placing herself within the regional environment, appropri-ating what urbanites like herself often dismiss as 'rural' symbols and trans-forming them into an aesthetic accessory for her 'big day'. Sunflowers, by comparison, are cultivated less in Greece but line huge areas along the motorway that runs through eastern Thrace in Turkey towards Istanbul. Bilge did not verbalize this connection, but her ideal bouquet was perhaps also a statement of aesthetic appropriation of what lies on either side of the state border. Cotton was not in season, however, and Bilge ended up with a bouquet of white roses.

In this book I describe the various ways in which people succeed and fail in putting together parts of their identity that others would see as mutually exclusive. I analyse the possibilities and constraints shaped by this mutual exclusivity. Komotini and its inhabitants are, due to the city's location (Map 1.1), marginal but also connected with the different states around them. My key informants in the town were a group of about twenty bilingual youngsters, like Bilge, in their twenties and early thirties, whose practices and discourse could be described as mediating between those of the Greek and Turkish local communities. By concentrating on this particular part of their lives (and those of their parents and extended families), I attempt to illuminate the processes through which concepts of

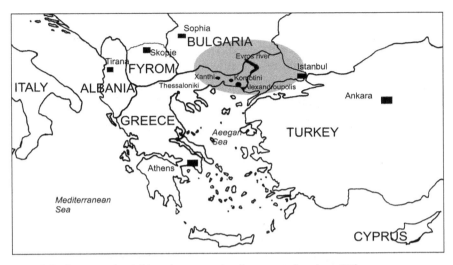

*Map 1.1 Greece and neighbouring states showing general region of Thrace
(shaded area)*

local importance ('Thrace', 'history', 'ethnicity', 'tradition', 'community', 'modernity') come to be perceived as Greek and Turkish, to be separated as such, and finally to be incorporated in my informants' counter-conduct (i.e. their 'struggle against processes implemented for conducting others' [Foucault 2007: 201]). These attempts are presented alongside those of people with whom I spoke less often and more formally, ranging from inhabitants of villages in the area who hosted me as a touring traveller, to local politicians and activists I interviewed, journalists I befriended as a social researcher, students and local Greeks I tutored in English, and others (dentists, hairdressers, shop-owners, traders) I got to know first as a client and then as an ethnographer. In such encounters, the border, as metonymized by Bilge in floral form, is referenced as the structuring principle of social relations and the framing principle of subjectivity.

Any study of such subjectivization processes, how one becomes Greek or Turkish and how one struggles against the conduct of Greek and Turkish subjectivities, is thus, again, primarily a study of borders. For both the subjectivization and the counter-conduct are inherent in the determination of 'Greekness' and 'Turkishness' and in the erection of that separation that defines one in opposition to the other. This is a figurative border then, but one that exists on the premise of the state border that separates cotton fields from sunflower fields, one mobile telephone network from another, the minority condition from hegemonic imaginaries. The 'border community' (Donnan and Wilson 1999) I write about is thus described not because it engages with 'others' across the border (in the kind of trans-border exchanges that border studies often concentrate on), but because it is governed as if the border surrounded it (which, until the mid-1990s, it did). A 'bordered population' might be a good way of describing the effect of the governmentality that I am tracing here. Its technologies, and the counter-conduct it generates, 'make, unmake and re-make' the border, destabilizing and reconfirming its presence, rendering its 'border-ness' not an essence, but rather a quality (Green 2010a). These technologies trace its contours away from the line in the river and into the conceptual line around neighbourhoods (Jansen [2010] traces a similar process in Sarajevo). The border then acts as the metonymic device for these technologies of governmentality: its designation is the critical event for the emergence of 'minority' as a specific subject of governmentality.

Interpellation into state subjecthood is one way of describing this process, but it is not merely this that I want to study. In a classic example of such interpellation, Althusser has imagined an individual who turns around on hearing a policeman call 'Hey, you there!' as becoming a subject at that moment.

> Why? Because he has recognized that the hail was 'really' addressed to him, and that 'it was *really him* who was hailed' (and not someone else). Experience shows that the practical telecommunication of hailings is such that they hardly ever miss their man: verbal call or whistle, the one hailed always recognises that it is really him who is being hailed. And yet it is a strange phenomenon, and one which cannot be explained solely by 'guilt feelings', despite the large numbers who 'have something on their consciences'. (Althusser 1971: 174, emphasis in original)

This turn at the policeman's hail might be the effect of subjectivization technologies stemming from a policing governmentality that renders the state border both a repressive and ideological apparatus (ibid.: 137). But for the people presented in this book there is a further layer of being cognizant of such technologies that complicates the mechanics of 'ideology'. It puts 'guilt' and 'conscience' into question by recognizing that there is something there indeed, but that this 'something' is not to be found in the stipulations of criminal law, but in the often implicit clauses that declare what 'minority' is. This 'something' is not on the conscience of the individual, but on the conscience (or the unconscious) of the law. In this sense, counter-conduct, stemming from the recognition of and reflection on the state's processes of producing difference (i.e. its bordering practices), is what destabilizes the border so that we may see it analytically as more than just a line.

This is what I mean by the capriciousness cited in this book's title. In proposing a view of borders as capricious I want to highlight the practices that make them so: unstable, fanciful, inconstant (OED 1993: 334).

I also want to indicate how these practices diverge from the 'slippery' nature that is often ascribed to borders and bordering apparatuses. What I have found articulated in counter-conduct of various kinds is not so much the failure to grasp the logic of bordering as a technique of governmentality but the very success of that grasp as one recognizes, refuses, struggles against, or accepts it. At the same time, there is an inconstancy in the way in which this is done. In this sense, capriciousness is a quality ascribed to the border through an agency that is limited, confined, frustrated, shifting and quavering, but nevertheless there. In constantly re-producing the differences that the border sustains in the interpellation of 'minority', the subjects that come into being through this interpellation do so in cognizance and with a reflexivity that 'majority' subjects (those who would be surprised to be hailed by policemen and who would therefore fail to turn around) rarely develop.

It is those moments of capriciousness in the erection of difference that I have tried to capture ethnographically. Capriciousness thus refers to the contradictory 'nature' of the border. It refers to the quality of the border – at points digital, at others analogical, at times hermetically closed and violently guarded, at others no more than, and sometimes not even, a line on the ground. It also refers to the qualities of the subjects that its existence conducts – citizens, travellers, migrants, those who are marginalized, illegal, established, exchanged, repatriated. It refers to the agency with which these subjects are conducted and counter-conducted – by reflecting on nationalist discourse and producing counter-discourses, by accepting the pathologization of the minority, by appealing to authorities through carefully phrased demands, by developing particular attitudes towards community and its rituals. Therefore it is not only borders that are capricious, but also, and mostly, people.

But it is also in the interaction between the two – borders and people – that capriciousness generates its affect (cynicism, frustration, indignation, injury, alienation, resignation, or ridicule). Caprice describes people's stance towards the differences that the border projects onto the world around, and inside, them. This is affect as distinct from feeling, as Deleuze and Guattari propose: 'Affect is the active discharge of emotion, the counter attack, whereas feeling is an always displaced, retarded, resisting emotion. Affects are projectiles just like weapons; feelings are introceptive like tools' (1987: 441). Inasmuch as the counter-conducts I analyse are 'affective' then, they are involved in this activity and this struggle. And yet, there is also an indeterminacy that imbues these practices, which Foucault, rightly I believe, initially wished to highlight. The 'battle' does not rage constantly, as resistance theory might suggest. The notion of 'capricious borders' therefore speaks to the imbrication of subjectivity over structures that spread over space on different scales (state borders, neighbourhoods, homes) and the governmental technologies that frame and animate this arrangement, but which are also questioned by it.

Capriciousness communicates the lack of determination in these relationships. Jean-Luc Nancy has employed the idea of the 'inoperative community' (1991) to relate a similar lack, outside the framing of borders. This framing is crucial to my purposes because borders are precisely what enable this non-operation of 'community'. In elaborating on this tension between indeterminacy and intention, I follow a theoretical trajectory that spans the deployment of Foucauldian governmentality across studies of two types of borders that often remain separate: the material (e.g. state), which figure prominently in ethnographic and political analyses; and the conceptual, which have mostly been treated in philosophical and literary modes. Straddling the two is a critical understanding of borders that has often made a convincing argument for politically committed theory. In following such insights I trace an analytical path from 'epistemic disobedience' (Mignolo 2009) to a focus on space (Massey 2005) as the site that qualifies 'agonistic democracy' (Mouffe 2000). From there, I turn to conceptualizations between the intimate and the political, as recently configured in the work of Stoler (2010) and Panourgiá (2009). In these terms, I seek to explore what Lemke identifies as 'the instability of the border between "life" and "politics"' (2011: 4). Through this trajectory, I am interested in tracing the techniques of subectivization, from the governmentality of population to the (non)operation of community.

Bare Names

My first encounter with the intricacies of 'community' was in October 1997, when, in preparing for my fieldwork, I imagined 'the minority' as a larger version of the population of people I had met in the Gazi area of Athens in the summer of 1996, who were internal migrants from Komotini. I had expected to find a similar but larger group in Komotini of what seemed to me then as downtrodden individuals, unwilling and scared to admit their Turkishness to an outsider. The Komotinians I met in Athens had insisted that they were Muslim and had described the language they spoke as 'Muslim' (*Mousoulmaniká*). By the time I actually arrived in Komotini, I had met Gümülcinelis (Komotinian Turkish-speakers) who had migrated to London and Turkey and I had been informed that the migrants in Athens were not Turks like them, but were rather 'Gypsies' from a neighbourhood outside the town known as a Roma area. As my first introduction to Gümülcineli society, this distinction alerted me to the fact that the minority in the Greek part of Thrace is far from homogeneous. Over the course of my fieldwork, this heterogeneity took on an ever complex form, as it spread from the level of ethnic distinction to a multitude of life circumstances (gender, age, political ideology, wealth, location of residence, profession, marital status, health, etc).

Confronted with Komotini's divisions on this primary level of ethnicity into Greek, Turkish, Pomak, and Roma, as I initially was in 1998, I turned my analytical gaze to the operations of difference, power, agency and marginalization, and it is these that my description of 'minority' attempts to capture. Through these operations, space, place, geography, land and location are also intertwined with understandings of history, family stories, origin myths and ethnicity, as well as gender and sexuality in order to form interpretations of belonging and being excluded from 'community'; this is what is recounted in the following pages.

Komotini (Map 1.1) is located in the western (Greek) part of Thrace, two hours' drive from the Turkish border (to the east) and four hours' drive from Thessaloniki (to the west). It is a town of around 50,000 people, half of whom are members of the Turkish-speaking minority and the other half Greeks. The Greek Ministry of Foreign Affairs' (MFA) website claimed in the late 1990s that 'the minority numbers approximately 98000 to a total of 338000 inhabitants of Thrace i.e. 29% of the [area's] population' (http://www.mfa.gr, accessed in August 2001). Over the next decade, the governmentality reflected in these statistics has shifted at least twice. Whereas in the late 1990s this statement was presented opposite Turkish estimates of 'nearly 150,000 Turks living in Western Thrace' (http://www.mfa.tr, accessed at the same time), by 2009 the statistical stakes were not those of numerical representation but of protection. Thus, the 'Turkey directorate' of the Greek MFA explained on its 'human rights' webpage in 2009 that 'in opposition to the fate of the Greek minority in Turkey, the Muslim minority in Greece is prospering and today numbers well over 100,000 members'.

This statement underlined the principle of mutual reciprocity (*arhí tis amiveótitas*) between the treatment of the Greek minority of Istanbul by Turkey and the treatment of the Turkish minority of western Thrace by Greece.[4] This is also emphasized on the Turkish MFA's website, which largely retained its text on the western Thrace minority through the years by comparison to Greece, claiming that the 'community constitutes the Turkish Minority of Western Thrace whose status is established by the Lausanne Peace Treaty of 1923' (ibid.). This is of course the document that established the reciprocity principle. According to this document, the Greeks of Istanbul are also *établis*, i.e. 'established before 30th October, 1918, within the areas under the Prefecture of the City of Constantinople . . . [and] considered as Greek inhabitants of Constantinople' (Article 2, Convention concerning the Exchange of Greek and Turkish Populations,

1923). The two groups have thus been the object of minority protection practices of each state, practices that are closely monitored by the other state, set up as each minority's 'protector'. In a later governmental shift on the Greek side, this 'logic of reciprocity' (*loyikí tis amiveótitas*) was recognized by the Greek MFA as 'outdated' (*parohiméni*) and a new approach was announced on its website by 2012 against 'attempts to ghettoize the minority', whereby 'the Greek state confronts [sic] the members of the Muslim minority and their issues in the same way that it confronts all Greek citizens'.[5] However, not all Greek citizens are afforded a section in the special issues area of the MFA; and prior to the austerity measures that have affected the vast majority of Greek citizens since 2010, not all were subjects of 'confrontation'.

And this is where the continuity of governmental logic is to be found. To the Greek state, the minority is and has been for some time, a 'foreign affairs' matter (as it is of course for the Turkish state which, however, also delegates Greek minority issues to the MFA). In effect, the Greek and Turkish states share an acceptance of the otherness of the minority that rests on notions of 'nationality' which are defined ethnically. In these terms, the rhetoric of both states is in agreement as to whether the minority is 'ethnically' Greek – it is clearly not, since it is a 'foreign affair'. However, as to whether it is ethnically one or three minorities, whether it is a religious or an ethnic minority, and whether it is wholly or in part ethnically Turkish, these are questions of heated debate.

Greek state discourse claims that 'there are no ethnic or national minorities in Greece, there is only one Muslim minority'.[6] Thus, the Turkish-speakers in Komotini are described as 'Greek Muslims' or 'Greeks, Muslim by religion' (*Éllines Musulmáni*, or *Éllines, Musulmáni to thrískevma*) and not 'Turks'. Furthermore, whereas 'Roma' and 'Pomaks' are formally identified as subdivisions within the 'Muslim minority', the existence of 'Turks' in Greece was categorically denied until 1999: they were at the time of my fieldwork called at best 'Turkish-speakers' (*Tourkófoni*) or 'people of Turkish origin' (*Tourkoyenís*). This debate over the minority's descriptive terminology has long roots, and was invigorated with the state ban in 1983 on the word 'Turkish' and its derivatives to refer to anything related to the minority. This ban was, however, substantially compromised when the later Prime Minister and then Greek Minister of Foreign Affairs, George Papandreou, proclaimed, in a much-discussed interview in July 1999, his support for the right to 'individual self-identification' (*atomikó dhikéoma ston aftoprosdhiorismó*) as regards 'the Muslim minority in Thrace' (*Klik* 12: 151–152).

At the time of my fieldwork at least, 'Turks' and 'Greeks' were not only mutually exclusive (at the state level), but were also oppositional terms. The large majority of my informants claimed they were Turks, that they were not Muslims, and, of course, that they were not Greeks. People who claimed that they were both or neither were criticized for 'projecting an image of the minority as in a state of identity crisis', even when these claims were first and foremost anti-nationalist. 'If a Greek nationalist asks me what I am I will say a Turk, if a Turkish nationalist asks the same question I will say a Greek, and to you I say I am neither' was the comment a friend once made to a TV journalist. Some of our mutual friends considered this comment 'utterly naïve because it presented the minority as confused about its identity'. Beyond the 'minority bind' revealed in the response, the question 'what do you feel you are?' that elicited it reveals the obsession of outsiders (locals, journalists, Greek and Turkish nationals) with defining 'the minority'. Indeed, to many local Greeks, the minority is 'officially' Muslim and 'unofficially' Turkish / Pomak / Roma (according to context). Alternative terms like 'Turkish Greeks' (*Turkoéllines*) or 'Greek Turks' (*Ellinóturki*), once suggested by a Greek informant, as references for the minority, sound utterly hilarious (they immediately provoked laughter around the dinner table of Greek interlocutors). As Gourgouris observes (1996: 267–282), the monstrosity of such suggestions functions in an interdependent relationship with the Greek national imaginary, where to be Greek is to entertain and reject the possibility of being a Turk.

What connects most of the people discussed in this book is the fact that they are inhabitants of Komotini, or Gümülcinelis, who prefer to classify themselves as Turkish, in contradistinction to other (lower-class) Turkish-speaking town dwellers whom they classify as 'Pomak' or 'Gypsy', often despite these people's refusal of such labels. It is because of this self-classification that I speak of them as 'Gümülcinelis', a localized identity category underlain by claims to Turkish-ness that are rather understated, treated as a matter-of-fact definition of ethnicity rather than celebrations of national affiliation. Thus, in reflection of local classifications, I will also speak of local 'Greeks' and 'Turks' alongside 'Gümülcineli' and 'Komotinian' and will use the more formalized distinctions of 'minority / majority' to invoke official terminology and the technologies of governance that arise from it.

The multiple distinctions within the minority are reflected on the level of occupation. Shop-owning Gümülcinelis form the largest part of the Komotinian minority's middle class, with the lower class mainly involved in cultivation and the well-off in white-collar professions, e.g. medicine, law, education, and journalism. Some families and individuals cut across these distinctions; for example, they might have a professional office in the town and grow tobacco in the villages. Tobacco cultivation was, in the late 1990s, by far the largest source of income among the non-urban minority population of Thrace. It was practiced in the mountains, where a large percentage of the minority lives. In the valley, inhabited by majority and minority alike, cotton was the preferred cultivation crop (these preferences, I should note, are largely set by the subsidies that the Ministry of Agriculture offers for each crop in each area and were shifting by the early 2000s). Overall, the difference in living standards between the minority and the Greek communities in Komotini, as well as in Rhodoppe in general are evident. Greeks own larger houses and more businesses and live in neighbourhoods and villages that are better served in terms of infrastructure. By contrast, many mountain villages and some households in the outskirts of Komotini are almost totally self-sustained. None of the Gümülcinelis in Greece could be called 'rich', and none of them own large businesses, or factories.[7] The discrepancy was in fact so great in the 1990s that it rendered western Thrace one of the most attractive European regions for EU structural funds. These improvements have had a limited effect on the minority but have seen the development of the road network and light industry in the area. The 1998 development report on the Rhodoppe prefecture includes no mention of the minority at all in its data (Αναπτυξιακή Ροδόπης [Rhodoppe Development Company], 1998).

According to local minority officials, such invisibility and the lack of development it portrays is partly due to the fact that individuals lack the knowledge, training, and networks that would allow them to apply for EU funding. In addition, the state projects that do get funded tended to concentrate, in the late 1990s at least, on the needs of the Greek population. For example, road construction has been one of the most visible areas of EU funding locally. Under this scheme, great improvements have been made to the highway linking the three main Thracian towns, as well as to roads leading to Greek valley villages (partly because these are also the main routes to local seaside resorts). However, the roads linking minority mountain villages to the towns as well as those between the villages, remained largely in a state of disrepair, and in some cases simply did not exist. In the year that I spent in Komotini, large amounts of money were spent on improving the town's main square and national monuments, while minority *mahalle* (neighbourhood) streets seemed to be in desperate need of improvement. This is even more pronounced in the villages just below the Bulgarian border, where transportation takes place on foot or by donkey. In these remote villages life appeared, in 1999 at least, to be centred exclusively on the cultivation of tobacco, and much of the villagers' contact with the outside world was limited to the visits of tobacco merchants arriving once a year to buy the produce. In these villages, the year was divided into (tobacco) planting, thinning, collecting, and drying seasons. The landscape was dotted with villages nestled in the forest, the two-storey stone houses and small strips of tobacco fields appearing suddenly opposite a bend on the road. For the last five decades, until 1996, these villages had been cut off from the rest of the region by a militarized border known as 'the barre' (*i bára*) that designated it as a 'surveillance zone' (*epitiroúmeni zóni*). This invisible (albeit formerly quite visible) screen rendered the mountain area out-of-bounds to the rest of the population, alienating them in a physical but also conceptual sense. Thus Pomaks, who inhabit most of these villages, are considered as others within the minority and their lifestyles (including religious heterodox practices) and identification (as being not quite Turkish) are considered suspect.

Yusuf, in his late fifties in 1999, noted the dropping tobacco prices with alarm while offering my partner some of his freshly processed 'first class' tobacco as we sat in the square of his village close to the Bulgarian border. As far as I have been able to elicit from other interviewees as well, the income gained through tobacco cultivation is often very low indeed – products are bought by wholesalers at specific times of the year and the income is usually just enough to keep the family going for the rest of the year. This perhaps explains why many minority members who have migrated to Germany and Turkey send remittances back to Greece.

Yusuf's comments seemed to communicate a different reality to the way in which Gümülcineli friends dismiss the mountain villagers as 'Pomak' and 'backward'. Within the context of global anti-smoking policies, Yusuf's pride in his first-class tobacco seemed out of step. His pressing concern about securing an income in the imminent future appeared to be symptomatic of a hand-to-mouth life behind the 'barre' that was beginning to resemble what Agamben described in his celebrated thesis on the camp as 'bare life' (Agamben 1998). When Gümülcinelis equate Yusuf's concerns about immediate sustenance with the 'backwardness' associated with a kind of 'Muselmann'-hood, they delegitimize those concerns. They instead consider identity-focused concerns (including religiosity and secularism), to be the true substance of political life. As another example of a capricious border (erected between Yusuf and young town-dwellers), it illustrates the fact that in Thrace, as much as in the philosophy of Agamben, *zoe* and *bios* cannot be separated (ibid.). This is where the biopolitical emerges.

Framing these biopolitics are of course the minority's relations with the Greek state, which are in turn framed by Greco-Turkish bilateral relations. In the 1950s, following the start of the Greek-Cypriot guerrilla struggle for Union with Greece, and the repercussions of this in Istanbul where nationalist Turks carried out what have reportedly been pre-planned attacks against Greek minority members and their properties (Öktem 2011: 44–45; Güven 2006), there was a large wave of emigration from Turkey to Greece, which was the precursor to the demise of the Istanbuli Greek community. This brought about a profound shift in

Greek state policy towards the minority (Iliadis 2006). In the aftermath of these events, and throughout the 1960s and 1970s, a period which saw the establishment of a right-wing military dictatorship in Greece, the minority experienced state oppression in the form of strict surveillance measures, restrictive policies in the spheres of education and property rights and the virtual absence of political representation. The summer of 1974, when Turkish troops launched an offensive in Cyprus, is a time that most of my informants remember because of the fear they felt. The government policy had, until 1983 when the 'independence' of the Turkish Republic of Northern Cyprus was unilaterally declared, wavered on the naming of the minority between 'Turkish' and 'Muslim'. After that event, it solidified on the categorical rejection of Turkishness. As one Greek local MP put it, this was 'in order to prevent the minority from doing what the Turkish Cypriot minority did in Cyprus' (Kipouros 1984).

Today, state structures are quite prominent on the Komotinian landscape. Government offices are located in the centre as well as on the outskirts of the town. Komotini's northern limits are marked by a military camp and the western limits by the humanities departments of the University of Thrace. At the city's eastern exit (leading to the town of Alexandroupoli and on the border with Turkey) one will find the prefecture administration office for Rhodoppe (the district of which Komotini is the capital) and at its southern exit the local branch of the national radio station. These were structures rarely accessed by the minority, at least up to 1999, which reveals a two-way problematic relationship. As far as the Greek government was concerned, the minority was largely invisible. At the same time, its relationship to the structures of power was so problematic, that this invisibility on the part of the minority was often desirable. My observations of local government establishments and minority politicians' offices showed that minority members rarely had direct contact with Greek officials and civil servants. Instead, they generally preferred to have their requests dealt with, to the extent possible, either by official minority representatives or minority professionals. This in turn means that firstly, such representatives are largely voted for on the basis of their ability to carry out these tasks and secondly, that when in office, their work centres around relatively minor tasks, stemming from their role as conduits between minority individuals and the state, thereby diminishing the possibility of their lobbying for more substantial policies that could redress many of the problems faced by the minority collectively.

Political science might describe this as clientalism, a symptom of underdevelopment and a correlate to corruption, to be addressed by the transparency of liberalism. A similar argument has been levelled at Greece as a whole to diagnose 'the Greek malaise' following the financial crisis post-2010. I find such descriptions inadequate because they misrepresent the inter-subjective relationships developed in the context of particular exchanges and power differentials, which fails to account for the liberal state's own implication in the process. Parliamentarians (MPs) may help individuals 'in return' for votes, but firstly, those individuals are requesting 'favours' (certifications, documentation, updates on applications to various government departments) that they are in theory entitled to but in practice barred from by the hurdles of bureaucracy. Secondly, it is usually a matter of everyday sustenance rather than privilege that is at stake, especially in the case of the minority (to secure recognition of a foreign university degree, medical cover, registration on a pension scheme, etc.). And thirdly, the allegiance of voters in these cases is inconstant precisely because their requests are legitimate, urgent and achievable by whoever happens to be in power. Therefore, what political science would diagnose as 'clientalism' is less about a hidden contract between voters and their representatives and more about the technologies of government whereby citizens become subjects of populations differentiated in terms of priority and de-prioritization: those that speak Greek and those who do not, those that have Muslim names and those who do not. This is what separates the minority condition from that of the general population: obstacles that are more widely faced by the minority when dealing with the state machinery, even if such obstacles are endemic enough to have been cited in discussions of the economic crisis as systemic failures.

When minority members come into contact with state structures, it can often become an occasion for individual criticism of the minority's treatment. Such instances may focus on visits to the hospital, where often the problem is not confined to the staff's treatment of individuals, but extends to the many obstacles faced in actually getting there (especially when coming from the mountain villages). Minority officials are often asked to handle cases involving the issuing of permits or identification documents or issues relating to fund releases for agricultural subsidies. Indeed, the latter seem to be the main source of state support for the minority.

Yet, the situation as recorded in 1999 was a far cry from the restrictive policies of earlier periods. The transformation of these policies was part of a more general shift in the Greek government's approach to the minority issue, inaugurated in the early 1990s by the call of the then Prime Minister Mitsotakis for equality in the treatment of all Greek citizens. This approach was condensed in the couplet *isonomía-isopolitía* ('civic and juridical equality' or, literally, 'equality before the law and state'), which still accompanies claims for improved conditions advanced by minority politicians. However, the limits of such claims were considerably reduced when the Greek government instituted a required minimum of three per cent for parliamentary representation, which means that minority MPs cannot be elected as individuals, but as members of national political parties (at a rough estimate of ten million for the whole population of Greece, a block minority vote of all purported 150,000 members would yield half the required three per cent). Most minority individuals with whom I spoke have no doubt that this change was instituted to prevent minority members who espouse Turkish nationalist ideologies from getting elected and causing the Greek government international embarrassment (which indeed one minority MP did in the early 1990s). Beyond the demographic logistics involved, this policy also exposes a more general approach of the Greek state to the minority, whereby complaints about the minority's treatment are viewed as being fuelled by Turkish nationalism and therefore illegitimate.

In fact, government officials (local and Athens-based) to whom I spoke during my fieldwork view Komotini as a particularly problematic area, primarily because of the location of the Turkish Consulate there. For these officials, as well as for many local Greeks, the Consulate is a source of Turkish propaganda, to which the minority is highly susceptible because in their view, it is 'illiterate' and 'backward'. It is a widespread belief amongst Greeks that the minority votes according to Consulate directions and that the Consulate pays its elite in return for their loyalty (pushing the argument of clientalism into the sphere of national sovereignty and national security). In this context, the minority members who speak against Turkish nationalism are mostly members of left-wing Greek political parties and are hailed by Greek intellectuals as heroic individuals who are willing to stake possible political careers on the ideology of Greco-Turkish friendship. In this sense, and despite tremendous differences in political opinion in Greece, there seems to be an overarching dichotomic securitizing discourse, where 'Greeks' and 'Turks', local or otherwise are primarily viewed as opponents, and where to be critical of one's own group is tantamount to showing support of the opposite camp, leaving the equivalence between ethnicity and political ideology intact.

Biopolitical Modes

For the minority individuals around whom this book is centred, 'community' is a constantly de-constructed and re-constructed entity where ethnic, class, and geographic divisions are drawn upon in the interpretation of one's position within power structures and in the process are themselves re-interpreted. In Nancy's terms, 'community' constantly 'co-emerges' with the subject (Nancy 2000). It is these relationships (normative, regulative, affective, and existential) that are at the heart of this book. Their exploration is undertaken in the following pages through an analysis of the governmental technologies (historiography, statistics, law, naming, mapping) around which the biopolitical order of the minority everyday is organized.

In what follows I explore three aspects of biopolitical governmentality that determine the processes of minority subjectivization and the modes in which counter-conduct takes shape and the 'community' emerges and is resisted. These are naming, genealogy, and state care. The first extends from the foundational question of naming the minority to toponymy and classifications of space and populations. Intimately connected to this is the aspect of genealogy under which racialized understandings of 'population' are seen to have been shaped by and to have also informed political disciplinary practices. These practices have revolved around a discourse of 'state care' (*kratiki storyi*) that included questions of how to educate, induce emigration, and control living standards and birth rates. These techniques are the focus of the three central chapters (four, five, and six). Prefiguring them, in chapters two and three, is a discussion of bordering and counter-bordering as practices that frame the field within which these technologies emerge and are encountered. In the last two chapters, I show how the sustenance and questioning of 'community' is informed by these aspects of governmentality, especially when they enter the sphere of religion and gender politics. In the conclusion I pose the counter-conduct of community as a question for anthropology. Finally, in the postscript I revisit the meaning of shifts in the bordering governmentality taking shape in western Thrace in recent years. Against the current background of what goes under the rubric of 'political instability' in Greece, the story I present might also invite reflection on how the premises of the governmentality that has diachronically targeted particular populations are being reconfigured to expand to the general 'population', which is now fiscally determined. At the same time the extent and limits of counter-conduct that I describe would, I hope, point to the possibility of also reconfiguring that 'population' into a constantly emerging 'co-mmunity'.

Notes

1. The reprint of the Lausanne Treaty and attached documents I have consulted are in Kantzilaris (2001). For the text of all other international treaties referenced in this book, I have consulted Toynbee and Israel (1967).
2. This is also to problematize the emphasis on the medical and the somatic in analyses of biopolitics. The works of Kleinman (1995; 1999) and Biehl (2005) readily

come to mind, as do others (Scheper-Hughes 2000; 2004; Corin 1990) who have participated in the groundbreaking volume on the ethnography of subjectivity (Biehl et al., 2007). Beyond anthropology, Agamben's writings on the hiatus between *zoe* and *bios* (Agamben 1998; 2002; 2005) corresponding to 'bare' and 'political life' (albeit in a reductive reading), where the figures of the Muselmann of the Nazi camps and the comatosed Karen Quinlan (Agamben 1998: 163, 185) loom large, have provided a key reference point where the somatic/medical focus is restricted to the presentation of 'bare life' at its extremes. Applying this to her analysis of state repression of the Greek left, Neni Panourgia has provided an illuminating critique of what this hiatus obscures (Panourgiá 2009: 104–114), which is precisely, in my reading, this imbrication of life by technologies of governmentality.

3. Both of these policies underline the fundamental differences in the position that 'Cypriot' and 'minority' occupy in the state imaginary, but I mention them as ways of showing that their existence nevertheless indicates a shared subjectivity which is defined in terms of a peripheral location to the national centre. Even though I studied in the UK and not in Greece, Greeks have reminded me on several occasions that 'we' (Greek-Cypriots) enjoy special privileges in Greece, such as easier access to universities, an argument that parallels frequent, and more hostile, references in the Komotinian local press to the 'injustice' of the university quota system (*posóstosi*) which has allocated 0.5 per cent of state university placements to the minority since 1996. The second example illustrates the differences more starkly: trainee officers in the Cypriot National Guard are chosen every year through competitive exams to receive special training in the Greek army schools (no such schools exist in Cyprus). By comparison, minority recruits are incorporated in army units across the country at lower ranks and very often in positions that do not bear arms. Both policies are based on the logic of setting, in very different ways, some populations apart from the majority – whether 'hosting' them at the top or pushing them to the bottom.

4. A recent volume (Akgönül 2008) has explored this 'principle of reciprocity' as the main legal frame determining state policies towards the two minorities.

5. Text copied from the English version of the website (http://www1.mfa.gr/en/issues-of-greek-turkish-relations/, accessed 3 January 2012), which largely remains faithful to the Greek original, apart from an omitted reference to the contested issue of the 'three parts of the Muslim minority' (*trión sinistosón tis Mousoulmanikís mionótitas*). In terms of web-browsing, the minority was located under 'foreign policy' – 'multilateral diplomacy' – 'global issues' – 'human rights' in 2009 (http://www2.mfa.gr/www.mfa.gr/el-GR/Policy/Multilateral+Diplomacy/International+Issues/HumanRights/THRACE+MINORITY.htm, accessed on 30 September 2009), while by 2012 it had migrated to 'foreign policy' – 'special matters' (official translation rendered as 'foreign policy issues') – 'issues of Greek-Turkish relations' (http://www1.mfa.gr/zitimata-ellinotourkikon-sheseon/, accessed on 3 January 2012). In the Turkish MFA website, the text on the minority is filed under 'foreign policy' – 'regions' – 'European countries' – 'Greece'. There, it is flanked by various translations of the main text in different languages and accompanied by two items on the Greek minority in Turkey, under headings that do not refer to 'minority' at all, but to the specific issues of the 'Greek Orthodox Patriarchate in Pnahar [sic]' and the 'Theological School in Heybeliada' (http://

www.mfa.gov.tr/turkish-minority-of-western-thrace.en.mfa, last accessed on 3 January 2012).

6. However, Stavros points out that Greek law does in fact recognize another minority: the Jewish (1995: 17).

7. There are, however, western Thracian Turks who have distinguished themselves in business and politics (sometimes in an infamous way) in Turkey.

CHAPTER 2

HERITAGE, HISTORY, LEGACIES

A Heritage of Community

One of the main streets of Komotini which runs through minority neighbourhoods is Egnatia, built on the ruins of the Roman thoroughfare that connected Byzantium (current-day Istanbul) to the Adriatic coast. Just beyond the points where Egnatia meets the city's Roman wall ruins, there is a square surrounded by a low concrete wall and fenced off with iron rails. In the square there are cypress trees, tombstones inscribed in Ottoman (an older form of Turkish written in Arabic script), and a dilapidated minaret the top of which has been broken off (Figure 2.1). This space is known to the minority as 'Selvili Camii' (the Cypress Mosque) but referred to by Greeks as 'the broken minaret' (*spazménos minarés*). Further down the road, at the edge of town, lies the area of Poşpoş, known as the site of the oldest mosque in Komotini. Now similarly in ruins, the Poşpoş *tekkesi* (shrine) is seen as constituting proof that Turkic groups settled in the area prior to the Ottoman conquest of the town, which took place under the command of the military leader Evrenos in 1363 during the reign of Murad I (Kiel 1983; Loupis 2001; Oğuz 2006: 32). Gümülcinelis know that the name Poşpoş is a truncated version of the phrase *postu boş* (empty *post*). The phrase makes reference to the empty seat of authority (symbolized by the chief's seat covered with a rug of animal skin called *post*) that characterized the Turkic tribe that first settled in the area. It was not that the tribe was egalitarian: on the contrary, its hierarchy demanded that the leader led the men to war and his empty seat signified the frequency with which this happened.

The story is one of the many that circulate within the minority but which remain fenced inside – it is a communal story of interest and concern to Gümülcinelis only, not Greeks. Likewise, the two squares, although highly visible, are unmarked and often unnoticed by passers-by.

Figure 2.1 Selvili Cami ruins in 2006

As well as dead clerics, they have also buried part of the town's history there. The Turkish name for Komotini itself has connotations of being buried. The name 'Gümülcine' is reputed to have come about as a worn-out form of the phrase *'gömülü içine'* which means 'buried inside'. This phrase refers to the town's physical positioning in a valley depression (six metres below sea level) between the coast and the mountains. Like Poşpoş, part of the town's history is also buried, inside the informal discourse of the minority. The morbidity referenced by the term 'buried', or the mutilation of 'broken', shows something of the minority condition explored in this book. Ballinger's Istrian informants, belonging to another Balkan border minority not far from Thrace, recognize their story as 'forgotten, cancelled, and buried' (2003: 11). Less explicitly here, the burial of knowledge about the origins of Turkish presence in the region is embodied in the broken minaret and the ruined *tekke*, which, by virtue of being unnoticed, becomes a reminder of what can and cannot be articulated about belonging in this place and this history. Knowledge (knowing the story) is a way of communicating this minority condition, if not yet reflecting on it.

In this chapter and the next, I intend to interrogate the process by which this burial comes about, to show the silences in the national story from which informal communal stories emerge, and the ruptures they effect in their articulation. Anthropology has shown that to piece together the stories that have fallen by the wayside of Greek national historiography requires attention to those lines that link 'Lesser Histories' (Vereni 2000: 56–60) to the grand narrative, puncturing this narrative in the process (Karakasidou 1997; Brown 1998a; Cowan 2000; Kenna 2001). That these lesser histories often draw their strength from the idiom of kinship (family stories) is indicative of the workings of politics in the production of subjects whose subjectivity is supposed to be biologically determined. Panourgiá has termed this 'political DNA' (2009: 214–216). Drawing on this, I present the stories cited below as the result of a biopolitics predicated on the assumption that birth (as a Greek or Turk) determines the espousal of a grand narrative. As a pointer to techniques of governmentality, these minority stories offer a first glimpse at how one counters the placing of the minority population into a national historiography that excludes them. In employing the term 'political DNA', Panourgiá draws attention to the paradoxes that a putative unified ethnicity of the Greek 'majority' has entailed in the context of the modern history of political fracture and 'civil war' (a concept that she also critically examines). In the context of my analysis of the minority condition, I take this as a point of departure for a further critique of the racialism that the concept of 'ethnicity' often entails. Thus, before returning to the distinction between 'political' and 'ethnic' identities, I take as a working assumption the proposition that 'ethnicity' is thoroughly invested in the political domain.

The Poşpoş story speaks to a Foucauldian conduct of 'population' through the multiple forms of counter-conduct it has inspired over the years. In terms of everyday knowledge, Gümülcinelis simply know a story that (Greek) Komotinians passing by the site – and ignoring it – do not.

But I want to mention two forms of counter-narratives to this ignorance. First is the politicization of discourses relating to the preservation of the site in the mid-1990s. Local authorities had destroyed parts of the Poşpoş *tekke* in 1989, claiming concerns over safety. In response, an official minority discourse developed that demanded the preservation of the site, consolidating its position as a collective minority counter-strategy against the Greek state's attempts to construct a particular historiography. Drawing on state promises to restore the site, which never materialized, conferences organized by Western Thracian Turks living abroad, together with members of the minority leadership considered to have links to the Turkish political elite, ensured that the restoration of Poşpoş *tekkesi* was added to the list of minority demands (ABTTF 2008). It remains a highlighted topic under the category 'destruction of cultural heritage [in Greece]' on the Turkish MFA website.

In this counter-discourse, Poşpoş seems to be a site of little relevance to Greece or to Greek identity, and thus its defence is argued on the basis of minority rights, not Greek heritage protection – as if its presence on a now Greek landscape is disconnected from Greek history. This understanding of minority rights informs counter-discourses on a number of issues, such as education, employment, land appropriation, and political representation. In doing so, it brings together the politics of minoritization of today's minority population, in rendering them 'Muslims' or 'Turks', and the politics of integrating diverse population groups into a 'majority'.

'Minoritization', Cowan notes, 'is a distinctive strategy within a global political field, that eschews territorial objectives and seeks rights within existing national borders; it may develop as a *reformulation of* and an *alternative to* an explicitly nationalizing project' (Cowan 2001: 156, emphasis in original). In this case, a parallel is set up that counters Greek destruction by accepting the very premises of the nation-state logic (that of unifying territory, history, and population) that produced it (Poşpoş is outside Greek history). This can only be the case if Greek history is seen as the history of a concept of 'Greece' in contradistinction to the territory of Greece. With relation to the Poşpoş grievance, this concept of 'Greece' is reproduced in formalized counter-discourse, which in turn re-creates the minority as being excluded from it. The minority thus becomes complicit in the mapping of history and place onto a national imaginary that reads ethnicity as congruent with landscape: the preservation of the monument rests precisely on its ethnicization as Turkish *topos*. In doing so, it eschews the possibility of de-ethnicizing the monument as heritage of 'this' place where 'this' can be thought outside the history-nation homology. The monument is rendered a marker of 'topographic desire' (the desire to occupy the site of the nation, where the question becomes 'which nation?'). This desire, Gourgouris explains, 'colonize[s] the site of the subject' and in doing so 'construct[s] the *native*' (Gourgouris 1996: 43, emphasis in original). The exclusions entailed in this construction often go beyond the 'which nation' question and are precisely what concern me in this chapter and the next. The question of who is a native of western Thrace is thus constructed as a corollary of the 'ethnicity' of place (read through the presence of heritage), rather than their own birth. A 'political DNA' links people to a lineage of place, not the other way round.

Consider however, a different strategy:

> I heard people say that years ago when bulldozers came to pull the minaret down they could not. They tried for a long time but they could not get to it – and they say it was as if a force was protecting the site, some kind of divine force they say, until the work men gave up and the bulldozers went away.

Selda, one of my female informants in her early thirties, married and an ardent secularist, told me this with some hesitation, not quite believing herself that the monument could have been rescued from Greek destruction by divine intervention, but nevertheless considering that the very existence of this story was interesting. Her story, insecurely positioned as part of 'the' minority story of Poşpoş (as Selda is uncertain of its legitimacy), speaks of a different kind of burial of knowledge. Although it is irrational as far as secularism is concerned, it does explain what saved the ruins that currently survive, and indicates the failures of local and national leaderships (Greek and Turkish) to protect the monument; it also indicates a subjectivity that wavers between belief in divine intervention, reverence of communal heritage sites, and disengagement from a 'they'.

It was a 'they' I had heard many times before in articulations of the distance between individual interlocutors and the conceptual 'minority' as a singular, unified population, representable by official discourse. Whose official discourse was of course always a stake in this 'they': the articulation 'they say' referred to members of the minority that accept the possibility of divine intervention unquestioningly. But the official discourse that maps this 'they' onto 'the' minority is the discourse of Greek nationalism, which presents the minority as blindly religious. In her emphasis on the 'they' Selda acknowledges and counters the sovereignty (be it Greek or Turkish) that creates this population (just as in other instances her 'they' would index Turkish official discourse where 'the' minority population would be assumed as espousing Turkish nationalism). Nancy's thoughts are illuminating on this point: '"In" the "NOTHING" or in nothing – in sovereignty – being is *"outside itself"*; it is . . . of an outside that it cannot relate to *itself*, but with which it entertains an essential and incommensurable relation. This relation prescribes the place of the singular being' (Nancy 1991: 18, emphasis in original). What is captured in the 'they', which I will continue to refer to throughout the book, is the counter-conduct of community at the centre of my analysis. In setting 'community' up as an exteriority, this 'they' also founds the singularity of the subject. And in doing so, it wants to evacuate the sovereignty that conducted this subject as a subject of community in the first place. In speaking of a 'they', community is counter-posed to the 'self', but 'community' is also recognized as being invested with a power to conduct a population and render it 'community'. At the same time, the self is not categorically positioned against community – exteriority is not contradiction, it is the foundation of a dialectic that in being worked out questions the sovereign power of putting bounds around 'community', fencing some people in and some out. The nuances involved in this discourse of counter-conduct are eschewed by analyses of 'resistance' that might instead focus on the normative level of 'rights', and lead us to consider the formalized discourse of the need to preserve Poşpoş as a Turkish heritage site as the only counter-position to Greek state practices of neglect.

If both the destruction of the site and the calls for its restoration indicate governmentalities that seek to create 'population' (in positing the minority as a unified entity), Selda's wavering hints at a different sort of counter-conduct, one that dis-assembles this 'population'. The family stories presented in the following sections elucidate this process of dis-assembly and tension with concepts of 'community' that inevitably frame them. In exploring the tensions between unity, multiplicity, and fragmentation that constitute notions of 'community' in the era of modern statehood, Nancy suggests that community 'emerged from the disappearance or the conservation of something – tribes or empires – perhaps just as unrelated to what we call "community" as to what we call "society." So that community, far from being what society has crushed or lost, is *what happens to us* – question, waiting, event, imperative – *in the wake of* society' (1991: 11, emphasis in original). This process of 'happening' is what I want to describe here, in order to show how 'question, waiting, event, imperative' ultimately come to constitute 'us' as subjects under question (our collectivity and allegiance to the power that conducts us as subjects being uncertain), subjects in waiting, wavering between community, individuality, society, and population.

Genealogical Legacies

Speaking of his likeness to his grandfather who 'liked drink and women', Celal traced the beginning of his *soy* (lineage) right back to Ridvan, his great-grandfather, 'where the *soy* [the consanguineal ancestral family]

Map 2.1 Regional borders in 1878 and towns mentioned in life stories

begins'. Ridvan lived in a village in what is now Bulgaria during the second half of the nineteenth century. He was one of eight children, and the father of Celal (the grandfather of the storyteller). Ridvan left the village in the late 1870s, after it had been incorporated in the recently autonomized territories of Bulgaria (map 2.1).[1] The rest of Thrace was still part of the Ottoman Empire, but was undergoing similar processes of autonomization, with elections for deputy councils. Ridvan followed a southerly migratory route, on which he met and married Fatma. She came from a village in the Rhodoppe mountains near the border that divided the Ottoman Empire and the newly autonomous Principality of Eastern Rumelia. They first settled in Kavala, in the region of Macedonia, before making a permanent home in Komotini. Celal (the grandfather) was born during his parents' stay in Kavala. Ridvan's settlement in Gümülcine (before its incorporation into Greece as Komotini) is thought to have been motivated by the violence that had gripped the region of Macedonia (extending to Kavala) around the times of the Balkans wars (1912–1913).

From 1913 to 1923, Gümülcine came under Bulgarian administration twice (October 1912–July 1913 and October 1913–August 1919), once under Greek administration (July–August 1913) before its 'liberation' in May 1920 and eventual incorporation into the Greek state in 1923, once under a French allied mandate (August 1919–May 1920), and twice under self-rule (August–October 1913 and October 1919–May 1920 in conjunction with the French Mandate).[2] These shifts were the result of volatile border-setting processes taking place in the context of the Balkan Wars (1912–1913), First World War (1914–1918), and the Greco-Turkish war (1919–1922). In the area through which Ridvan and his family moved during this period, these processes must have been experienced as a series of violent events of different intensity ranging from war and occupation to skirmishes and intimidation.

Ridvan's flight is thus probably revealing of the micro-politics of deciding where 'safety' lay amidst constant border shifts prompted by and inducing shifts in the calibration of 'ethnicity'. Deciding what one was and plotting this on a demographic map, waging war over who would rule these demographically-defined ethnic subjects, and debating their right to exist on this or that side of the border, were all technologies used in this calibration, means of deciding what difference consisted in and how much difference the nation-state would tolerate. They were ways of conducting, in the sense of managing, ethnicity. For people who set off looking for safety, these forms of conduct would have induced localized attacks and friendly warnings that were then negotiated amongst family and friends. How much fear was tolerable? How many stories of flight before one was on the road? How close to power did a warning need to be to be believed? How totalizing was mass flight? How far was far enough in the flight to safety? Knowledge of the micro-politics that negotiated these questions has been buried with Ridvan, Fatma, and Celal. What is known is that Ridvan's brothers, who left Bulgaria at the same time, followed a less elaborate route, settling in eastern Thrace and Bursa. Were these locations perhaps a more 'correct' choice for settlement, if seen with the benefit of hindsight, given their eventual incorporation into the Turkish state? Did Ridvan's settlement in Komotini ultimately result in a permanent state of displacement? These are implicit questions circumscribed by the logic of the nation-state, which the story's development – again implicitly – answers in the negative (thus also putting this logic under question). Komotini was not the wrong choice as place of residence because there Ridvan's descendants should have a place – and if they do not, the onus is not on them but on the process that decides who should and should not have such a place.

This makes it possible to celebrate the lives that Ridvan and Celal (senior) lived in Komotini subsequently to displacement as part of the family's heritage. In the story, Celal grew up in Gümülcine and soon began to make his living as an owner of sheep and cattle, which brought him wealth. Celal is remembered as a great hunter and the expeditions he organized in the mountains were lavish affairs with all the trimmings: horses, dogs, expensive guns and lots of entertainment (primarily involving alcohol and sex). This 'must be a family trait', Celal junior surmised, since his namesake's mother Fatma is described in similar terms, with her most celebrated qualities being traditional male ones of resolution, determination, perseverance, and courage. Her most renowned pose is in a photograph showing her dressed in full hunting gear, riding next to her husband. In this masculinist account, Celal's wife's woes over her husband's 'naughty' habits, another 'family trait' that Celal junior inherited, seemed out of place: 'she cursed my grandfather on her deathbed', he remembered, laughing. Read as a form of counter-conduct to the minority status he inherited, gender is used as a marker of a 'political DNA' that situates him in this location as descendant of resolute and courageous, if also profligate, people – not victims of war and oppression. In choosing one genealogy over another, Celal points subtly to the aporia of whether that ancestral settlement in what is now a Greek *topos* (a place in the national imaginary) was ultimately a dis-placed choice. In the nonchalance of his laughter, the gender politics that characterize his genealogy of preference is equated to the ethnic politics that would characterize a genealogy of victimhood, and together both are mocked. At the end of the story, habits are passed on as life continues, the mountains of Rhodoppe are now homely hunting grounds, and Bursa (where Ridvan's relatives sought refuge) a place 'over there' home to relations one seldom sees.

İsmail is another ancestor, of a different family, who followed a similar trajectory. He left Bulgaria when he was very young, in the 1870s, and initially went to Yanya (current-day Ioannina, north-western Greece), where a Greek family adopted him. His granddaughter recounted how, 'luckily', they respected his religion and arranged for him to have a *sünnet* (circumcision). He worked as an apprentice and eventually became skilled in skin processing and dyeing. When violence spread to the area, he was warned by Greek friends that he should leave otherwise his life would be in danger, so he set off for Gümülcine, where the Turkish community was growing. There he married Zehra, who was a Pomak and also an immigrant from Bulgaria, and they had four children. He continued tanning, but also began tailoring, making *potur* (men's trousers, usually made of stiff black cloth, baggy at the hip and narrower at the bottom). He probably married a Pomak because no Turkish Gümülcineli bride would marry an outsider (and a tanner to boot), his great-granddaughter joked. İsmail's story is again one of displacement and emplacement, this time in a way that also crosscuts presumptions of ethnic purity. In pondering the possibility of becoming Greek through adoption ('luckily' averted), and acknowledging the part-Pomak ancestry of the family, the contingency of

İsmail's descendants being here and now (and being minority subjects) is acknowledged. The micro-politics of violence (the reasons that led him to part from his family, the form which his 'adoption' took and how it related to his lowly profession, the circumstances of his departure from Ioannina), just as in Ridvan's story, are long buried and impossible to explore.

At around that time (1880s), Hasan also migrated to Gümülcine, with his wife. They left their house in Felibe (current-day Plovdid, in Bulgaria). In Gümülcine Hasan got a job in an oil factory on the outskirts of the town, as a security officer. His granddaughter, Ayşe, who died in 1995, would often recount a particular story about him to her own grandchildren. In 1913, when the Bulgarians took control of Thrace, or sometime after, Hasan's friends decided to play a joke on him. They ambushed him as he was returning home from the factory one night, and without letting him see them, they passed a ring fixed onto wooden planks round his neck and led him into the town. Thinking that they were really Bulgarians, and that his life was seriously in danger, Hasan had wet his pants by the time he arrived into the town, which caused great amusement to his fellow townsmen for a long time after.

Under the Treaty of Bucharest (August 1913), Bulgaria gained access to the Aegean through the control of the region of western Thrace (Map 2.2). Bulgarians had been in control of Gümülcine since October 1912, with the exception of a month-long period of Greek control (July–August 1913) and two months of self-rule under a 'Provisional Government of Western Thrace', inaugurated by a Turkish-Pomak rebellion (August–October 1913). Bulgarian control was re-established again in October 1913 when self-government was dissolved with the Treaty of Constantinople/Istanbul (September 1913), which transposed the provisions (mostly in terms of territorial adjustments) of the Treaty of Bucharest (signed between Greece and its allies and Bulgaria) onto the plane of Bulgarian-Ottoman relations. Hasan's fear of the Bulgarians might be due to the heightened measures of repression that occurred after Bulgarian control was reinstalled, or – as will be seen below – the result of his experience of seeing his son-in-law die during a Bulgarian attack in 1913 (presuming the incident recounted by his granddaughter took place after). Why his 'friends' thought this was an appropriate prank to play in this context, the specifics of his relationship with them, or whether Hasan had additional reasons to fear reprisals against the Muslims by the Bulgarians at this point remain buried parts of the story. For whatever reasons, despite this fear, Hasan did not take up the right granted him under the Treaty to emigrate to Ottoman lands within four years. Under the Treaty of Istanbul, this was a clause that introduced displacement/'relocation' as a technology of nation-state purification and

Map 2.2 Border shifts in western and eastern Thrace 1913–1923

'population exchange' as the instrument of this purification in terms of management on the level of realpolitik.

Similarly, İbrahim, who was at that time a local (and on which basis his descendants claim 'real' Gümülcineli ancestry), remained in Komotini, despite the fact that he had been an Ottoman civil servant during the late nineteenth century, travelling extensively throughout the Empire. After years of travelling, he returned and settled in Gümülcine, marrying locally and building the house in which I interviewed his great-granddaughter in the late 1990s. His family was one of the richest in the town, but of his four children only one, Osman, stayed in Gümülcine; the others emigrated to Eskişehir and Istanbul, both of which were places where he had served for long periods. Osman's sons used their share of the wealth to become richer and his daughter married into a wealthy Istanbuli family (patrilocal marriage residence being the norm among western Thracian Muslims).

Taken together, the stories of Rıdvan, İsmail, Hasan, and İbrahim speak of the complex and now largely irrecoverable ways in which shifts in the borders of states seeking to consolidate their sovereignty in the region during that era of nation-building prompted shifts in the movement (and immobility) of people, who were seeking 'safety', 'rights', 'freedom', or perhaps life, livelihood, or laughter. At the end of the Balkan Wars two new *mahalles* (neighbourhoods) formed in Komotini to accommodate Turkish newcomers who, having left areas designated as Bulgarian after 1870, found themselves under Bulgarian rule again. These mahalles etched into the urban landscape even more starkly the ethnic segregation that attended the nationalist governmentalities of population.

Counting prospective subjects was developing into a 'war of statistics' (Michailidis 1998), with local and foreign commissions producing figures that would be debated in the diplomatic battles over treaties. This economy of population was less benign than Foucault might have anticipated in describing it as the welfare sought at the end of the equation linking people, territory, and production. It was guided by the goal of achieving ethnically pure majorities from which minorities could do nothing but detract.[3] Matching these majority-minority sums with concerns over resources (e.g. access to the Aegean) would yield the legal instruments (treaties) that subjected the population to decisions about whether to leave or to stay, firstly by allowing or disallowing residence and secondly through the rights conferred on 'settled', 'repatriated', 'established', or 'minority' populations. Through these stipulations, populations were created and then rendered particular kinds of subjects.

As such mechanisms of subjectification (*dispositifs* as Foucault would say), these treaties established a particular linkage between knowledge and power that subjectified not only the populations referenced in their articles. They also subjectified future populations that would only become subject populations once new border shifts, outside the legal and territorial bounds of the treaties at hand, had taken place. Recall the definition used for the population that was to be exempted from the compulsory exchange convention attached to the Lausanne Treaty of 1923: 'All Moslems established in the region to the east of the frontier line laid down in 1913 by the Treaty of Bucharest shall be considered as Moslem inhabitants of Western Thrace' [Article 2, Convention concerning the Exchange of Greek and Turkish Populations, 1923]. However the (Bulgaro-Ottoman) Treaty of Istanbul, for example, may have affected Hasan's decision to continue living under 'the Bulgarian yoke' at the time of its conclusion, it was the Treaty of Athens (November 1913), signed between the Kingdom of Greece and the Ottoman Empire in order to transpose the Treaty of Bucharest in bilateral relations, and of no significance to Hasan in 1913, that would classify him and his descendants as *établis* ten years later, when Bulgarian would give way to Greek rule. When the Treaty of Athens was implemented, a governmentality of population was implanted in the region that would form a basis of conducting that population as 'minority' when the Lausanne Treaty indirectly made reference to it a decade later. Shifts in the regional order took place in the meantime, as new and old states drew and re-drew their borders (Old Greece, new Greece, Ottoman Empire, Turkey), each time subjectifying peoples anew, yet always on the back of previous *dispositifs* of subjectification.

Displacement and Un-mixing

The effects of the application of these governmentalities were exposed much more dramatically in a first-hand story I heard about pre-1923 displacement. I met Eleni, a Turkish-speaking Christian Orthodox, in May 1999. Although most Turkish-speaking Orthodox Christians who settled in western Thrace after the region's 'liberation' by the Greek army in 1920 were Karamanlıs (mainly refugees from the Kayseri area), Eleni was a Gagauz – a member of a much smaller group inhabiting a couple of villages in Rhodoppe, and a few villages in the neighbouring prefecture of Evros. Speaking in her Turkish mother tongue, she explained that she was born in 1905 in a village in eastern Thrace. She remembered going to Bulgaria (under the control of which western Thrace was then), when she was eight (1913), to escape the war (for which she used the old word *cenk* rather than the more current *savaş*). Her father was fighting in it, so her mother left with the children, and they did not hear from him again, presuming he had died there. They stayed in Bulgaria for four years, until the end of the First World War. In 1918, Eleni's family were told that they could return to their village in eastern Thrace, which they proceeded to do. The family stayed in the village for six months and then moved back into Bulgaria, where they stayed for a couple of months before returning again. At this point the Greco-Turkish War (1919–1922) was underway, and the Greek army was advancing towards Istanbul (it eventually stopped at Dedeağaç, now Alexandroupoli, the capital of the western Thracian district of Evros, when Turkey asked for an armistice). With the signing of the Treaty of Sèvres in 1920, which gave Greece control over most of eastern Thrace, the decision must have been taken to move back into the family house (Map 2.2). Their next move only happened in 1923, when the boundary shifted again, bringing eastern Thrace under the control of the Turkish state, with the Treaty of Lausanne (July 1923). The Treaty also made compulsory the Muslim-Christian population exchange between Turkey and Greece, which meant that about 200,000 Christians living in the Ottoman Empire were to be forcibly moved to Greece in exchange for about 350,000 Muslims living in Greece who would move to the recently established Turkish Republic. This was in addition to a further estimated million Christians who had already made the move prior to 1923 to escape hostilities (Hirschon 2003: 14–15).

At this point, Turkish-speaking Orthodox Christians found themselves at a difficult crossroads. Eleni explained that they had to choose between giving up their language and giving up their religion; they chose the first – '*dilimizi verdik, dinimizi vermedik*' (we gave our language, we did not give our religion), as she put it. That is how they ended up coming to western Thrace as refugees with the population exchange (seemingly having chosen the classification of 'Christian' over 'Turkish') and settling in a mixed (Greek and Turkish) village in the valley of western Thrace. Because her father had died during the war, her family found it difficult to cope with the hardship of the initial period. They eventually built a house in the village, where other Turkish-speaking Orthodox had already settled. She married and had four children; she lost one, but the other three continued to visit her. Her husband had died long ago. She was the only one in the village who spoke the old Turkish dialect and who could speak of those times from personal experience.

Against the background of the nation-state governmentality, shaped by the periods of war in which her family displacements took place, Eleni's story speaks of an uncertain positioning towards the political DNA that concepts of ethnicity sought to ascribe to individuals at the time. Was Eleni's mother a Turkish-speaking Christian Orthodox, 'Greek' or 'Turk'? Were the repeated movements to Bulgaria indicative of an Exarchist (and therefore 'Bulgarian') or Patriarchist (and therefore 'Greek') identity? For whom, indeed, had her father been fighting at the front? What Eleni articulates would indicate that her eventual 'Greek' ethnicity was decided on the basis of contemporaneous political context and the seemingly accidental categorization as an exchangee. Moving to the closest non-hostile state in the midst of a growing and pressing convergence between religion and statehood in Ottoman eastern Thrace, which until 1919 shared borders with Bulgaria but not Greece, was probably less about being Bulgarian, Greek, or Turkish than about moving temporarily, until 'normality' was restored. For Eleni, becoming a subject of the 'Convention concerning the Exchange of Greek and Turkish Populations' (January 1923), appended to the Lausanne Peace Treaty (July 1923), was more a matter of having happened to be at her native location at that particular time than about being represented in the category of 'Greekness' that the Treaty set up. Eleni's subsequent rationalization – of preferring to give up language over religion – seems, in this context, to be an attempt at legitimizing (albeit in heroic terms) the choice that was enforced upon a wartime widow looking to protect her life and her children. It is an articulation of counter-conduct that speaks of the difficulties of ethnic 'un-mixing' that Hirschon problematizes (2003: 3–12) in the discourses that take nation-state concepts of 'ethnicity' for granted. To Eleni's mother, such unmixing may have appeared more in terms of an emergency that threw her life into dramatic disarray than the norm of governing population (rationalized by those drawing the boundaries). Eleni thus emerges as a biopolitical subject, in the sense of having her life conducted differently in myriad micro-ways in the everyday because of who the law made her in 1923. Furthermore, her story speaks of the burial of a subjecthood that has now become irrecoverable in Thrace: that of the Bulgarians (one of which Eleni might have become, had circumstances been different) who have been completely erased from the western Thracian landscape.

Hints of this burial are to be found in some villages, whose churches stand out in their straight-lined, cubic architecture from the domed 'Greek' churches. One such village is next to Ali's, a man of about the same age as Eleni, who remembered the 'coming of the refugees'. His own village is wholly Turkish (i.e. not 'mixed'), and is located in a cluster of mostly Turkish villages. However, in the past, he remembered, there used to be a number of Bulgarian villages in the area. Then a lot of the Bulgarians left, soldiers came and left, and finally they all left. Then the Greeks (refugees) came. The progressive evacuation of Bulgarians described by Ali is likely to refer to the period of the Balkan Wars, the Bulgarian occupation of the First World War, and the ceding of western Thrace from Bulgaria to Greece agreed under the Treaty of Neuilly-sur-Seine (November 1919). Under that treaty, 'Bulgarian nationals habitually resident in the territories assigned to Greece [excepting those who became resident in these territories after January 1, 1913 would] obtain Greek nationality ipso facto and [would] lose their Bulgarian nationality' unless they chose to opt for Bulgarian nationality within a period of two years from the agreement of the Treaty, upon which decision they were expected to 'transfer their place of residence to the State for which they have opted' within twelve months (Articles 44 and 45). How exactly this 'voluntary exchange of populations', as it problematically came to be known, modelled on the 1913 Treaty of Istanbul (Meindersma 1997), worked in practice so that no Bulgarians are now to be found in western Thrace, is a question that pertains to the 'crude' forms taken by 'state power over the individual' (Hisrchon 2003: 27).[4]

Exception and Event

This 'stripping down' of life involved in what proved to be a non-choice thus appears to have been far from voluntary, and far from exceptional. In this context, the compulsory exchange of populations under the Treaty of Lausanne, which turned the tables and excepted not those who chose to move, but those who chose to stay, represents the apogee of this process. For whereas, similarly to the Treaty of Istanbul, the Treaty of Sèvres (1920) also provided that '[p]ersons over eighteen years of age losing their Turkish nationality and obtaining ipso facto a new nationality under Article 123 shall be entitled within a period of one year from the coming into force of the present Treaty to opt for Turkish nationality' (Article

124) and that such persons 'must within the succeeding twelve months transfer their place of residence to the State for which they have opted' (Article 126), the Treaty of Lausanne stipulated exactly the opposite. To be precise, the Treaty's main text normalized this practice of voluntary displacement, in stipulating in its Article 31 that '[p]ersons . . . losing their Turkish nationality [according to the Article 30 because of habitual residence 'in territory . . . detached from Turkey'] and obtaining *ipso facto* a new nationality under Article 30, shall be entitled within a period of two years from the coming into force of the present Treaty to opt for Turkish nationality', and in Article 32 that these persons 'must, within the succeeding twelve months, transfer their place of residence to the State for which they have opted'. This referred largely to territories outside the Greece-Turkey dispute: territories ceded to colonial powers (Cyprus, Egypt, Sudan, Libya, and some Aegean islands under Italian control) and territories already incorporated into other Balkan states (Bulgaria, Romania, and Hungary). Furthermore, subsequent litigation exposed the weakness of this formulation when a former Turkish resident of Palestine claimed British nationality (*The King v. Ketter* case of 1939, cited in Quingley 2010: 40–41).

The 'Convention concerning the Exchange of Greek and Turkish Populations' of January 1923, annexed as item VI to the Treaty is of a very different disposition. It provided that '[a]s of the 1st May, 1923, there shall take place a compulsory exchange of Turkish nationals of the Greek Orthodox religion established in Turkish territory, and of Greek nationals of the Moslem religion established in Greek territory' (Article 1). This stipulation was the critical event that established 'population' in Greece and Turkey as imagined 'pure' populations. The concomitant critical event for the establishment of population in western Thrace was the Convention's second article which reads:

> The following persons shall not be included in the exchange provided for in Article 1:
> (a.) The Greek inhabitants of Constantinople
> (b.) The Moslem inhabitants of Western Thrace.
> . . . All Moslems established in the region to the east of the frontier line laid down in 1913 by the Treaty of Bucharest shall be considered as Moslem inhabitants of Western Thrace.

This event was noticeably absent from the Gümülcineli stories I collected. Yet it was not that it was not acknowledged as a critical event in terms of how Gümülcinelis understand their identity today. Selda has kept her great-grandmother's *Certificat d'Etabli* (Figure 2.2), passed on to her from her mother, safe among old family photos and protected in a special folder. She considers it important for her own place in the

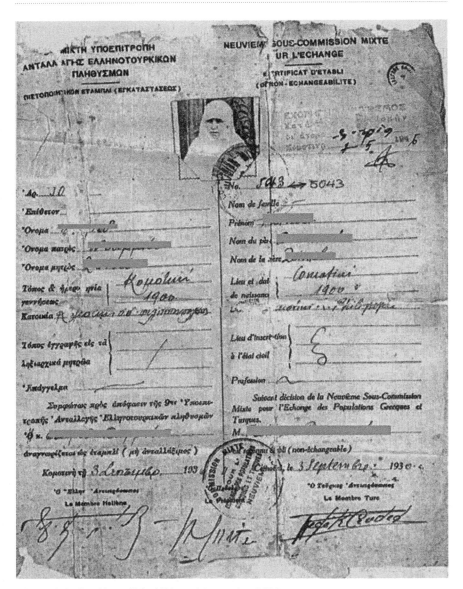

Figure 2.2 Certificat d' établi issued September 1930

minority's large-scale history, but she has no stories passed down, funny or otherwise, about how exactly her great-grandmother acquired it. Was the process complicated? Did she wait in queues? Who filled in the form? If an official, was this official memorable? Did her husband provide it on her behalf? Another great-grandfather's certificate posed a bigger puzzle:

on it, he was declared to have been born in 1879, yet Selda remembered that he had died in 1975 in his seventies. 'He gave the wrong date to the authorities', her mother explained, 'to avoid the military. He was actually born in 1900'. In 1923, an 1879 birth date would have made him forty-five, the cut-off point for conscription. What made the authorities believe that a twenty-three-year-old was forty-five opens another series of questions about the process of certification. How he managed to conduct his life as a Greek citizen perpetually over-aged by twenty-one years (and was this a life immersed in counter-conduct?), is a different series of questions about the relations between the state and minority citizens that pertained during his lifetime.

The lack of emphasis in stories on this critical event of 'establishment' underlines the gap between the normality of staying, and the many minor 'abnormal' things that people did to cope with that 'normality'. It must be remembered that this normality was formulated as 'exception'. Under the Lausanne Convention, *établis* were established not so much as 'natives' (their 'establishment' having been decided according to the political criterion of the Treaty of Bucharest), but more as 'exceptions to the exception'. In fact only a year later, the interpretation of how to define the category 'established' would be a matter of legal questioning before the Permanent Court of International Justice in relation to the Greeks of Istanbul (*Greece v. Turkey*, Advisory Opinion No. 10, 21 February 1925). Questions would be raised about whether 'Article 2 of the Convention was a mere exception to Article 1, or whether, on the contrary, it laid down the principle of non-liability to exchange within its own sphere of application' and about 'the grammatical meaning of the word "established", more particularly as compared with the word "domiciled"' (§ 16). Determining 'establishment', was, in other words, about regulating, that is conducting legally, the exception of remaining in one's home within the exceptional context of being forced to abandon it. Such regulation was necessary because the exception to the exception did not equal 'normality'. In fact, a special regime of governance was needed to maintain this distinction between double exception and normality. This was the rubric under which 'minority' was conducted.

The 'normality' of exception, experienced by the masses who were displaced together with Eleni, featured as a critical event in the stories I collected in the villages of the western Thracian valley, which accommodated these refugees. One of these villages was Ali's. Ali remembered the coming of the refugees to the village, the squalid conditions, and the hardships inflicted on both locals and newcomers. The latter had nowhere to stay and the government made the villagers put them up in their own houses, he said. They stayed for months, until new houses were built for them, and they then moved to the new villages.

Because most of the refugees that arrived in northern Greece (primarily from eastern Thrace) were settled in rural areas, the demographic ratio changed more spectacularly in the valley than the town. In rough estimates, the number of Greek villages in the Rhodoppe prefecture rose from fifteen to forty, most of them being formed from new settlements (*ikizmi*). As this took place over the subsequent decades, one might suppose that for a number of years refugee accommodation would have been a sore point for guests and hosts alike. Reports of that time describe refugees living in schools, monasteries and sheds, threatened by disease, facing 'hardship and death', to the extent that the High Commissioner for Refugees at the League of Nations Fridtjof Nansen lobbied the League to approve a loan to Greece to alleviate the situation and humanitarian organizations for assistance (Divani 1999: 69–71). With the exchange agreement not yet in force, the Muslim inhabitants of northern Greece who had not yet made the move to Turkey had already been rendered conceptually an obstacle to Greece's ability to respond to the dire situation and 'anxious telegrams were reaching Venizelos in Lausanne asking for the Convention to be effective from the date of signature, not ratification. If the Muslims did not leave their houses and fields imminently, where were the refugees to be housed?' (ibid.: 7).

It might therefore be surmised that the *établis*, like Ali, would have been seen by the state, in the local context at least, not as 'established' but rather as exceptional obstacles to refugee settlement. This was the point at which 'rooted-ness' was reconfigured on the basis of ethno-national terms instead of geographic ones, when it came to mean the opposite of physical/'natural' connections. Ali pointed towards the neighbouring village and said that it used to be a Bulgarian one, which was abandoned before the Greeks moved in. It seemed to me that there was a sense of resentment in what he described but he did not want to be questioned further. 'The village you asked for is down there', he said, 'and I have to tend to my work now'.[5] Burying is a choice which is configured within the same false parameters of 'freedom' that decide who belongs and who does not (and who is given an option and who is not), and when exactly disinterring the story might jeopardize that belonging.

The village 'down there' is in fact a double village, in the sense that the Christian and Turkish mahalles are at a considerable distance from each other so that the village is in fact encountered as two clusters of houses. The Turkish part is on a hill, overlooking the Greek one. Adnan is one of the very few Turks who have stayed in the village. He is in his late forties and although he does not remember the Bulgarians or the arrival of the refugees from his own personal experience, he is well aware of the nuances of Greek experience. He jokes about the fact that half the Greeks in the village do not like the other half, by virtue of being Sarakaçan and Karamanlıs respectively. Karamanlıs are Christians from Anatolia who speak Turkish but use the Greek alphabet. For this reason, their identity is considered somewhat suspect by the Sarakaçans, who up until the 1940s were transhumant shepherds, before the government gave them incentives to settle in villages. Because the Sarakaçans are considered as 'locals' and because there have been various campaigns to present them as 'pure Greeks', and especially in Thrace as 'pure Thracians', they consider themselves as more patriotic than the Karamanlıs, which Adnan finds quite amusing. Not far from his village, the landscape on the side of the old highway takes on an exhibitionary aspect as one drives along. A cluster of model Sarakatsan huts are on show, announcing the musealization of Thracian traditional life – and by implication pointing to those who 'traditionally' (i.e. rightfully) belong here and those who do not. Here, the 'accident' of the Sarakatsans having been the first group to be ethnographically studied in Greece (Campbell 1964) suddenly gains an exclusionary undertone. Adnan used the same trope I had seen accompanying implicit references to the vexed question of belonging amongst my Gümülcineli friends – laughter – only this time he articulated it explicitly: 'They will sometimes say to us "if you don't like it here go back where you came from" – well, this is where we came from, and if anybody is from over there [points east, to the direction of Turkey], it's the Greeks themselves! We have roots here (*köklerimiz burdan*).'

This statement shows quite clearly the ramifications of recent history on present-day Thrace – the exception to the exception countered by the paradox of displacement. It underlines every one of the stories so far presented.

From the North and from the East

While the First World and Greco-Turkish wars were raging, the families of Celal, İsmail, Hasan, and İbrahim were growing; they had eleven children in total, most of whom had been around at the time the stories above were unfolding. All were first-generation Gümülcinelis growing up in a place that they called their own, in opposition to their parents who had got to know Gümülcine in a very different way. Celal was slowly building his fortune through animal trading and meat selling. İsmail was raising his three children; the eldest of these was actually his nephew, whom he undertook to look after following the death of his sister-in-law.

Hasan's daughter, Emine, had been born in Gümülcine around 1886 and had been known in her youth as '*güzel Emine*' (the Beautiful Emine), which, in conjunction with her father's white-collar job, must have made her a highly desirable bride. She married Salih, a few years her senior, and together they set up a restaurant. Emine spent most of her time over the fire, preparing meals and coffees for the patrons. According to her descendants, this job ultimately killed her in 1910, after she had suffered many years of lung disease. She had by then given birth to one daughter, Ayşe who would recount Hasan's funny story to her own grandchildren. In fact, Ayşe knew her grandparents much better than she knew her parents since Salih did not live long enough to bring up his daughter. In 1913, when the Bulgarians occupied Thrace, they attacked him one night and hurt him so seriously that despite the family's efforts to heal his wounds by wrapping him in animal skin, he did not survive. Ayşe was then six and this was one of her earliest memories, yet this was not a story that she recounted as often as that of Hasan's (presumably later) encounter with the fake 'Bulgarians' of his friends' hoax. She was raised by her grandparents and stepmother, whom Salih had married out of obligation and need. She was his sister-in-law, widowed when Salih's brother died a few years before Emine's death; in marrying her, Salih did what was then usual practice, and he also needed somebody to look after Ayşe who was only two.

Ayşe got married about a decade after her father's death, to Halil, who had recently returned from the front, fighting for the Turkish army in the War of Liberation (*Kurtuluş Savaşı*) against the Greeks. Although Halil was awarded for his contribution to the war over the previous six years, with a comfortable house and plenty of land in Turkey, he preferred to return to Gümülcine, now under the Greeks, and live on the family land. There are no stories of discrimination towards him but his years of service with the Turkish army mean that he is still treated with great caution by his descendants and is rarely mentioned. The 'Declaration of Amnesty' attached to the Lausanne Agreement, which allowed him to live the rest of his days as an *établi*, stipulated that

> No person who inhabits or has inhabited Turkey, and reciprocally no person who inhabits or has inhabited Greece, shall be disturbed or molested in Turkey or reciprocally in Greece, under any pretext whatsoever, on account of any military or political action taken by him, or any assistance of any kind given by him to a foreign Power signatory of the Treaty of Peace signed this day, or to the nationals of such Power, between the 1st August, 1914, and the 20th November, 1922. (Article 1)

The Amnesty Declaration appears to have interpellated both him and his descendants as subjects who had once been hostile to the state – tied by a 'political and military' DNA that is best left buried. 'He got the amnesty but we don't talk about it', Selda's aunt explained with a wink, correcting the fragments that her niece was trying to piece together for me – humour surfacing again to smooth the glare of unearthing history.[6]

Explaining her use of 'political DNA' in her analysis of the historical persecution of the left in Greece, Panourgiá states that '[w]hat I mean by this is that the Greek state has, from the beginning of the Leftist movement, articulated a thought about the Left that rests, on the one hand, upon understanding kinship as a purely biological category and, on the other, on a notion that social and political behaviour are overdetermined' (2009: 214). In this chapter, I have invoked the notion not simply as a substitute to 'ethnicity', but as a means of underscoring the fact that such overdetermination has been linked ever more tightly to that of ethnic difference. An amnestied Greek citizen has been subjectified as first 'amnestied', then 'citizen', and perhaps never 'Greek' – and this subjectification is continued through to his descendants in the knowledge that this is a buried story. The descendant of an *établi* has kept her grandmother's certificate as a family heirloom, testifying to a matrilineal subjectification into citizenhood. A minority villager refers to ancestors in order to articulate rootedness to a now Greek place. In contrast to the idea of 'becoming' that the Greek left has appropriated in its counter-conduct to the state (Panourgiá 2009: 215), the stories I have recounted here converge on a counter-conduct that accepts the logic of genealogy as a mode of political subjectivity. Yet in accepting that one is born into the 'minority condition' (unlike one who becomes leftist through endurance of oppression and torture), and in articulating that acceptance through humour and laughter, a 'minority' population is set up that cannot quite encompass that multitude of divergences from 'the' minority story that that humour and laughter brush aside. Buried minority stories thus emerge as asides to the 'main' minority story – a story of 'established' Turks and communal rights (e.g. over heritage, as described in the beginning of this chapter), a story that is unconcerned with the displacements (territorial, legal, genealogical, affective) that preceded this 'establishment', and which only 'partial' family stories can articulate. Through the humour of story-telling, hybridizations and other complexities that the main story would also silence, appear. Such are the affective relations of appreciation and respect of a Muslim boy's genealogy in the arrangement of a religious rite of passage by Orthodox foster parents (whatever the specific configurations of that relationship might have been at the time). Such is also the resolution of a purported incompatibility between Pomaks and Turks that marriage in the aftermath of war 'necessitated'. Together, these asides form the ground on which the distanced 'they', through which a person is alienated from 'community' without abandoning it, develops.

As I explore this development in the rest of the book, I will be returning to the legacy of the critical event of the establishment of 'minority' as the community in question, a community conducted in specific ways and counter-conducted in multiple forms. The following chapters thus explore how 'roots' came to signify relations other than those of living on the land, through a process of nationalization that delegitimized such physical bonds, thereby rendering them 'out of place'. This was the same process that re-invested with meaning the locations signified by the 'here' and 'there' of a villager pointing eastwards to articulate 'rootedness'. As a result of this process, the 'North' and the 'East' were displaced from signification as locations intimately connected to migrants and refugees of previous decades, becoming instead the locations of the Greek state's two gravest threats (Bulgaria and Turkey). In the following pages I will explore the process of un-doing and re-fashioning history, space, and ethnicity along the same axes that redefined 'roots' and 'enemies'.

Notes

1. The Exarchate was granted autonomy in 1870 and the Principality of Bulgaria was established with the San Stefano Treaty (March 1878), which ended the Russo-Turkish War (1877–1878). Its territory included parts of Thrace and Macedonia (including Kavala) but not Komotini. The Treaty was revised by the Berlin Treaty (July 1878), which returned most of Macedonia and Thrace gains to the Ottoman Empire and established Eastern Rumelia (roughly in the region of northern Thrace) as an autonomous province (which would be annexed by Bulgaria in 1885). Bulgaria gained full independence in 1908. Here, and for the rest of the chapter, information on the general history of the Balkans has been collated from a number of authors, including Castellan (1996), Llewellyn Smith (1998), Pavlowitch (1999), Glenny (2000), Mazower (2002), and Gerolymatos (2002).
2. See Yaz (1986: 113–174), Oran (1991: 27–38), Akgönül (1999: 20–24), Divani (1999: 167–192).
3. One might also wonder here about Foucault's analysis of racism and the implications of his emphasis on denizens of 'majority' populations (see also Stoler 1995).
4. Petitions to the League of Nations, as Cowan reports for the 'Organisation of Exiles and Refugees from Thrace in Bulgaria', continued until at least 1927. However, as the problem was considered to have been 'solved', such complaints were dismissed as being guided by nationalist interests (Cowan 2007: 38–39).
5. It is noticeable that national identities seem here to be defined by movement. Thus in terms of my previous discussion, 'Bulgarians' figure as people who lived in specific villages, but most importantly who left, whereas 'Greeks' are those who came. In one sense, then, Ali is articulating a concept of 'nationality' that seems self-evident, but Eleni's case shows it is not.
6. I have in mind Ballinger's discussion of the tropes used to discuss 'the nontransparency of [violence being remembered]'and her problematization of concepts of unearthing, exhuming, disinterring, and bringing to light 'buried histories' (2003: 14). The following quotation is poignant: 'the violent event persists like crushed

glass in one's eyes. The light it generates, rather than helping us see, is blinding' (Daniel, quoted in ibid.). The employment of humour at such moments, which I have highlighted throughout this chapter, is indicative of both the uneasiness that this unearthing causes (as a Freudian account would suggest) and a recognition of articulating such uneasiness as possible counter-conduct. There is a depth of interpretation here, in other words, that humour enables without explicitly laying open all the analytic parameters – this is an issue I have explored in a different analysis of humour as a strategy of countering nationalism (Demetriou 2004a).

CHAPTER 3

COUNTER-BORDERING

Tempestuous Borders

One of the things that I hope to have shown in the previous chapter is the extended duration of the Great War for the region of western Thrace, which experienced the repercussions of violence much before 1914 and long after 1918. The Balkan Wars were succeeded by the First World War, succeeded in turn by the Greco-Turkish war, resulting in an almost uninterrupted decade of fighting. The scars of that fighting have undoubtedly left their mark, prefiguring the 'crazed network of trenches' (Macmillan 2001: 1) that scarred Great War battlefields in western Europe. Military history has it that the First Balkan War 'would be won and lost in Thrace' (Hall 2000: 23). The battles that extended Bulgarian control to the outskirts of Istanbul (Kırkkilise, Lüle-Burgaz, Çatalca, Edirne) raged in eastern Thrace. Western Thrace was taken by the Bulgarians in one bloodless sweep, between 22 and 26 November 1912 (ibid.: 42–43), explaining perhaps why Gümülcineli families like Hasan's and Ridvan's remained settled while eastern Thracian families like Eleni's embarked on their long pursuit of safety. But if the western Thracian landscape was spared the deepest scars of fighting during those wars, the constant shifting of borders marked it many times over. In each one of the treaties (London, Bucharest, Istanbul, Athens, Neuilly, Sèvres, Lausanne) that ended one cycle of fighting only to start another, lines on maps that became state borders on the ground were successively erased and re-drawn in ways that either directly or subsequently, affected western Thrace. Each treaty used the same phrasing to task scientific committees ('boundary commissions') with the 'trac[ing] on the ground of the frontier . . . follow[ing] as nearly as possible the description given [in each Treaty], taking into account as far as possible administrative boundaries and local economic interests' (this phrasing taken from the Lausanne Peace Treaty, Article 5). Such clauses lent scientific credence to the translation of the linguistics of geography (found in the description of borders under territorial clauses) into the materiality of boundary markers that did not always prioritize 'local economic interests', and other kinds of interests even less so. They instead ran across grazing grounds, between inter-marrying villages, even on the crests of waves in the rivers and lakes which the new borders now crossed (see also Tsibiridou 1994; Green and King 2001; Myrivili 2004). In the first two decades of the twentieth century, western Thrace experienced the ebb and flow of sovereign claims and compromises. The dizzying sketching and erasing of those borders, some lasting years, some only a few months, some never making it to the ground, is a prime illustration of the illusory fixity of boundaries that de-solidify the ground, making it look like a 'liquid land' (Cocco 2006: 8), bearing the temporal traces of 'tidemarks' (Green 2009).

The previous chapter showed that on the crest of those political waves of belligerence and negotiation rode people who left their native homelands to wander through the shifting geographies of the nation-state, settling in what would subsequently prove to be unsettled territories. This human flotsam and jetsam of the various wreckages of nation-state experimentation is what made western Thrace the Greek land it is today. The process of solidifying this Greekness is what I turn to in this chapter. From the perspective of the nation-state, these people may have been 'driftwood' to begin with (e.g. when the refugees were piled into makeshift homes and the voluntary exchangees were still deciding whether to relocate), but when the tide settled, the political work of constituting population had to begin. This is the focus of this chapter, which reviews the ideologies that drove policies of making the *établis* exception fit the norm of population. In doing so, the chapter traces the process by which borders on the ground bifurcate from lines of territorial consolidation into boundaries of racialized differentiation, frontiers of nationalist ideology, and limits marking the extent to which these can be questioned. During the process, the deceptive 'choice' offered to the flotsam of the displaced gave way to the agency of co-optation and counter-conduct that subjectified Komotinians and Gümülcinelis alike. Intellectuals, academics, historians, alongside state officials, teachers, members of cultural associations, readers of newspapers, audiences of varied events, as well as radicals and others, all took part in (even when resisting), this nation-building effort. This chapter tells their stories.

How Things Came to Be: Greek Stories

Greek historians of the region usually begin their story in antiquity, when Thrace used to be inhabited by *Thrakiká Fíla* (Thracian races).

These people were classified as 'barbarians' in relation to Athenians and Spartans, but were nevertheless Greek. 'Barbarian' is a historically loaded term that transposes insider/outsider distinctions onto conceptualizations of identities in antiquity. It is a term, as Greek schoolchildren often learn, referring primarily to the language that outsiders used in antiquity, which to the refined ears of Athenians sounded like a continual repetition of the syllables 'bar-bar'. Stilpon Kyriakides (1887–1963) is one of the leading figures in the formation of local historiography along these lines. He was a Greek Komotinian folklorist who wrote extensively on Thracian history and culture, and for this reason was honoured with having his name given to the street passing in front of the current Law School of the University of Thrace and his bust grace one of its junctions. Although Kyriakides was born in Komotini, he moved to Athens with his mother to attend secondary-school there, as the educational standard in the capital was higher. He went on to study philology at the University of Athens before moving to Germany, where he received instruction in the scrutinizing methods of Byzantinology and Ethnology oriented towards establishing continuities between ancient and modern civilizations. He returned to Greece as a promising scholar to assume prestigious positions in the local academia.

In his lectures to the Komotinian public, Kyriakides went to great lengths to prove that these local 'barbaric' races were in fact civilized and that they accepted the Achaic invasion as a civilizing mission (1993: 9–10). Nevertheless, he maintained that the failure of Thracians to 'wholly assimilate the Hellenic civilization' eventually caused the Achaeans to drive them to the north. Thus, he assures his audience in Komotini in the 1950s, they can be certain that 'we are not Hellenized Thracians. I strongly rather believe that we are Hellenes of Hellenic descent' (*then ímetha dhiladhí exellinizméni Thrákes. Polí mállon pistévo óti ímetha Éllines ex Ellínon*) (ibid.). As will be shown in chapter five, official historiography has reserved a special role for these Thracian races that links them to part of the minority population, the Pomaks. This image, of an Athens-educated professor returning to his native town to lecture local Greeks on its history, is one that captures well the dynamics between contemporary peripheral and central identities in the search of a unifying discourse of ethnic beginnings and ethnic continuity. His opening remarks indicate that the audience attending Kyriakides's Thrace lectures in 1953, 1954 and 1959 largely consisted of eastern Thracian refugees. His emphasis on homogeneity and common descent, as well as his passing references to his own ties to the town and the 'locals', address this nation-building ideal of unity. They also underline the righteousness of the incorporation of Thrace and its people (through bonds of history and race) within the national body. This role, of being the conduit of nation-building between state and public, places Kyriakides within the school of public intellectuals who produced scholarly works in order to prove the national thesis (of continuity with ancient Greece).[1] For these intellectuals, western Thrace presented a particular problem because of the need to incorporate (or otherwise place) the minority within the national body – something that at the height of the Cold War and the crushing of the left after the Civil War (1944–1949) was more of a priority for the region than it was for the central Athenian government and academia.

One of Kyriakides's recurring appointments in the 1950s and 1960s was on the board of the Thessaloniki-based Institute of Balkan Studies. The Institute was founded in 1953 with Marshall Plan funds and a mission to extend the work of the Society for Macedonian Studies (*Etería Makedhonikón Spoudhón*), of which it continued to be a branch until 1974. The Society for Macedonian Studies was founded in 1939 by a group of intellectuals based in Thessaloniki, amongst whom was Stilpon Kyriakides, who had by then been appointed to the Byzantine department of the city's Aristotle University as a specialist in ethnology and ancient Greek life. According to the official current interpretation of the Society's aims, the founders' key concerns were to 'raise the educational, spiritual, and cultural level of the Macedonian people', while the institution's 'strategic aim . . . was from the beginning, and remains forever, the defence and showcasing of Greek Macedonia'.[2] This interpretation is indicative of both the changes and continuities in the nationalist orientation of specific branches of Greek scholarship, especially in the region of northern Greece. On the one hand, the Hellenization of Macedonia as a newly acquired region within Greece (under the 1913 Treaty of Bucharest) was focused on the education of its public into Greekness and the linkage of the regional past to the nation's present and future. These aims may have been superseded by the solidification of national borders over the years but they resurfaced within a new climate of nationalist fervour which rendered 'Macedonia' a disputed location and a concept claimed by different nation-states. This peaked in the post-socialist era, but had been an issue much before the breakup of Yugoslavia. These differences and continuities have been noted by a number of anthropologists (Danforth 1995; Cowan 2000; Brown 1998b) but the role of state intellectuals and academic organizations such as the Society in sustaining them has largely been ignored.

The Institute of Balkan Studies remained for a long time at the forefront of Greek research in the fields of archaeology and history in the Balkans. Its aim in the early 2000s was 'the systematic investigation of the conditions prevailing in the sensitive area of the Southern Balkans both before and after the Macedonian Struggle' ('Macedonian Struggle' being the Greek designation for the 1904–1908 conflict between Greece and Bulgaria over control of the Macedonian region which was ultimately divided between Bulgaria, Greece, and the Serb, Croat and Slovene Kingdom).[3] IMXA, the Institute's acronym, stands for *Ídhrima Meletón Hersonísou tou Émou*, designating the 'Balkan' area through the ancient Greek name of the mountain *Émos*, and thereby emphasizing claims to a Hellenic Balkan heritage. In the long list of publications that span the period from the 1950s to the present, studies of this heritage abound – they include ethnological and historical studies of Greek groups of the region (from Albania to Egypt), studies of the Macedonian Struggle and the Balkan Wars, studies of regional ancient and religious Greek heritage, and studies of post-1923 refugee groups who have settled in Greece. These titles provide an indication of Greek attempts to rediscover, classify, and ultimately claim the Balkans in the intellectual sphere (Todorova 1997: 117–160).[4]

Significantly, many of the Greek studies about the minority bear the stamp of the Institute. An early example is a study on 'The Muslim minority of western Thrace' (Andreades 1956). One of the first Greek publications on the minority, this study is instructive of the intellectual milieu within which the minority population was conceptualized and governed. The author, having served as the commander of the royal gendarmerie of Xanthi, had by the time of publication been promoted to lieutenant colonel. His years of service are cited in the introduction of the book as a claim to legitimacy, having provided him the opportunity to witness 'from close-up the ways of life of the Muslims and to form friendships with many of them' (ibid.: ix). This is a point repeated by Kyriakides in his preface to the volume, albeit subtly juxtaposed to the axiom of objective truth. He thus continues with an emphasis on the Institute's concern 'to be absolutely certain about the precision [of the information]', which, he informs the readers, led to the provision of a legal scholar to work alongside Andreades and ensure, together with Kyriakides, 'thorough scrutiny and verification through on-site examination' of the data (ibid.: vii).

This data ranges from demographic statistics, to reviews of legislation relating to the religious administration and the organization of the minority's education, an overview of their economic situation and voting rights, and a countering of arguments presented in the Turkish press about alleged rights' abuses against the minority. The longest part of the book is a chapter entitled 'The state's affection towards the minority' (*i kratikí storyí ipér tis mionótitas*) which describes the welfare policies implemented during the period 1923–1954 in areas such as land redistribution, rehabilitation after the occupation and civil war, social welfare, healthcare, and agricultural credit (these will prove significant in later chapters). The semantics of this framing are telling: the word *storyí* (affection, or 'loving care') connotes motherly care, placing the state in a kinship relationship with the minority that develops out of the work of nurturing. So far, this constitutes a handbook on the government of population that corresponds to the eighteenth-century notion of policing as aiming at public well-being as Foucault describes it (Foucault 2004: 334). The use of this discourse in twentieth-century Greece might be attributable to the time-lag between the two countries' state-building projects. But confining oneself to this explanation would be rather simplistic if not orientalist.

The operative difference is that the book is not only about the government of population in the general, and therefore, not about this particular notion of policing. This 'handbook' seeks to account for a particular governmentality applied to a particular population. Against the critique of Turkish propaganda, it is difficult not to see in the claim to parenthood based on the caring labour of the state a 'wink' at Turkey's 'biological' parental claims (the genetics of ethnicity). In fact, a mere year after Thrace's General Commander Fessopoulos had circulated a memo instructing prefects in Evros, Xanthi, Drama, and Kavala to refer to the minority not as 'Muslim' but 'Turkish', Andreades criticizes this policy. In the requests that Greece so willingly, and in contravention of the Lausanne Treaty, acquiesces to in the name of 'Greco-Turkish friendship', Andreades discerns a Turkish plot to achieve 'the practical recognition of an ethnic minority in Greece' (*émbrakton anaǧnórisi ipárxeos en Elládhi ethnikís mionótitos*) (ibid.: 10). This intervention goes to the heart of the politics that frame the book, a politics acknowledged in Kyriakides' preface, through an appeal to precisely the scientificity that IMXA holds dear: 'As the information provided in this book is thoroughly validated, we believe it is able to show to the civilized world how Greeks really behave towards their Muslim co-habitants and to dispel ill-intentioned sowing of lies (*kakóvoulous spermoloyías*) by certain unrestrained Turkish media' (ibid.: vii). Read in conjunction with the fact that an English translation of the book was published in the same year, it seems that the audience the publication aimed at was not only domestic (consisting of Greek intellectuals and the wider majority public), but also international, consisting of people, in power perhaps, belonging to the community of civilized nations, who would be able to judge right from wrong, 'care' from 'ill-intentioned lies'.

In the politics of this preface, we begin to get a glimpse of the more contemporary and less affectionate forms of policing that the book inadvertently evidences: a policing that unfolds in the context of the post-war era of consolidation of nation-state borders through inter-state diplomatic encounters that posited Greece as Europe's bulwark against the Communist threat, and within which 'Greco-Turkish friendship' (which Fessopoulos' memo is believed to have propounded) sat uneasily next to the nation-state ideology to which Andreades remains faithful. Is this critique also indicative of splits developing within the repressive state apparatuses at this point of upheaval within the executive branch (elections having been called in 1950, 1951, and 1952)? Fessopoulos, a military leader in the Asia Minor expedition (1919–1922), was also head of the General Security Service (*Ipiresía Yenikís Asfálias tou Krátous*) unit in 1927, that focused on 'all forms of propaganda propagated against the security of the state and suggesting ways of neutralizing them'[5] prior to its development into the CIA-modelled Central Intelligence Service, KYP. By the time he wrote the memo, he had been moved to the post of Commander for Thrace, having led other attempts to set up a national intelligence unit.

In writing the memo, Fessopoulos combined his functions as intelligence officer, military man, and diplomat. This combination speaks well to the different policy aims that the conduct of the minority population negotiates (in this case, 'Greco-Turkish friendship' and thwarting claims to the minority's ethnic difference). Critiques of notions of 'diplomacy' that reify particular concepts of statehood (recognized as the post-Westphalian nation-state) emphasize the need to reconceptualize 'diplomacy' as 'homo-diplomacy', that negotiates knowledge of the Self and of the Other (Constantinou 2006). If such homo-diplomacy is to be seen as a form of counter-conduct, this negotiation is its main characteristic. As a technique of government then, the Andreades-Fessopoulos disagreement on the naming of the minority is only one of the most formal instances where the analysis of statehood and subjectivity is complicated. It is complicated firstly in the sense that the analyst's position explicitly informs the analysis of state conduct (Fessopoulos also wrote a book about the situation in Thrace, and published it from his own funds in 1957). Secondly, it is complicated in the sense that it shows that the relation between 'state' and 'subject' is not a straightforward one of two homogeneous entities one placed on top of the other in the structure of power. Each is far from homogeneous, and their interactions, vertical and horizontal, also impact on how power is understood to work. If this would make Fessopoulos a homo-diplomat, in the sense of mediator between 'the people' and the powers that be, he would be no more so than Machiavelli. The complication arises in the fact that Andreades is also claiming a homo-diplomatic status. So the question is not about differentiating a benign homo-diplomacy from its sinister version. The question remains the tracing of those entangled strands of policy that govern populations in multiple and even contradictory ways, yet leave the modes of subjectification (the premise of 'minority' and the binaries on the basis of which minoritization takes effect) intact.

Since the 1950s Fessopoulos' memo has received ample citations in the literature, Greek, Turkish, and international, which tries to puzzle the question of the minority's legitimate description (Muslim or Turkish). It is sometimes cited to show that at points even the Greek state considered the minority Turkish. At other times, it is cited to show that negotiation of state positions in the name of 'Greco-Turkish friendship' has only benefitted Turkey and weakened Greece's claims. In this sense, Andreades' critique seems relevant to this day. In a synchronic sense, it also hints at the wider power structures within which studies of the minority were framed at the time. Assuming that Fessopoulos' position would have been superior to that of Andreades during their service in Thrace, the latter's 'thoroughly verified' analysis of 'scientific facts' reveals a politics of positioning academia in a place from where it might have been possible to 'police the police', so to speak (presuming this secondary policing also emanated from within the police). More authoritarian aspects of policing thus begin to emerge, which develop as the (internal) critique of inter-state 'friendship' politics turns to the 'real' enemy (Turkey). In Andreades' arguments against Turkish claims of abuses of minority rights, we get a glimpse, through refutation, of the adverse effects of these 'affectionate' policies on the daily life of at least part of this population, policies that caused it to migrate to Turkey, selling its land assets and abandoning its occupations (ibid.: 51–59). As I turn in later chapters to these technologies of biopolitical governance, the development of more opaque aspects of policing will become evident. But as a precursor to that, Andreades' study exemplifies the connections between the barest forms of governing the life of the minority population, the cultural-intellectual premises on which this biopolitics was legitimized, and the global context of inter-state relations that enabled and constrained such politics.

Other Times, Other Sovereigns

In his archaeology of the *raison d'état*, Foucault locates the beginnings of diplomacy, as the precursor to the political order of policing-as-care, in the Westphalian era (2004: 285–306). Read as a metonym for the ordering of sovereignty that preceded the governmentality of inter-state diplomacy which arrived with the nation-state era, it might be posited that the 'Westphalia' of Thrace happened at that critical juncture of 1923. But this cannot be said without considering that it took place within the global context of colonial and neo-colonial relations that the real Westphalia set in train. The tension between the governmentality issuing from the rubric of Greco-Turkish friendship (developed in the 1950s within the context of the NATO alliance) and the anti-Turkish precepts of national ideology that we saw unfold in the previous section developed in the frame of these colonizing relations. The questions of sovereignty (concerning the primacy of the national state, vis-à-vis inter-state relations, and the international order, as well as the primacy of state interests over the East-West balance of power) thus emerge as the larger stakes in what might seem by comparison a mere squabble over the naming of the minority. Fessopoulos' memo was less about Greco-Turkish friendship than it was about the maintenance of power balances within NATO. This, in turn, was important in ensuring the strength of the Alliance over the Soviet bloc in world order. As we will see, the danger of communism, in world politics, as at home, was never far from the minds of either Fessopoulos or Andreades.

But the fact that this 'squabble' has left a legacy stretching to the current day, equating the very mention of minority with espousal of state politics ('Muslim' for Greece, 'Turkish' for Turkey), demonstrates the relevance of those stakes beyond the communist era. 'Greco-Turkish friendship' is still often presented as crucial to an East-West balance that is now configured along the contours of a liberal EU (and Euro-America more widely) and an 'unstable Middle East'. To examine the politics of naming the minority then, is to trace out the power grids that the minority, as subjectified population, is enmeshed in. As I will show in the rest of the book, this enmeshment becomes evident not only during instances of inter-state interaction (e.g. when Greece and Turkey pursue policies of 'protection' based on claims to kinship), as during instances of (homo-diplomatic) daily interactions, when individuals (officials as well as lay people) assume the role of mediator between two adversarial sides.

In this section, I want to exemplify one such instance where minority members mediate between the 'two sides' of discourses about historical beginnings and sovereign claims. In re-interpreting official discourse on these points, lay members of the minority become 'homo-diplomats' and in the process, show this homo-diplomatic interpretation to be another characteristic of 'the minority condition'. The discourse within which this mediation unfolds is a story that links medieval sovereignty with current questions of inter-state relations. As such, it is a perfect example of counter-conducting the population that the stories expounded above seek to conduct (through Kyriakides' tracing of an unbroken line between 'Thracian races' and Pomaks, and Andreades' solidifying of the line of separation between Greeks and Turks). Celal told me the following story by the seaside one evening, while cooking some freshly caught fish. I had already heard parts of it from other minority friends, and I had read other parts in various minority publications or in scholarly studies. I therefore use Celal on this occasion as the mouthpiece for several viewpoints that converge on a 'homo-diplomatic' counter-conduct:

> Thrace was incorporated into the Ottoman Empire in 1363. Turkic tribes arrived
> from the East – you know, Asia Minor was actually called that because it reminded
> tribal Turks of the steppes deep in Asia that once used to be their home. Their

entry into Europe followed two routes, parallel to the Black Sea coast. One was from the north, through Russia and down into the Balkans. The second one was from the south, through the Caucasus and current Turkey. At the point when this movement happened, the *Bizans* (Byzantine) kingdom was concentrated around Istanbul, Selanik, and the Morea. The Balkans, including Thrace and southeastern Europe, largely belonged to the Serb kingdom. Thrace was conquered by the great-great grandfather [Murad I] of Fatih Sultan Mehmet [conqueror of Istanbul]. At that time, the only Muslim tribes in the area were the *Peçenek*. The subsequent spread of Islam to the area was primarily related to the fact that under Ottoman law, Muslim subjects paid less tax than non-Muslims. In fact, religion had much less significance for these early Ottomans than it did for Christians. You must realize that the reason Turkey is now almost completely Sunni is that Sunnism was the religion of the bureaucracy. Until the great rise of the Ottoman Empire, most of its subjects were Alevis, who were only later given incentives to adopt more orthodox [Muslim] practices.[6]

In a softer, more serious tone, he added:

Also, something that you won't find in books, and it is obvious why Turkish historians would not want to talk about it, is this: ever since the split of the Roman and Byzantine churches, Christians were trying to unify under one Empire. With the conquest of Istanbul that hope was shattered. However, when Kânuni Sultan Süleyman [the Magnificent, great-grandson to Fatih Sultan Mehmet] tried to expand westwards into Italy, the *Bizans* approached him and made a deal. They offered their assistance in the campaign, if Süleyman would be baptized and conquer Rome as a Christian. This would unite the Eastern and Western churches under one Christian empire. Süleyman in fact agreed, but unfortunately died before the campaign was over and Rome was never conquered. He did, however, conquer an Italian fortress, which is evidence enough for the existence of the scheme. Why else would he have gone up there? And why would Ottoman Greeks call themselves *Rum* and nothing else? They considered themselves Romans.

At first I noted the story as a remarkable myth of origin; I was slightly taken aback by the exoticism that seemed to make the story remarkable (the medieval imperial frame, the secrecy of the pact, the placing of the storytellers in the number of the select few who possess knowledge of it), but astonished by the irreverence it communicated towards the orthodoxy of the competing nationalisms (for example, the idea that the Byzantines would have been reduced to consorting with their conquerors, and the mightiest of Sultans to agreeing to join the ranks of the remnants of those he had conquered). As I kept re-analysing it over subsequent years, a meta-narrative began to take shape, one that speaks in much more depth to the minority condition.

The first of the strands that needs to be untangled in order to explain this is historical. The Ottoman forays in the region of Rome that occurred during the reign of Süleyman the Magnificent (1520–1566) were the siege of Vienna (1529) and the war with Venice (1537–1540) (Faroqhi et al. 1997: 424–431; Inalcik 1997: xvi, 271–774). At the time, western diplomats believed that his ultimate aim was to reach Rome (Finkel 2005: 128). On the question of hybridity and relations between conqueror and conquered, Inalcik contends that after the conquest of Constantinople Mehmet II (Fatih Sultan Mehmet) 'received tacit acquiescence from the Greeks, Armenians, Bulgars and Tatars' (Inalcik 1997: 271) and asserts that '[w]hen the sultan destroyed the Latin colonies or compromised with them to buy time, many felt that he had restored the old Byzantine imperial tradition for the benefit of the indigenous peoples' (ibid.: 271–272). The conquest of Rome had been cited as forming part of his aspirations as well, and his adoption of the title Kayser-i Rûm (Caesar of Rome) after the conquest of Constantinople has been noted (Somel 2003: lxxx). Of the earlier time of Orhan's reign (1324–1362), when Ottoman-Byzantine diplomacy began to unravel, Finkel states that 'John Palaeologus, aspiring to unite Byzantine and Ottoman territories, married his daughter Irene to Halil – in the hope that Halil would succeed his father [Orhan] . . . But the plan came to nothing, for it was Halil's older brother Murad who took their father's place' (Finkel 2005: 17). Celal's story is therefore a blending of myth and history, a metaphor through which an understanding of communal identity may be communicated. This understanding reveals an aspect of political subjectivity where the negotiation between subjectification and counter-conduct takes place.

The two sections of Celal's account celebrate two genealogies that counter-narrate the Hellenic purity traced by Kyriakides in his genealogies of Pomaks (as descendants of 'Thracian tribes') and modern-day (Greek) Thracians (as descendants of the Achaeans). For the first, we have a counter-genealogy of Thracian tribes who are Turkic (the Peçenek), and for the second a counter-genealogy of Sultanic sovereigns. Both genealogies problematize the very basis of purity that Kyriakides' story seeks to demonstrate. The Peçenek appear within a social system that is determined by the sovereign-subject hierarchy, something that remains muted in Kyriakides' description of the tribe-conqueror relations after the Achaean 'civilizing mission'. The Peçenek are thus mentioned alongside other groups who are equally subjected to their sovereign, and subjected through far less benign means than the 'gift' of civilization. These groups are converted through monetary coercion (taxing non-Muslims), and are co-opted by an elite minority that managed to assert demographic control through 'incentives', turning the Alevi majority into a minority. This cynical narrative, aimed at answering the reflexive question of Celal's own communal genealogy, counters in the starkest terms the celebratory tone of Kyriakides: the minority in western Thrace today is heir to groups that have been minoritized through the ages through conquest, coercion, and co-optation.

And yet, this is not a counter-narrative of disenfranchisement. A celebrated past is recoverable through the grand genealogy of Sultanic sovereignty in the second half of the story. This genealogy follows a territorial trajectory that starts in Thrace (therefore emphasizing its Turkishness even before the fall of Constantinople), continues to Istanbul (the current Turkishness of which is now undisputed, but which also, we are reminded, was won through the greatness of its conqueror), and ends, albeit without success, in Rome (which assumedly might have become Turkish had its prospective conqueror not died).

Central to all of this is the name. But the answer to the question 'how is the minority to be defined?' is not explicit. Instead, it is articulated through the reciprocity of naming those other *établis*, the Greeks of Istanbul. Considering that the specific conversation was carried out in Greek, Celal's use of the Turkish word *Rum* to name them becomes particularly poignant. His rhetorical question – 'why do Istanbul Greeks call themselves *Rum*?' – therefore reveals an implicit questioning of authority. In calling the Istanbul Greeks *Rum*, the name used in Turkish to describe Greeks under Turkish sovereignty, Celal was deciding their identity for them, even if he was presenting it *de facto* as their choice. He used neither the Turkish term *Yunanlı*, used for Greeks in Greece, nor the Greek *Hellenes* (*Éllines*), the most commonly used word in Greek to describe Greek nationality – also a classicizing word for 'Greeks', bearing allusions to ancient Hellas. This mirrors the strategy by which nationalist Greeks, like Andreades, decided his Muslim identity for him.

In fact, in conversations that addressed the question of the naming of the minority explicitly, Celal, and many other Gümülcineli friends, would often use the argument of their atheism to delegitimize the religious descriptor 'Muslim' as an accurate depiction of their identity. Celal thus identified the problem of religion as the underlying dichotomy of Turkish identification, and he stressed the unimportant character of religion in early Ottoman times. The existence of a conflict within the minority between religious and secularist circles had been used by Andreades to criticize what he saw as a Greek policy of favouring the latter (in the name of inter-state 'friendship') to the detriment of abiding by the religious definition in the Lausanne Treaty. In a different reading of this friendship, Celal questions the Islamic faith of Süleyman the Magnificent, portraying him as 'almost a Christian'. This merges the Islamic and Christian worlds along ethnic lines, allowing his own ancestral past to claim a presence in both ancient Greek and early Ottoman worlds – at other times he would emphasize the fact that many Sultans' mothers were actually Greek. Thus, he does not question the fact that he is a Turk, but rather whether a good Turk must be a religious, or even pure-blooded, Turk.

Celal's story thus counter-conducts historiographical truth (did the baptism pact really take place?), purified genealogy (were the Sultans pure Turks?), and judicial naming (which is the most legitimate minority descriptor?). Besides these, it also counter-conducts the concept of sovereignty, on which Andreades' argument of 'state care' is based (Greece's responsibility towards the minority emanates from its sovereign right to control this particular territory absolutely and without interference from Turkey). Celal's sovereignty is instead about conquest achieved not through 'civilization' (as in Kyriakides' Achaean case) but through the opaque politics of secret pacts that blur the hierarchies between victors and losers (did the Bizans outwit Süleyman?) and evacuate the importance of the name (was it ultimately important that he conquer Rome 'as a Christian'?). In this description of sovereignty, a different kind of '*storyi*' (care) is articulated: that of a sovereign concerned to extend his 'gift of law' to his subjects (Kânuni Sultan Süleyman translates as 'Suleyman the Lawgiver'), even if it means changing his own Sultanic name (the exact opposite of the granting of rights to the population on the condition that the population be named in the way the state decides). The relationship between subjects and sovereignty is inverted and also complicated. Is Süleyman ultimately a sovereign beyond the concrete borders of the Greek-Turk opposition? Would there still have been winners and losers among Ottomans and Bizans had Rome been conquered and who would they have been?

All these counter-interpretations amount to a counter-conduct of this opposition in what might be described as a reconciliatory frame – the ideal of Rome's conquest would have legitimized hybridity. But this is not an idealistic reconciliation of frictionless coexistence. It is a reconciliation of cynicism, secret pacts, adversarial diplomacy, and indifference to the lower strata. It is a counter-conduct that remains without effect but yet does so not because of an underlying naïveté but because there is no effect to substantiate, no correspondence between knowledge and power (the story is articulated almost in secret). And yet it is a productive counter-conduct in the sense that it offers a reflection of the minority condition (rendering it a process of countering rather than a static 'condition').

I would argue that this is an instructive point that is often missed in discussions of agency that emanate from the effectiveness of 'resistance' (taking Scott [1987] as a foundational argument). It is equally a point that remains underdeveloped in the Foucauldian categorization of counter-conduct. In his examples of religious revolt, secret societies, military insubordination, and Soviet dissidence, Foucault essentially enumerates types of counter-conduct that are distinguished on the basis of their relation to governmentality (2007: 196–202). The notion of 'counter-conduct' is offered there as an alternative to 'dissidence', 'diso-bedience', 'insubordination', 'revolt'. With regard to the first in particu-lar, Foucault says that

> there is a process of sanctification or hero worship which does not seem to me of much use. On the other hand, by using the word counter-conduct, and so without having to give a sacred status to this or that person as a dissident, we can no doubt analyse the components in the way in which someone actually acts in the very general field of politics or in the very general field of power relations; it makes it possible to pick out the dimension or component of counter-conduct that may well be found in fact in delinquents, mad people, and patients. (ibid.: 202)

While agreeing on the analytic potential of counter-conduct, I believe that this framing retains a focus on effect ('someone actually acts') that obscures the conceptual significance of counter-conduct. It therefore remains uncertain whether counter-conducts that are not threatening enough to warrant incarceration (I am thinking of the institutionaliza-tion of delinquents, mad people, and patients, and the exile of dissi-dents) would be of the same order (this threat also seems decisive for the treatment of religious sects and secret societies). But if the threshold of 'threat' is on the level of the conceptual and not of the practical (as Foucault makes clear) then the analysis of counter-conduct should not be driven by the question of what responses counter-conduct elicits through the governmentality of repression, but by what it reveals about the gov-ernmentality in which it is immersed in the first place. So Celal might not be a dissident, but his counter-conduct emerges from the biopoliti-cal condition of his minority everydayness. He does not offer a utopian alternative, nor does he pose a threat to the state; yet in a soft tone he counter-conducts a population within and outside history, within and without genealogy, neither Greek nor Turk, but also both.

Imaginaries of Coexistence

If hybridity (the merging of oppositional identities into one sovereign and potentially one genitor) is a principal feature of Celal's counter-conduct, multiplicity is one that I have heard articulated much more often in Komotini, by both majority and minority members. I refer here to the classic liberal view of multiculturalism as the coexistence of distinct groups that together, and in harmony, create a 'mosaic'. Komotini in the late 1990s was teeming with this discourse. Its multiculturalism was pro-jected as a unique trait by local authorities, which organized food festivals to highlight it (Demetriou 2004c; Yiakoumaki 2006). In the brochure that accompanied one such festival, multiculturalism was likened to a bouquet of flowers, a well of traditions, the light shining on commensal tables once the curtains of separation are drawn aside (Anonymous 1999: 4, 5, 7). Philosophy has exposed the de-politicizing cul-de-sacs of this discourse and its postmodern variants. Examples are Žižek's critique of 'identity politics' where subjectivity becomes exploded into infinite facets of 'identity' that exist in their own right and outside a necessary structure of power (2000), Mignolo's critique of the Euro-centrism of those identity politics (2002), and Mouffe's critique of liberal, consensus-led antagonism (2005). On the local level, examples of multicultural discourse have been analysed as instances of state- and elite-led subjectivization (Tsibiridou 2006) and driven by EU politics of integration (Yiakoumaki 2006).

These limitations (obfuscation of conflict, retention of the premise of purity/boundedness, disregard of class and other power dynamics, confinement within a liberal ethics, etc.) also instantiate, I would argue, the biopolitics of the ordinary that frames the minority condition in western Thrace. In the culinary exhibition of the festival, taste was described as 'the mirror of ideologies, ways of life and worldviews' (Anonymous 1999: 6). It became a medium of affect, in other words, that transformed daily sustenance into an aesthetic device for differentiating between 'ways of life'. This is, however, ultimately a thoroughly political differentiation that is already assumed in the classification of each of these ways of life. Throughout the catalogue, different types of cuisines are exemplified, including a multiplicity of 'Greek' ones (Cappadocian, Sarakatsan, Pontiac, Eastern Thracian, Eastern Rumelian) and the three minority ones (Roma, Pomak, Turkish). The afterword, signed with the name of the restaurant that presumably sponsored the catalogue's publication, concludes with an analysis of what makes a perfect cuisine:

> The place then, that is the land and the sea with their products, their smells and their colours, give birth and define the main cuisine. The gastronomic cell is the place and not the nation, because this [the nation] usually covers many gastronomic areas without affinity between them. *Therefore, [we are for] cuisines local and not national.*

> On the other hand, cooking as a cultural phenomenon, which is related to the perfection of diet, presupposes non-moving, stable populations with a permanent residence. Moving populations, warriors or nomads, are at a gastronomical disadvantage because they lack the ability to work the land on a regular and systematic basis and do not have the material resources that would allow them to execute complicated recipes. (ibid.: 41, emphasis in original)

What is articulated here is nothing less than a regional racism that critiques national unity only to seek perfection in the stasis of settlement. The evaluation of who, in the local context of Komotini, can claim to have the perfect cuisine is related to national discourse, undermining the critique of nationalism expressed in the previous paragraph: warriors and nomadic groups (who are underdeveloped in culinary terms) bring to mind Ottoman conquerors (and the Turkish minority that descends from them, perhaps also the Pomaks) and itinerant Roma (whose descendants in western Thrace are believed to have only recently become settled). The reference to complicated recipes similarly conjures up images of the Greek Istanbulite cuisine, widely considered to contain the most complicated of 'Greek' dishes. It is the cuisine of a people whose settlement in 'the City' (as Constantinople is often referred to in Greek) spans millennia and whose demise under the Turkish Republic has often been lamented through the cinematography of food (film being only the most spectacular of a number of cultural tropes in which this has been done, most memorable of which are the highly popular 1980s TV series 'Loxándra' and the 2003 Greek-Turkish production 'A Touch of Spice'). The culinary distinction then that is communicated in the separation between 'warrior', 'nomads' and 'settled' populations is no less than cultural hierarchy. The catalogue of the late 1990s is not very different from Kyriakides's 1950s description of the Achaean 'civilizing mission' against the 'Thracian tribes'. Such was the biopolitics of food sponsored by the state in 1999.

The return to the idea of the civilizing mission is not accidental here. Mignolo locates a major shift in the concept between the Spanish and British imperial projects in the Americas. Through a reading of Kant, he argues that the Spanish mission claimed legitimacy on the basis of the universality of religion, while the British one staked its legitimacy on the universality of the nation-state (2002). The 'civilizing mission' is in other words the idiom of subjugation legitimized by universal ontologies. Thinking of neoliberal globalization as another phase of the universalist colonial project, he advocates a 'diversality' (a concept of the many that nevertheless maintains something of the common in contrast to 'diversity') against the 'universality' propounded by United States capitalism and its understanding of 'human rights' (ibid.: 174–184). This, he further contends, becomes possible through the re-appropriation of concepts that coloniality has rendered hegemonic (e.g. 'human rights') by the subaltern; what is required is 'border thinking', i.e. the crossing of those conceptual borders that define colonial power as the possession of knowledge (ibid.: 172–182). Border thinking therefore emerges as the key strategy for negotiating coexistence between the one and the many, unity and difference, subjugation and confrontation. Border thinking is the beginning of an emancipatory project of coexistence.

If food is the parody of such coexistence, the appropriation and redefinition of the concepts that have founded the nation-state's knowledge of itself (genealogy, sovereignty, naming, care), articulated in Celal's story, may be the step across Mignolo's thought 'border'. Thinking 'unity' and 'multiplicity' otherwise than what is presented in the naïve celebration of the Komotinian food mosaic are the stakes of Celal's counter-conduct. Such 'epistemic disobedience' (in the analysis of what the minority's difference consists in) reminds us that although

> [t]he differences between bio-politics in Europe and bio-politics in the colonies lie in the racial distinction between the European population (even when bio-politically managed by the state) and the population of the colonies: less human, sub-humans . . . it is also important to remember that bio-political techniques enacted on colonial populations returned as a boomerang to Europe in the Holocaust . . . This consideration shifts the geography of reason and illuminates the fact that the colonies were not a secondary and marginal event in the history of Europe but, on the contrary, colonial history is the non-acknowledged center in the making of modern Europe. (Mignolo 2009: 16)

This not only implies that the Zapatistas or Maori anthropologists (to whom Mignolo makes reference) cannot be treated as emblematic of an 'ultimate' subaltern (ibid.). It also implies that the European subaltern cannot be idealized in the Jew, the Muslim, or any minority bounded by the unitary 'the' (which is of course very different to saying that the governmentalities of oppression, like colonialism, the Holocaust or the War on Terror do not share affinities, which they do). This goes for Celal (and the individuals whose voices he transmits), which methodologically begs the question of other forms of counter-conduct, i.e. those that Celal does not represent, perhaps also outside 'the minority'.

Consider that of Andreas, a Komotinian urban planner with a good historical knowledge of the town, who is identified as a leftist and who maintains good relations with minority colleagues and left party members. In his version of local history, space and migration are determinants of the town's very specific identity. When I went to visit him, on advice from his minority colleagues, for an 'expert' articulation of this story, he produced a series of sketches tracing the changing borders of Komotini and its two 'ethnic' sides at particular points in time, explaining, as he sketched away, the significance of each addition (Figure 3.1). These maps had chronological titles, each year representing the period of greatest demographic change, resulting from the historical event that marked each of those years: 486, when Thrace came under Byzantine rule after being captured by Theoderic (also Mitchell 2007: 118); 1453, when Constantinople was conquered by the Ottomans (a metonymic date for the fall of Byzantium, not its Thracian dominions); 1870, when the Bulgarian Exarchate was established; 1878, when the principality of Bulgaria was established; 1920, when Greeks took control of Komotini;

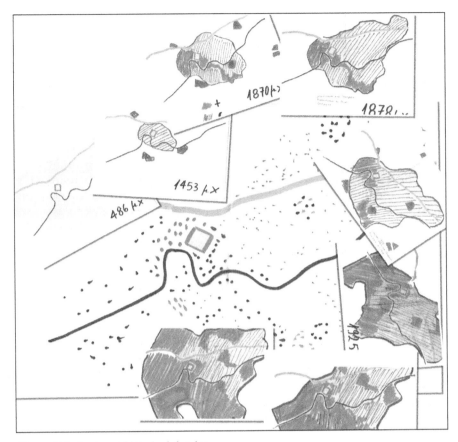

Figure 3.1 Andreas' historical sketches

1925, when the 1923 exchangees were settling in western Thrace; 1976, after Greece entered the era of *metapolitefsi* (the term used to refer to the period after the fall of the 1967–1974 junta); 1999, the 'present' of the sketches. On these sketches Andreas had drawn the river (on the banks of which the initial settlement was established and which was paved over in the junta years) and the first features of civilization: Egnatia street, and the Roman town walls. To show populations, he used the colours blue for Christians (block shading in the figure above) and red (line shading in the figure) for Muslims and traced coexistence effectively through spatial separation. He explained that Roma Muslim populations were settled outside the town's boundaries in pre-Ottoman times and that Ottoman settlements developed around them. After 1878, Muslim neighbour-hoods expanded due to the in-migration of Muslims from Bulgaria, as well as 'a few Bulgarians' (suggesting a more complicated view of

Bulgarian independence). In 1920, the Christian areas shrank because of the flight of Greeks during the Bulgarian occupation of 1913–1919. From 1925, these areas expanded, first through settlement of refugees and later through development.

In comparison to the dilution of antagonism that the food festival's recipes of multiple cultures demonstrate, the complex inter-ethnic relations in the town are reduced here to the familiar Greek-Turkish binary. This can be interpreted as another implicit form of critique, or confinement to older narratives. I would posit that it comes from a certain kind of knowledge, acquired through Andreas' professional engagement with Komotinian urban space and punctuated by his political engagement with minority members on the one hand and leftist critique of nationalism on the other. As a result, the sketches engage with concepts of 'conquest' and 'independence' through the prisms of 'flight' and 'refugee settlement'. They also depict population and spatial expansion as a result of contest for space (Greek flight for 1913–1919, Greek encroachment into Turkish neighbourhoods post-1923).

In mapping the town's history, Andreas' sketches re-present the exercise of boundary-drawing – they seek to place two groups in mutually exclusive locations, ascribing 'ownership' to space within the frame of political, administrative, or ethnic likeness and unlikeness (Green 2005: 29–35). From cadastral surveys to tourist guides, what maps map above all is people onto territory through a process in which power works to define 'people' in particular ways and turn 'territory' into a 'natural' homeland (see also Cohn 2000: 8–32). In the case of Thrace, it should be remembered that the most well-known historical maps were produced in the late nineteenth and early twentieth century, when sovereignty over the region was most under dispute. These maps were ethnological and sought to show the presence of ethnic groups, each time differently defined, in particular locations. Andreas' sketches conform to this frame of representation in mapping out Greek and Turkish spaces in blue (for Greek) and red (for Turkish, defined as 'Muslims' in the first and 'people of Turkish-origin' in later sketches) even as they point to the inconsistencies it narrates (populations come and go, there are overlaps and intra-communal differences). Overlapping is acknowledged, albeit minimally and confined to 1925 onwards, its occurrence designating 'mixed' neighbourhoods that seem to have dwindled over time.

There is an implicitness in this counter-narration which subscribes to state forms of knowledge, while also acknowledging that there is more to the celebration of multiculturalism as an aspect of the nation-state project. This is more forcefully brought out in the last sketch, which most closely mirrors the 'mosaic' concept. In trying to summarize the movements depicted in the previous drawings, Andreas plotted on a new sketch 'ethnic groups in Komotini until 1925 and 1940' (central sketch in Figure 3.1). This double dating reflects precisely the limits of nation-state multiculturalism. In 1925 the Gypsies living in the town were moved to a neighbourhood outside it, Andreas explained. The phrase 'until' enables the representation of the Bulgarian and (most of) the Greek groups on the same sheet, exposing, as it silences, the fact that by the time Greek refugees moved in, the Bulgarians had gone. The year 1940, on the other hand, indicates the obliteration of the Jewish population from the town's landscape. The research I carried out in the town's land registry indicated that some Jewish families sold their possessions during the occupation and left, while others survived the concentration camps and returned to sell their property and relocate to Athens or Thessaloniki (presumably, still others were deported, never to return, and without surviving descendants to claim the properties). The dates mark the deletion from Komotinian space of the two groups that were forcibly removed. Thus, just as '1940' points to the universally acknowledged violence of the Holocaust, 1925 hints at the largely unacknowledged violence of the displacement of the Roma population outside the city borders in the aftermath of Greek refugee influx from the east, and the earlier flight of Bulgarians. Ethnic presence is noted in a matter-of-fact way and the absence of violently evicted groups, such as the Roma, Bulgarians, and Jews, is made apparent. Critique is not verbalized – the violence implied in that absence is not commented upon explicitly – but this form of 'noting' provides a potential basis for questioning the taken-for-granted nature of the presence of various groups inhabiting Komotini in 1999. By showing how things were not always so, a space is opened for a questioning of what brought about particular changes.

In very different ways then, Celal and Andreas counter-narrate the state's historiography of Komotini. In doing so, they point to questions that this historiography leaves unanswered. Yet they also represent the predicament of articulating such critical discourse in the Komotinian context. They both speak from the position of their respective identities, Andreas as Komotinian, Celal as Gümülcineli. From these positions, they endorse the view of the town as inherently divided between two mutually exclusive ideologies, spaces, identities and histories, and embody the knowledges of majority and minority: Andreas has probably never heard the story of Süleyman, and Celal has probably not elaborated it to his Komotinian friends – but Andreas has obviously had occasion to share his knowledge of the town's development with the minority colleagues who suggested that I speak to him. The 'burial' of history therefore comes to mark the border that needs to be thought across: majority-minority.

As I continue to explore this border, I will attempt to pick at its many bifurcations into a border between ways of being. These often unstable shifts from one register of difference to another circumscribe minority subjectivity in the process of their being encountered in the everyday. They are the border's caprice. Bringing together the main themes of Andreas' and Celal's stories, space and naming, I start by exploring the former as a key domain where this capriciousness unfolds, framed by the politics of naming. Naming thus comes into view as the first of the three modalities of governmentality that shape 'the minority condition'.

Notes

1. I mention this continuity as the underlying concept. The nuances with which it was interpreted by various schools of intellectuals from the nineteenth century onwards have been the focus of examinations by Gourgouris (1996), Lambropoulos (1988), and Tziovas (1986), among others.
2. http://www.ems.gr/home/istoria.html, last accessed on 23 January 2012.
3. Information accessed on 26 October 2001 on http:// www2.hyper.gr/imxa/ research.html (now unavailable). In later reformulations, this aim is described as the promotion of 'a better understanding of the developments which have shaped the current situation in south-eastern Europe, and [collaboration] with the international and Balkan scholarly community' (http://www.imxa.gr, last accessed on 23 January 2012). In these conciliatory terms, a securitizing nation-state ideology (where the protection of the nation from external and internal enemies would be primary, and the point of history would be to maintain those relations of enmity in the interests of security) gives way to a neoliberal logic of funding, networking, and cooperation.
4. In this long list, the name of Stilpon Kyriakides features a number of times, in studies that he compiled himself and in works that he prefaced as President of the Society for Macedonian Studies. Another name that stands out is that of Apostolos Vakalopoulos, through his eight-volume history of *The Greek Nation, 1453–1669* published between 1961 and 1988. Vakalopoulos, whose terms at the Institute coincided with those of Kyriakides, shared the same classicist approach to knowledge as an objective reality attainable through meticulous research, while the vital importance of nationalist ideology was placed beyond scrutiny. The relationship between the two authors speaks as much to the technologies of linking research to state policy, as it does to the workings of 'political DNA' as a factor in the sustenance of these technologies. Apostolos Vakalopoulos' son, Konstantinos, whose 'Northern Hellenism in the preamble of the Macedonian Struggle (1878–1894)' was published in 1983, shared the same approach to nationalism as his father and 'inherited' placements at IMXA and within Greek academia. By contrast, Kyriakides' daughter, Alki Nestoros, devoted her academic career to questioning the politics of Greek ethnology (Kyriakidou-Nestoros 1986), rooting her enquiries in the paradigm of critical reflexivity. Her positions in the Greek academy may have mirrored her father's, but it is telling that she did not hold a position at IMXA. For a more detailed exploration of these genealogies, see Demetriou (2004b).
5. This phrasing is part of the official historiography of the current Intelligence Service, as presented in their website, http://www.nis.gr/portal/page/portal/ NIS/History/BeforeEYP (accessed on 7 February 2012).
6. Note that neither Celal nor any of the other storytellers are Alevi.

CHAPTER 4

NAMING AND COUNTER-NAMES

Spatial Bilingualism

What does it mean for a town's name to exist in two registers – Komotini in Greek, Gümülcine in Turkish? In a place where the naming of a group (Turks? Turkish-speakers? people of Turkish origin? 'A' group or multiple?) has been a topic of legal, administrative and political debate, what is the import of naming space? These questions are the subject of this chapter. So far, cartography has been explored as a device of subjectification. Where ethnological maps established populations of ethnic, religious and linguistic majorities and minorities, peace treaties offered them choices (or failed to do so) of establishing lives anew within the former, or becoming established where they were rooted as the latter. These treaties sought to attain the homogeneity that newly drawn borders dictated to nation-state governmentality. And when this homogeneity proved elusive, other populations were brought in (Asia Minor refugees), settled from the mountains (Sarakatsans), moved out of urban areas (Roma), sent to an occupier's camps (Jews), or repatriated (from the former Soviet Union). The numerical conduct of population (how much 'minority' was tolerable when) was inextricably linked to the space being claimed as national.

The concepts of sovereignty, genealogy, naming and care have determined the modalities through which this conduct was actualized and the forms that counter-conduct took. The following three chapters will elaborate on the last three: naming in the present chapter, genealogy in chapter five, and care in chapter six. As a strategy of population conduct, naming becomes a device for bordering – ordering people on this side of the border or the other (Turkish-Greek, included-excluded, central-marginal). Along with other devices of governmentality that unfold in the domain of space (urban planning, construction of monuments, property allocation, policing), naming is a biopolitical technology that interpellates people in their daily itineraries as national subjects (e.g. 'refugees', 'Greek', 'majority') or as something less (e.g. '*établis*', 'enemies', 'minority', and more recently also 'migrants', 'asylum-seekers'). But those who are being conducted can also re-draw, to varying extents, that border. Here, I show how the issue of naming works on the level of the street, to emplace individuals in a Greek-named street, a Turkish-named neighbourhood, and a bilingually-designated town. Language is particularly important in counter-conducting such emplacement.

I focus specifically on what I call 'spatial bilingualism': the ability of Gümülcinelis to conceptualize place on two different registers – Greek for the level of the street, Turkish for that of the neighbourhood. Fanning out from linguistic competence, this spatial bilingualism also enters the political domain of inter-personal contact. In linking the politics of naming to the experience of space, 'spatial bilingualism' offers us a way of understanding the ordinariness of nationalism in the workings of a governmentality that conducts the minority as compliant, marginal, or excluded. It connects languages of cartography (lay, official, region-specific, or street-level) to practices of naming (towns, neighbourhoods, streets), embedding power relations (framed by nationalism, capitalism and communalism) into the spaces one walks through, lives in, avoids, or bypasses.

The analysis of space through concepts of representation (of which language can be considered one) has been criticized for de-prioritizing space over time and de-politicizing it (Massey 2005). Massey has drawn on Foucault and Derrida to explore the politics inhering in landscape-as-text where the aim 'is to challenge the pretensions to closure of the text' (2005: 50). Such deconstruction begins with the strategies used to 'tame space' (ibid.: 122–125):

> [c]onceiving of space as a static slice through time, as representation, as a closed system and so forth are all ways of taming it. They enable us to ignore its import: the coeval multiplicity of other trajectories and the necessary outward-lookingness of a spatialised subjectivity. In so much philosophy it is time which has been a source of excitement (in its life) or terror (in its passing) . . . Conceptualising space as open, multiple and relational, unfinished and always becoming, is a prerequisite for history to be open and thus a prerequisite, too, for the possibility of politics. (ibid.: 59)

This holds for philosophy as it does for the state and it is in this sense that Massey turns her criticism to Laclau as a way of 'open[ing] space itself to a more adequate political address' (ibid.: 48). The conduct and counter-conduct of naming is one way in which space is opened up to such address.

Greek toponymy exists in Komotini in that particular form exactly because Komotini's Greekness is a fact perpetually in need of proof (and therefore, to follow a Derridean approach, always under question). This proof is manifested on a daily basis in how people speak about the town, how local officials mark claims to Greekness on Komotinian streets, and how its Turkish-speaking minority is pushed out of official constructions of urban place such as street-naming and cartography. This chapter examines the ways in which Komotini's Greekness is constantly put into question through space.

During the first days of my arrival in Komotini, I walked through the streets trying to understand the translation from representation (the town map) to materiality (streets, houses, parks, etc.). During those walks I was struck by the names I came across (all communicating a sense of purified Hellenization), the ways in which they were communicated (explanations on street plaques functioned as educational devices) and the actuality of the border everything referred to (the materiality of the difference between Greek and Turkish neighbourhoods). Later, I heard people use street names inspired by national heroes, national topoi and national ideals, without being conscious of the signifieds they were articulating – this in itself was not surprising. But the differential references to streets and neighbourhoods were more so. In noting the difference in the ways my Gümülcineli friends named places amongst themselves and in conversation with Greeks, I realized that such inter-personal communication was in fact grounded in the politics of place (by which I mean 'space' understood as domesticated and tamed). My friends rarely spoke about space amongst themselves in terms of street names and always primarily in terms of neighbourhood. Thus, my Gümülcineli friends often talked about Kır Mahalle, using the Turkish name ('the Countryside Neighbourhood', denoting an older placement 'in the fields' and away from the town), but would translate it to Greeks as *Filippoupóleos* (the name of the main street running through it, after the Greek name of the town of Plovdiv, in Bulgaria). It seemed as though spatial understanding operated on two levels, whereby the two languages were also tied to different 'semiologies of orientation' (Mounin 1980). Here these semiologies did not merely point to the politics of the official and the lay (ibid.: 491–492) – in the context of minority governmentality they also pointed to the politics that make the minority condition ordinary (Figure 4.1). They are inextricably tied to a politics of space- and place- making. This includes, on the one hand, state attempts to nationalize Komotinian space and, on the other hand, minority practices of navigating between nationalism and communication. This communication involves subscribing to a nationalism that considers the Turkish presence in the town as an aberration on one extreme and communicating with people who may or may not subscribe

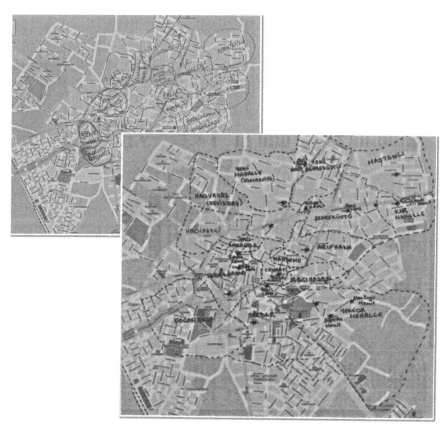

Figure 4.1 Rough and official mahalle boundaries superimposed on official town map

to this nationalism but have no alternative linguistic reference on the other. Whether or not to insist on the name 'Kır Mahalle' and when to name it 'Filippoupóleos' are decisions that result from such navigation. Their articulation thus points to the dynamics of bypassing, just as one is aware of, strategies of taming space. In this sense, this articulation is an instance of the workings of the governmentality of space.

In reading these decisions in terms of counter-conduct, I return to that 'old and largely discredited field of toponymy' (Goodchild 2004, quoted in Rose-Redwood et al. 2010: 455). In doing this my aim is to recover the possibilities of 'agonism' (Mouffe 2000) that contests over space and its naming bring into view. Indeed, I would also see in the notion of agonism developed after Lalcau and Mouffe's *Hegemony and Socialist Strategy* a lack of emphasis on the spaces such agonism unfolds in. In the current conjuncture, such spaces are clearly not the cafes, the streets of protests, or the squares of the 2011 'Occupy' movements because what one finds there are basic forms of agreement, not the radical disagreement of agonism (except of course at the moments of police confrontation). In Mouffe's version of democracy the spaces of such radical disagreement are (or rather should be) the spaces of governmentality: the parliaments, the law, the media. But those possibilities for connecting these two spaces (bringing, for example, protesters and their issues into parliament, in an agonistic, rather than a formalistic, sense) I would argue, are recoverable through a re-reading of those old forms of subjectification that the nation-state has used and of the ways in which such subjectification is negotiated and resisted. To open up the cafes and public squares, in other words, parliament and the law need to acknowledge what exclusions they have been inscribing on the streets. This inscription is what I examine below.

The Biopolitics of Naming

Greece has reportedly been the first modern European nation-state to employ 'the "nationalization" of toponymies as a symbolic homeland-building measure ... [when, in 1830] Turkish, Slavic, and Italian place names were Hellenized' (Rose-Redwood et al. 2010: 460). After Athens became the capital of the newly independent state in 1834, the Royal Committee and city council undertook to replace 'barbaric' place-names with Greek ones (Bozos 2004; Bastéa 2000). The same happened during the period of expansion in the territories that were incorporated over the next century. By the 1920s, when western Thrace became Greek, the techniques of toponymy were developed and perfected. The nationalization of Komotinian space thus began with naming, almost as soon as the Greek army walked into the town in 1920 and proceeded as an extension of those military claims.

Nevertheless, the shift effected in that naming was not as abrupt or as totalizing as might be expected of changes to the regime of sovereignty. The slate was not vigorously wiped clean and written anew. Instead, it harked back to previous conceptual and phonetic forms. Village name conversions have particularly interested me since I first came across them because of the clear links between old Turkish and new Greek names that could still be discerned in the majority of cases. The committee responsible for converting Turkish village names into Greek ones included the same state intellectuals who sought to prove the area's historical links to Greekness. One of these was Stilpon Kyriakides. In a lecture he gave on the naming of the town of Komotini long after the work of the committee was done, he sketches out the ideological concerns that must have guided this renaming work. Delivered to his townsfolk at the Komotinians' Club in 1966, the lecture argued that the town's name had never been Turkish. The switch from the Turkish 'Gümülcine' to 'Komotini' signalled the restoration of the town's Greek essence, since the Turkish name derives from the Greek word '*Kumutziná*' denoting fields belonging to the wife of a Roman soldier of rank, a '*Komítissa*', or to a person called *Kumutzís*, in what could be seen as a way of embodying Komotini's Greekness in its name. With this claim he refuted etymologies linking the town's name to Turkish words such as *kömür* (charcoal) and *gömüllü* (buried) (1966: 52–55). Such claims to Greekness through etymology had been part and parcel of the nation-building process, as Wace and Thompson showed in an early publication that described the strategy as 'political philology' (Wace and Thompson 1914: 9).

This strategy of nationalization clearly followed earlier tracts. The name 'Ellinohóri' ('Greek village') is found both in the peninsula of the Peloponnese (Corinthia prefecture), where the War of Independence began in 1821 and where the first capital of the Greek Kingdom was located, and in the eastern-most prefecture of Evros in western Thrace. It is a name that attests to the process that rendered these villages Greek, expunging some other identity that might have been present in the past. The Ellinohóri of Evros was reportedly previously named Bulgarköy ('Bulgarian village' in Turkish) – what exclusions this earlier name might have pointed to remains unknown. In the scientific and meticulous renaming of village names in western Thrace, rules of transliteration and translation were followed closely. The village Kızıllar (loosely translated as 'Reds') was renamed Kizári, which has no meaning in Greek, but is the grammatically correct form of the word stem converted into neuter singular. By comparison, Hacıköy ('Village of the Blessed', designating those who have travelled on the hajj to Mecca) became Ayohóri ('Village of the Saints') in translation. Mis-translations are also found, for example in the conversion of Sınırdere ('Border Stream') into Névra ('Nerves'), possibly because *sınır* (border) was confused with *sinir* (nerve). Also underlying this conversion was a concern with idealization, whereby this newly incorporated geography was rendered beautiful. Thus, one finds such village names as Oréo (Beautiful), transliterated from the latter half of Yassıören (Flat-built), or Évlalo (Sweet-voiced), translated from İnehanlı (possibly related to *inilti*, meaning 'echo') and Égiros (the tip of the poplar tree) from Kavaklı, the Turkish name of the tree.

These conversions are now to be found in lists of old and new names that circulate amongst minority members. My own copy was given to me by a minority official who consulted it from time to time when liaising with Greek authorities on individual grievances. The request of an old man hailing from the village of Hacımustafaköy ('the village of Hacı

Mustafa', designating the honorary title of hajj traveller bestowed upon a certain Mustafa at some point in time), for example, would be written down in the official language of Greek petitions, which requires that information such as name, age, place of origin, etc. is placed in the opening paragraph. When this information was being typed up, the list may have been consulted to check that Hacımustafaköy is indeed Ámfia (referring to the vestments used by priests during church ceremonies, a name that seemed to be inspired by the Muslim practice of assigning specific head coverings to differentiate hajj travellers from commoners) – and usually the list would prove correct. In those moments, the conversions, from the name that village inhabitants used to designate their location to the 'place of origin' communicated to officialdom, would be rendered biopolitical techniques, on which access to licenses, grants, benefits, or health care might be decided.

At those points, naming, perceived by the state as a connector to national allegiance (as we have seen in the dispute over the naming of the minority), made the difference between hardship and the improvement of one's living standard. The state's investment in those conversions was as political as it was economic. Use of the correct name indicated compliance with the governmentality of population conduct on the level of space. For despite the merits or shortcomings of any specific application, it could be said with some level of certainty that a hypothetical official faced with an application that stated an 'origin' in a Turkish-named place would be compelled to read in this name a failure of citizenhood, an outright failure to be conducted into a Greek minority population, resulting in the removal of all possible claims to other citizenship rights. Language functioned to place such origins 'over there', beyond the state border, even if the location designated was actually 'over here' (according to the logic dictating that Turkish locations should exist only in Turkey). Staple nationalist rhetoric responds to minority claims with the statement 'if you don't like it here go back to Turkey' – this is the argument that Adnan (chapter two) responds to in reference to the minority's historical bonds ('roots') to western Thracian place (a space, that is, inhabited and culturalized by specific people who on this basis claim it as 'theirs'). Unless this 'place' is communicated in Greek (and therefore Hellenized, even by those 'rooted' in it but who designate it otherwise), such 'rooting' remains precarious, with deracination always a threat (through lack of access to welfare for example, or even lack of access to citizenship at the most extreme). Naming thus makes the place a political and material object, it does not simply effect the transposition from signifier to signified (I have in mind Deleuze and Guattari's critique of semiological precepts here [Deleuze and Guattari 1987: 83–122]). Hacımustafaköy and Ámfia are not signifiers of the same location if one of those places is the location of citizenship rights and the other locates its lack. Yet both together, and in their inter-relation, are conduits of the minority condition. I think this is what Massey means when she criticizes 'a problematical geographical imagination . . . [where] [t]he couplets local/global and place/space do not map on to that of concrete/abstract' and proposes that '[i]f space is to be thought relationally then it is no more than the sum of our relations and interconnections, *and the lack of them*' (Massey 2005: 184, emphasis added).

Analysing similar toponymical conversions (this time from Greek to Turkish) in northern Cyprus after the war of 1974, Navaro-Yashin claims that sovereignty bifurcates in the encounters between officials and the mentality of government they serve. In these encounters, she shows how sovereignty is practised not along a single, pre-ordained route, set by 'the' government. Instead,

> sovereignty is worked upon through a network of people engaged and engaged upon through materialities (for example, tools of cartographic measurement, instruments of aerial military photography, calculating devices for geographical maps, documents of title deed, the office building of a Maps Department, or methodologies for assigning value to distinct properties). The practiced network between human and instruments, then, is what makes sovereignty. (2010: 133)

The materiality of sovereignty I talk about here is perhaps less militarized and less contested than that of the Turkish Republic of Northern Cyprus (TRNC, an unrecognized state which is 'occupied', 'governed', or 'protected', as the rhetoric may have it, by 40,000 Turkish troops), but its binary bordering effect (Greek is here, Turkish over there, Greek naming in applications examined, Turkish naming thrown out) is perhaps even more totalizing (Greek village names in northern Cyprus may be used even amongst Turkish Cypriots in explicit attempts to resist the imposition of Turkish names, or indeed, even by officials). The Hellenization of village names in Thrace has been more certain (names changed once and for all), more scientific perhaps (the committee tasked with name changes took less time to complete its work than its TRNC counterpart, which spent two decades on this), but the biopolitical objectives – to insert toponymy in the mechanics of governing the everyday – were no less clear, perhaps even more so.

The settlement of Greek refugees from eastern Thrace was another technique based on the same logic of governmentality. The newcomers in the 1920s were settled in villages that had been renamed with a view to Hellenizing the Thracian landscape. Elsewhere in Greece, and particularly in the north, new settlements arose to accommodate these refugees, which were named after their original places of habitation. For example, Néa Kessáni, 'New Kessáni', in the Thracian district of Xanthi, was named to memorialize the town of Kesáni/Keşan in eastern Thrace. Néa Smírni (New Smyrna) sprung up south of Athens, after the city of Smyrna/İzmir on the Asia Minor coast and Néa Éfesos, after the town of Éfesos/Efes (near current-day Kuşadası on the same coast) became the name of a village near Katerini, south of Thessaloniki.

These newcomers were not only settled in newly-named places, they were also often given new names themselves. This is because the process through which settling refugees was registered required that individual names included both a birth name and a family name. Reportedly, many refugees did not possess the latter. Thus, local knowledge has it, Thracian surnames often have the ending '-akis', recognized as a Cretan name form, because the registration of refugees in the area was done by a Cretan regiment which liberated the town (and which is commemorated in 'Sintáğmatos Kritón' street). The officers, charged with registering refugees after their flight from Asia Minor, found themselves offering surnames to people who had none, as a first step to making them Greek citizens, and drew on their locally specific experience of Greekness (such as in the form of relatives' or friends' surnames) as they did so. In the 1920s the state, and its military and intellectual representatives, therefore named both people and place, and in the process Hellenized and humanized them.

By the 1990s, when I walked through Komotinian streets for the first time, plaques did not only communicate knowledge that national subjects were supposed to have (one did not simply read 'Athens street' [*odhós Athinón*] on a street name plaque), they also included the explanation 'the capital of Greece' (*protévousa tis Elládhos*) at the bottom. A didactic function was communicated in those plaques, which had less of an educational and more of a scolding tone about it: Athens is this nation's capital, the plaque seemed to announce, and everyone should know this, even if they do not know it as 'the birthplace of civilization' (as school textbooks teach), or the ancient city-state. By the same token, names of towns in current Turkey or Bulgaria were commemorated as 'homelands' to Greek communities – one read the phrase *haméni patrídha* (lost homeland) under the name of *Makrás Yéfiras* Street (from Üzünköprü, in eastern Thrace) or *Ardhá* after a tributary to Evros river, located in Bulgaria. Eighty-seven of the 195 street-names listed in the 1936 Komotinian street guide are names of geographical locations in Greece, Asia Minor and Bulgaria; the rest celebrated Greek personalities and military men, Greek ancient tribes, or indicated important locations in the town. In 1999, the street plaques containing the phrase *hamenes patrídhes* were found in the same vicinity as street names celebrating locations that are part of the Greek State, like *Thásou* (Aegean island), as well as locations outside Greece and with no clear claims to 'homeland' identity. Ankara (*Angíras*) street was found in a neighbourhood of eastern Thracian 'lost homelands', suggesting perhaps that on a different historical grid (for example, if the Greek Asia Minor expedition had succeeded), it might also have been a 'homeland' – even though the plaque failed to explain this reasoning.

Asked about these didactic explanations, informants claimed that they were added 'at the time of the Sadık events' (*tóte me ta yeğonóta me ton Sadhík*) in the early 1990s when Sadık Ahmet, a local minority politician who espoused Turkish nationalist positions, was campaigning vociferously against the Greek government for the rights of the minority. He was elected as an independent MP in the elections held in June and November of 1989 and April 1990 (resulting from the repeated failures of the winning conservative party to secure a parliamentary majority). Between the second and third elections, on 26 January 1990, Ahmet was convicted, together with another member of his 'Friendship, Equality and Peace Party' (Dostluk, Eşitlik ve Barış Partisi – DEB), for disturbing the public order with election material that emphasized the minority's Turkishness. In a trial that had been characterized as 'unfair' (Helsinki Watch 1990), defendants were told by judges to 'go to Turkey' when they said they were Turkish. At the end of the trial Ahmet reportedly stated that his 'message to the minority in Western Thrace is that they should not forget they are Turks' (ibid.: 18). Two days later, a Greek mob ran through the shopping streets of Komotini, smashing the windows of minority-owned businesses. They were followed by a slow-moving police car who failed to intervene (ibid.: 20–23). Compensation promised by the state had still not been paid out by 2006 (OSCE 2006). At the same time, the Greek state added didactic explanations to street name plaques, and raised the threshold for parliamentary entry to three per cent (Law 1907/1990), one percentage point higher than the highest demographic estimates of the minority population (whereas the previous system under Law 1847/1989 set instance-specific thresholds for each prefecture that depended on the total number of valid votes divided by the seats allocated to that prefecture).

In the spatialization of biopolitics, didactic name plaques 'scold' unruly subjects who 'should really be in Turkey' but are instead in Greece, teaching them to behave like Greek citizens – and disciplining them through law and the political process when they do not. The repercussions of this move, traced by Massey, from the representational level of space (naming) to the phenomenological one (of actual streets) are destroyed businesses, loss of income, lack of compensation – all things that transform daily life into a 'minority' life irrespective of the ideological leanings of the person who leads it (were all 400 minority shop-owners supporters of Ahmet?)

An allusion to such repercussions cannot be missed in similar naming strategies across the border in Turkey: following Ahmet's death in 1995 in a car crash, Turkish authorities gave his name to the street in front of the Greek Orthodox Patriarchate in Istanbul (whose minority community dwindled after the 1955 pogroms that took place there) (Aarbakke 2000: 626). Gümülcine Street is located in the Black sea coastal city of Samsun, where Atatürk launched his military campaign (1919) which crushed the Greek army and eventually established the modern Turkish state (ensuring that *Angíras* Street did not refer to a Greek 'homeland'). Another street in that city bears the name 'Drama', a town west of Komotini, from which Muslims were forcibly exchanged under the Lausanne Treaty. Like in the Greek case, toponymy has been part and parcel of Turkish state-building both in efforts to obliterate 'otherness' from former multi-ethnic landscapes (Öktem 2004) and in efforts to commemorate 'lost homelands'. What remains to be analysed is how biopolitics operates in these spaces.

On a symbolic level, this biopolitics takes a gendered form, whereby the masculine notion of time (history) is seen to conquer the feminine notion of space (Massey 2005: 29). The streets become the 'Greek body' – political and civic, ethnic and religious. In its various manifestations this remains a virile body, moulded by men (as those who give the street names), and celebrating male achievement and male presence in the nation – Bouboulína, a female heroic figure of the independence struggle, normally depicted as possessing male courage and stature, is the only woman immortalized in Komotinian street names.

But as much as events of recent history have solidified the borders that toponymy put into text (between 'Greece' and 'elsewhere'), they have also shown that those borders have, at other times, been less solid (non-didactic, less scolding). In fact, they have been rather porous. Research in the town's land registry has revealed that the locations of fields have remained unchanged until quite recently in relation to village and street changes, and that the change from Greek transliteration of Turkish names into purely Greek forms has been very gradual. This kind of transliteration differs from that employed in village name changes in that it is the exact transfer of sounds into the Greek alphabet, without any attempt at Hellenization in terms of grammatical correction. For example, a field location called 'Kuru Çayı' was referred to in exactly the same way as late as 1979 and a place called Dar Sokak (Narrow Path) survived in its transliterated form as late as 1987; but this was not always the case, as since 1983 a location called 'Kurt Beyli' was translated into the Greek 'Likótopos' (Wolf-Place). Those spaces of wilderness that were 'non-places' were allowed to remain un-Hellenized, highlighting the link between civilization and 'proper' naming.

Such policies of naming, renaming, forgetting to name, reshuffling names and educating the population on the politics and histories of names, which maintained the currency of Komotinian toponymies, complimented other technologies of governmentality. The attempt to settle 'Greek' refugee populations in this demographically 'suspect' territory, repeated in the 1990s with the policy of settling 'Greek-origin repatriates' from the former Soviet Union, could be seen in this way. Together with the naming of streets and other urban planning projects, these settlement policies provide examples of technologies that create and reproduce 'Komotini' as 'Greek' but also as a place the Greekness of which needs repeatedly to be confirmed. Both processes have been predicated on the paradox of the identification, on the part of the name-givers, of Komotini as (thoroughly and justifiably) Greek and their concern that in fact it was not quite so. There has always been an implied exterior that has needed to be 'tamed': this exterior was the established minority.

Governing the Untamed

Komotinian streets are only labelled if they lead into other streets. Dead ends do not have names: they are simply called *Adhiéxodos A, Adhiéxodos B* ('Dead End' A, B), followed by the name of the main streets they branch off from. These dead ends are found in the oldest neighbourhoods and are presumably the result of house division through connecting yard doors, 'neighbour's doors' (*komşu kapı*), which are a feature of Turkish houses. These doors functioned as corridors of intimacy, allowing women to move from one house to the other without being seen by the public world outside the high walls that separate front yards from the street. With many *komşu kapı* now built in, dead ends are a reminder of an ordering of space which is shaped by concepts of femininity and patriarchal concerns about honour, whereby gender segregation is naturalized. Despite the fact that minority gender relations may now be differently ordered, what remains are the links of this segregation to the ethnic segregation of the townscape at large.

The lack of names for these roads thus seems, if not calculated, at least symbolically significant. In terms of gendered dynamics, the ordering that takes place here seems to emasculate minority space. Dead-end streets serve minority members almost exclusively and, therefore, are not 'public' spaces. Hence, not naming them reinforces the image of the minority as secluded and marginal while at the same time stressing the exclusion of the minority from the formal nationalist image of Komotini. As streets without names, dead ends are places outside the scope of nationalizing strategies, and are subject to different techniques of governmentality. They are illustrative of where the state draws the line in bringing Turkish neighbourhoods into its symbolic compass. The ambivalence governing the relationship (respect for communal privacy, recognition that Greek formal rhetoric is unable to account for the minority, denigration of the minority into an 'alien' element) extends beyond spatial arrangement. It forms the basis on which minority conceptualizations of space are predicated, and whereby inter-communal spatial communication becomes possible.

Dead ends are spaces of exception that constitute the law of street-naming and space-making. They offer a way of ordering what are otherwise abject spaces, spaces that become encultured through processes (minority rituals, daily lives and social relations) that the Greek majority is largely absent from. Dead ends can thus be seen as a technique for subsuming differentiated Turkish neighbourhood names into the undifferentiated concept of '*Tourkomahallás*'. This is a designation used by many Komotinians to refer to the town's 'Turkish neighbourhood' (used in the singular, but denoting all minority areas). Dead ends mark out Turkish neighbourhoods as unknown and unknowable. They 'bury' a specific kind of spatial knowledge in the minority condition.

The names of the mahalles on the other hand, that Gümülcinelis use to communicate space amongst themselves, reveal a social history of Komotini that is, to most Greek Komotinians, lost. For example, the mahalle known to minority individuals as Tabakhane (usually shortened to Tabana – 'Tanning place') is located on the part of the river where most tanning activity used to take place. Şehreküstü ('above the town') indicates that the old borders of the town used to be below this mahalle and that it was built before Yeni (New) Şehreküstü. Kır Mahalle was evidently built in an area that was considered as 'countryside', therefore the area must have been built up rather recently, and similarly Yenice indicates construction after Yeni Mahalle (New Mahalle). Mastanlı would imply that its first settlers immigrated there in the 1870s, since it is the name of a Bulgarian town in the district of Kırcalı/Kardzhali, which lies directly north of Komotini. Arifhane (Arif's place), Aşçıhasan (Hasan the cook) and Kocanasuh (the Great Councillor) are presumably named in honour of specific personalities of those mahalles. The fact that Cemaati (Religious populace) is the name given to the mahalle around Yeni Cami (the New Mosque) would imply the historically correct fact that Yeni Cami is actually older than Eski Cami (the Old Mosque). In turn, the fact that Eski Cami is located near the Poşpoş area might imply that it was built as a replacement of the old mosque that must have functioned as the basis for calling Yeni Cami 'new'.

Most Komotinians (Turks and Greeks) would be able to answer questions about the meaning of most street names and most Gümülcinelis would be able to deconstruct the Turkish names of mahalles and explain their origin (and it is this practice that I partly recounted and partly mimicked in the previous paragraph). However, explanations on plaques go mostly unnoticed, as do Turkish explanations. Naming space is an automatic choice, implying that the 'political' has become tacit knowledge. Or as Green and King suggest, it would be possible to take social interaction as an indication of regionalization and of the power relations inherent in it (2001: 265–271). In this sense, one type of space stands out in particular: that which is generally avoided or unused.

The daily trajectories of most of my Gümülcineli friends included their homes, work, parents' or in-laws' houses and sites of entertainment. Unintentionally, they did not frequent Greek areas, just as they did not frequent mahalles other than those of the close family. By implication, the communal division in space prevented inter-communal co-presence (Greeks did not need to go to Turkish mahalles, and Turks did not need to go to Greek ones). Even when work was located in Komotini's 'mixed' busy centre, Greek and Turkish shop-owners would mainly socialize with their 'communal' neighbours. Unsurprisingly, the coffee shop next to the *müftülük* (the religious administration office) only hosted minority men while Çukur Kahve ('the coffee shop in the ditch') was known as an 'upper-middle class' spot (frequented by men in their fifties and sixties and occasionally Greek students). Places of entertainment were similarly segregated with the notable exception of one bar (Alávastro, whose story I have examined elsewhere [Demetriou 2002: 231–245]) which had a mixed clientele of minority youngsters and Greek students.

This rigidity of divisions also pervaded the use (and non-use) of space. Thus, daily journeys to nearby destinations would be made on foot, longer ones by car, and some would be avoided altogether. Yet, there is a sense in which distance was judged on the basis of what particular places connoted as much as it was on quantifiable elements. On the occasions where I visited houses in Kır or Yeni mahalles with friends who lived in the centre (a considerably higher-class location), we usually took taxis, or drove there, despite the accessibility and proximity of these areas. Still, there were other mahalles which were clearly 'out of bounds', such as the Roma mahalles of Alan Kuyu (a shanty area next to the site of the weekly market) and Kalkanca (a neighbourhood on the outskirts of Komotini, formally considered to be a different area, an *ikizmós*, which was established after the relocation of the 'Gypsies' from the town to the outskirts in 1925). Kalkanca has been given a Greek name – Ífestos – after the Greek god of fire who is usually depicted in the process of metal-working, testifying to the racialism of name-givers who associated the Roma with this profession.

Kalkanca is known by Gümülcinelis as a place of 'trouble', where there are often fights between (usually young) men and which is frequently visited by the police. 'It is our very own Harlem here', Bilge once joked:

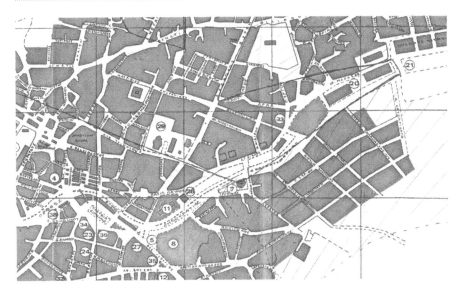

Figure 4.2 Section of Komotini street map

'Even the police are scared to get involved when a fight is on, they always come after everything has calmed down.' Some Gümülcineli men enjoy all-male drinking outings (*muhabbet*) to Kalkanca, hiring Gypsy *davul* (drum) and *zurna* (flute) players. Women, on the other hand, refuse to join such outings, sometimes blaming the area's reputation, but most often citing distance as a problem and explaining that 'it is too much hassle getting there'. The divisions that inhere in the politicization of Greek and Turkish space in the town are here reproduced within the minority group along cultural, class and gender lines.

Alan Kuyu ('Field Well'), another Roma mahalle, was considered to be outright dangerous. When I first announced that I had 'passed through' the area, I was told that one should be careful in that place and that if I wanted to see it again, my friends would arrange for somebody to drive me through one day. Curious about what this 'seeing' entailed, I accepted the offer, and found myself literally looking through the car window, as co-passengers repeated exclamations about the dirtiness, the squalid housing, the neglect of children who stood barefoot on the road side and stared back at us, the unemployment and alcoholism of the men, etc. It is indicative that on maps of Komotini Alan Kuyu is marked as fields rather than an inhabited area, that the spaces between houses are not considered streets (or even dead ends) and that there is no Greek name for the neighbourhood (Figure 4.2). In this sense, the derision implied in the use (by Greeks) of Kalkanca rather than Ífestos is turned into plain denigration in the case of Alan Kuyu since there is not even the availability of choice to be considered. Bordering thus becomes a technique for classifying 'others' as more or less distant on the basis of the conceptual distance of their 'otherness'. Thus, from a Gümülcineli perspective, Greeks are left out of the picture, whereas 'Gypsies' are far away. The Roma group that is most rigidly bordered is geographically closest, because it is most clearly 'Gypsy' – living on the border of deprivation, in an area outside the concerns of the local authorities.

By comparison, Pomak mahalles are rather recent. Although they have Turkish names specifying their former rural uses, such as Harmanlık (Place of wheat/chaff separation) and Bağlar (Vine-fields), in Greek they are simply known as *ta afthéreta* ('the houses without building permits'). People living in these Pomak mahalles would point out with resentment the fact that the municipality had supplied them no water and electricity until a few months before the elections, but it had labelled the streets long before that. In these three abject places, the border, unmarked and erased from maps, is read on an ethnic register, marked by the capricious shifts between inclusion, denigration, and racialism.

Counter-conducting the Spatio-lingual Border

If the governmentality of minority topography is characterized by the taming of space, this taming has not only generated by-products in the abject spaces that remain untamed. It has also produced specific kinds of counter-conduct that persist in the daily interactions of majority and minority. For most Gümülcinelis, mahalles are categories used in everyday speech and rarely represented in written form. This double register operates in the two different languages simultaneously, thus exposing several characteristics of the way in which the two communities interact. It shows the separation that pervades daily interaction, as well as its adjustment, which allows Turks to function within their group and in relation to Greeks, and the inability of formal discourse to regulate all aspects of social life. Turkish-speakers thus still refer to Leofóros Iróon as Yeni Yol (New Street), which seems to imply that it pre-existed the name conversion of the 1920s (initially into Stratónon – Barracks' Street – after the military barracks set up there by the Greek army), and that the state efforts to inscribe Greekness failed not only on the level of what they excluded (mahalles and rural space), but also in cases where street space had been socialized and linguistically domesticated before the conversion. However, few if any local Greeks are familiar with this name and when referring to the street in conversation with Greeks minority members always use the term *Iróon*. In effect, minority members are fluent in two spatial codes, whereas Greeks usually in only one. I often heard younger Greeks, in their twenties and thirties, refer to the northern part of the town as one location, a '*Tourkomahallá*'. Very few of these young Greeks seemed to know any names for the different mahalles, even though many had minority friends. And when I named mahalles in Turkish to my friends, they exclaimed that I had become 'a local'. The political significance of such exceptions is shown in the following example.

After many attempts to find a taxi, Meral managed to stop one and I hopped in with her son. She greeted the taxi driver in Greek and gave the street address, whereupon three-year-old Enis asked rather assertively what the man had replied. Meral whispered that he should save his questions until we reached our destination, but Enis insisted even more loudly. The taxi driver turned around, smiled and gave a translation in Turkish of what he had just said, that he was not quite sure where this street was. Then he turned to Meral and asked in Greek whether this street was in *Yeni mahallá*, to which Meral replied (in Greek) positively. She later related the incident to friends, stressing the driver's failure to be upset at Enis's rudeness, and her amazement at his knowledge of Turkish and of the Turkish name of Yeni Mahalle in particular.

In this instant of inter-personal exchange, the taxi driver was using the 'other' spatio-linguistic code (Turkish) to facilitate a particular form of communication with a child as much as with his mother. Verbalizing *Yeni mahallá* in Greek was a technique to ensure that his interpretation of the spatial code Meral had translated for him (street address) was indeed correct. But in translating the code back to hers (specifying a neighbourhood), he was also exposing the limits of national mapping (for those who do not live in them, Turkish mahalle streets are not so familiar) and substituting it with the verbalization of his own distinct and personal identity – as a local who knows 'the other', both spatially and linguistically, and a professional who not only guesses correctly, but also puts aside nationalistic priorities for the benefit of a client. This suggests that in addition to the existence of the double register, which otherwise seems linguistically confined, there also exists the ability to shift and switch between languages and between the codes (in this case spatial) that accompany them. Counter-conduct is not only expedient; it is also a surprising aspect of inter-personal relations. Difference is acknowledged, but the linguistic border can, capriciously, also be broken down. And space can be opened up to situational shifts.

In this counter-conduct, the 'burial' of knowledge I wrote about earlier is momentarily ruptured. Those moments of inter-personal communication become occasions for resurrecting linguistic and spatial knowledge that is supposed to be 'intimate', in the sense of being ethnically confined. Such ruptures are then indeed ruptures of intimacy, undertaken in the frame of a broader 'cultural intimacy' (Herzfeld 1997). In Herzfeld's analysis of this concept, such intimacy is shared within the group and is used to point out the 'native'. The rupture effected here then, is that of re-bordering that 'nativeness' not around the nation-state, but around the Komotinian and Gümülcineli townscape. Space, in other words, becomes the medium of a specific form of counter-conduct that in the previous chapter was identified as 'border thinking'. But as in Celal's case, such ruptures are enabled by an 'intimacy' (a secretive form of communication in that instance) that maintains the majority-minority border. In this case, it is the gender dynamics pertaining to the privacy of conversations with women and children, in turn predicated on the knowledge of majority-minority power dynamics: i.e. that the child will eventually grow up to speak the language and to communicate space in the Greek form – to be, in short, a 'proper' citizen, like his mother. Would this rupture have occurred if his father had been present? I am uncertain. Would it have happened with a monolingual Turkish-speaking mother? She would most likely not have taken a Greek taxi in the first place. In these cases, the minority counter-conduct of knowing space in particular ways, verbalized here by the taxi driver, would remain fenced in. But it is on the basis of its existence that instances of 'majority counter-conduct' (in their rare occurrences) gain force.

And this is the crux of the gesture as counter-conduct – for it is in the crossing of the codes that nation-state subjectivity is counter-conducted. To assume that the taxi driver's ethnicity also ethnicizes his conduct, and thus analysing it as a form of 'Greek counter-conduct' would be to essentialize and ultimately maintain the border (between Greekness and Turkishness) that street names conduct. The comparison between the historiographical counter-conducts of Celal and Andreas arguably did just that. But here a different possibility emerges. The rupture of population conduct effected here, occasioned by the inter-subjective dynamics in the taxi, is communicated to friends and may lead to further articulations of the Turkish spatial code in correlation with the Greek one. Space therefore goes beyond the boundaries the nation-state seeks to impose on it. The outcome is not the counter-conduct of the Greek taxi-driver, but the counter-conduct of driver, Meral, and Enis together, and without that combination it would not emerge as such. This is one way in which space is 'opened up for political address'.

Reconfigurations of Place

And yet, this is not where the conduct/counter-conduct dialectic is exhausted. For on this plane of inter-subjective relations a neoliberal taming of space has recently been taking shape. When I returned to Komotini in 2004 construction sites were to be found in all of the Turkish mahalles and the majority of the Gümülcinelis I spoke to had stories to tell of the sale of the family house in exchange for flats in a building block (*andiparohí*), which had recently been agreed with one of the developer companies active in the town. In most cases, the companies were based in other northern Greek towns and the deals involved the exchange of the land for about 30–40 per cent of the building to be erected. The demolition of Turkish houses in order to build Greek apartment blocks was rarely related to me with resentment by minority informants. Meral would guide me through the history of such buildings in a very matter of fact way, and friends would announce deals with Greek contractors to build blocks on their land with mixed feelings (of joy because they would receive their own floor and of frustration because they felt they could have got more out of the deal). Meral had herself moved into one of these flats, in a block inhabited by both Greeks and Turks.

'Respect for privacy' was often mentioned in discussions about coexistence in the building: in-laws and parents could now more easily be kept at a distance but issues concerning the possession of keys had to be negotiated, neighbours' habits and complaints were related with humour or frustration. In contradistinction to the implications of ghettoization that this carries in the 'private' minority areas of dead-end streets, where the state is unwilling to name and thus encompass the minority in its *topos*, this concept of 'privacy' provides a code through which individuals can relate, or avoid relating, to each other. Friends have often described with some amusement their experience of attending tenants' meetings, emphasizing the micropolitics of this new form of inter-ethnic coexistence, with questions or phrases showing Greek neighbours' limited knowledge of minority realities, arguments that cut across ethnic differences and ones in which such difference played a role. The opening up of dead ends and the building of blocks of flats is thus indicative of a shift in the logic of governmentality: it is no longer focused on the production of the nation through exclusion, but, rather, is driven by neoliberal market logics.[1] But that does not mean that the state withdraws and its place is taken by the market. Rather, the changing conceptions of 'privacy' are to be seen as indicative of a change in governmental practice. As Lemke states, '[t]he neo-liberal forms of government feature not only direct intervention by means of empowered and specialized state apparatuses, but also characteristically develop indirect techniques for leading and controlling individuals without at the same time being responsible for them' (2001: 201).

In other words, what appears here as a receding of the state, in terms of the biopolitical power exercised over the minority, is itself a technique of government, resulting not in the exclusion of the minority but in the 'shifting of regulatory competence of the state onto "responsible" and "rational" individuals' (Lemke 2001: 202) – in this case, property development companies and minority individuals exchanging their plots and houses for flats. This in turn inaugurates a different kind of biopolitics, where these individuals are faced with life choices that are political, including ones about their identities as middle-class Greek citizens over their identification as minority members – for example, whether they should send their children to Greek rather than minority schools on the basis of offering them a better education and career prospects, or when they will have to move into new houses. These choices entail a different concept of 'responsibility', tied to different material conditions. This shift of regulatory competence away from the state might indeed lead to that successful 'social integration' of individuals like Meral that has elided Greek minority policies for the last few decades, so that now minority women (and men) can fluently converse across linguistic and spatial codes and inhabit 'mixed' apartment buildings. It may alternatively preface the agonism of radical disagreement that would allow the connection between the spaces of protest and the spaces of governmentality that I alluded to earlier to be achieved without the violence that the 'Sadık events' (as precedent of this connection) necessitated. Still, a question needs to be asked about the future of less 'responsible' minority individuals, such as those living on the other side of town, in houses they have built without planning permission and on land that is fast becoming sought after. The implications of this question extend to the governmentality of ethnicity (predicated on notions of genealogy) and of land ownership (predicated on the notion of state care), which are examined in the next two chapters.

Note

1. Such shifts in minority policies have been related to wider EU-induced policy shifts, such as decentralization (Anagnostou 2001). Changes in place-making could be subsumed under these shifts in the sense that EU structural funds aiming at the development of the region, which was until recently branded the 'poorest region in the EU,' have contributed to the booming of the town's property sector.

CHAPTER 5

THE POLITICS OF GENEALOGY

Genealogy and the Dangerous Border

I have so far argued that the borders drawn by naming are primarily read as 'ethnic'. They create a division between the Greekness of over here and the Turkishness of over there. They are drawn on idealist assumptions of absolute binaries that render intelligible concepts such as 'nation' or 'the law'. Yet as soon as they are in place, an exteriority surfaces that questions them, undermines them, makes their counter-conduct possible, multiplies them, or reinforces them. What is at stake in the name of a border is ethnicity, but that ethnicity is in turn an index of sovereignty: who speaks what language, and when, in order to name a place, to describe themselves and others, are questions that are less about the subjective and individual free will to choose where one 'belongs' and more about the state's rightful claim to 'own' those subjects. 'Kin states' are thus less about kinship and more about enmity – they are the 'enemy' states for those into which 'kin subjects' are incorporated as citizens. This makes ethnicity part of what Panourgiá describes as the workings of a 'political DNA' in Greece: the conceptualization of genealogy as a marker of political affiliation (2009). But the homology is not neatly sealed, like a DNA strand. Leftists in Greece have been rendered 'dangerous citizens' on the paradigm of ethnic difference that is calibrated on the friend-enemy distinction. Their 'treason' was predicated on the existence of collaborator states 'over there'. A political DNA may be immutable (as for example when a family is labelled 'leftist'), but it is its leakage, within the nation but also beyond it (e.g. marrying into that family, or joining the Communist Party), that renders a citizen 'dangerous':

A person who posits a danger not because of the acts that she commits and the gestures that she makes, but because she (and those like her) thinks such acts and imagines such gestures. Her body, as flesh and bone, enfleshes the danger that she has come to embody and represent. Her presence becomes dangerous for the polis, as she is always suspected of thinking up thoughts of exploding (the categories, the borders, the classifications, the complicities, the secret treasuries of) this city. (ibid.: 7)

It is in one sense an inwardly inflected explanation, where 'danger' is contained in the body (a female body that should be domesticated, it must also be noted), with its gestures and its thoughts. But at the same time it is the possibility of this body multiplying into others like it and exploding (through its acts and thoughts) across 'categories, borders, classifications, complicities' that prompts its subjugation. The body is an internal threat (for this city) but only because of the possibility of reaching across an exterior. In the case of the left, the exteriority of the Soviet Union, and now terrorism (multiply-defined, as Panourgiá also shows), is the condition of possibility for the threat being pre-empted in the repressive measures against it.

In the Foucauldian move from the political economy of European power balances to the conditions of its production that founds governmentality, the body shifts from being an objective marker of difference (poverty, illness, defect, crime) to an effect of the governmentality that defines what poverty, illness, defect, and crime are and what they look like. This is the move that Panourgiá presupposes. Race, ethnicity, colour, origin, civilization, roots, heritage, extraction and so on are all tropes that have been employed and criticized in the analysis of just such shifts from marker to effect. To read them then as an effect of biopolitical power is an obvious starting point – and this is indeed what race studies have been doing for some time. But to read them after the migration of biological concepts into other domains of the political (e.g. right-left in Panourgiá's use of 'political DNA'), is to reinsert into the equation the connections that still elide both theoretical (in the 'disciplining' of ethnic/race studies, gender studies, post-colonial studies) and political work. It is to take 'race', 'ethnicity' and so on, as the effects of a governmentality that has not only produced racial and ethnic difference, but has also rendered it a metaphor for the multiplication of that difference into whatever needed to be disciplined and subjugated. It is, in other words, to reconnect the differences (race, gender, colonial history) through the modes of their disciplining.

These connections between theory and practice that this insertion enables are what I have previously alluded to in reference to Mignolo's 'thought border', where he problematizes the fact that relations between emancipatory struggles are mediated by the West (2002). The integration of these critiques into those of the capitalist project has not always been obvious but remains an influential and, I believe, productive argument for insisting on those connections. Nancy Fraser, for example, makes a convincing argument for second-wave feminism when she says that 'the cultural changes jump-started by the second wave, salutary in themselves, have served to legitimate a structural transformation of capitalist society that runs directly counter to feminist visions of a just society' (2009: 99) and that for this reason a reorientation of feminist thought and praxis is necessary. This is a different argument to that of 'intersectionality' which subsumes a range of differences (class, ethnicity) under a main category of concern (gender).

Closer to my concerns here, Stoler locates the relevance of her examination of the construction of race under colonialism in the '[opening] up of new spaces for thinking the present, prompting deeper genealogies that course between imperial moralizing missions and contemporary humanitarian interventions . . . [such as] detention centers for unwanted immigrants in France, refugee camps for Palestinians displaced by the Israeli state, and barbed-wire and fenced reserves for native Americans and Australia's indigenous population' (2010: xii). The connection between such older forms of governmentality (imperial moralizing missions) and newer ones (humanitarian interventions) is exactly the issue at stake for me here. The morphing of borders from devices that cordon off the minority to devices that incarcerate migrants is one aspect of the capriciousness that western Thracian borders exhibit (see post-script). This capricious aspect calls on views of the political which, rooted in genealogy, have given rise to multiple, and at points contradictory, techniques of governing the minority population (and later migrant populations).

This chapter is thus concerned with elucidating this capriciousness by exploring the genealogical thinking that underlies its emergence and maintenance. If the minority has been, and by some still is, treated as a 'fifth column' on Greek soil, this is only through the ways in which biology comes to bear on politics. A distinct race or ethnicity is the last thing that the Greek state has officially accorded the minority (it has diachronically insisted that 'no ethnic minority groups exist in Greece') – yet it has constructed exactly that in order to prove the point: the Pomaks as ethnically distinct from 'people of Turkish-origin'. My examination of Pomakness in this chapter traces this logic of genealogy as a device of biopolitical governmentality that has been coursing between constructing ethnicity and treating it as natural.

Kin States, Friendly States, and the Politics of Blood

In an earlier work (Demetriou 2004c), I argued that Pomakness is a 'slippery' category of identification, caught up in the contest between Greece and Turkey about who has a say over minority affairs – who, ultimately, 'owns' the minority. This presents a slightly paradoxical situation, as Pomaks were not always seen as coming under the protection of Turkey as a 'kin state', at least not solely. They have also been seen as somehow related to Bulgaria, although no organic links are discernible in the same way as pertain to Turkish minority members' links with Turkey (e.g. being a preferred location for long- and short-term migration, the home of close and distant relatives, the country many leading minority members have studied in, and of course, the cosignatory state to the Exchange of Populations Convention). In this sense, the relation of Pomaks to Bulgaria has over the years been a cause of exclusion rather than empowerment – those viewed as Pomaks were excluded from structures that sought to limit the power of the minority as a whole, as well as from structures that required a claim to 'Turkish' identity. In this, of course, the status of Pomaks in Bulgaria as a problematic (and therefore discriminated) minority group (see Brunnbauer [2001] and Poulton [2000] among others) played a significant role – Bulgaria could never have been a 'kin state'.

The paradox is that an equally important role was played by the Cold War context that placed Bulgaria in the position of an enemy state, with whom all potential links were suspect, even links that could not actually develop. The threat here was perceived in the possibility of Pomaks developing ties to the (same? other?) Pomak group across the border. History was seen as instructive. The 'so called "Pomak republic"' known as the Tamrash Republic, was established in 1878 in a region of Rhodoppe covering a number of Pomak villages which had refused to be governed by the Eastern Rumelia province (formed under the San Stefano Treaty upon Bulgarian independence), and survived until the incorporation of Eastern Rumelia within Bulgaria in 1886 (Todorova 1998: 304). Its existence seems to have made the argument of a feared resurrection of a Pomak state convincing even after the Cold War. During fieldwork, references to a vague 'Pomak state' still survived amongst educated Greeks who laughed off the possibility but nevertheless employed it to explain the salience of anti-Pomak Greek nationalism of earlier times.

On that legacy, Andreades' volume is instructive. References to Pomaks are scant in the book, yet the concerns he expresses over 'state security' converge on two issues where Pomaks are seen as important actors: communism and religion. Within the large appendix of letters from minority associations communicating with the Greek state (which Andreades probably secured in his military capacity) are many documents protesting against the Greek state's preferential treatment of the Kemalists within the minority and the concomitant inattention to matters pertaining to religion. In a letter dated August 1955 the 'Union of Muslims in

Greece' asked for a replacement of a *medrese* (religious high school) that had opened in 1949 in the town with a 'proper' religious high school that could constitute 'an anti-communist hearth, to fill the gap that has formed within the Muslims of western Thrace through the lack of such a centre, able to effectively defend against the united front of communists and atheists, as is the case in all the countries' (Andreades 1956: 74, my translation). The school in question, which could not respond to this need, is Hayriye, the only religious high school in Rhodoppe at present, and one which is today strongly associated with Pomakness. To trace the ways in which this association between the politics of religion and the politics of ethnicity has shaped views of Pomakness, one must view genealogy as a political category which has been shaped by the shifting distinctions between friend and enemy. More importantly, these distinctions are not 'local' but formed within global power balances, and in view of the friend-enemy distinctions (politics) that emplace 'all the countries' within a system of western democracy.

As argued in chapter three, Fessopoulos' turn to 'Greco-Turkish friendship', which elicited Andreades' criticism, was chiefly related to the communist threat in this larger context: that in which Greece and Turkey cooperated as NATO allies standing at the gates of the Soviet bloc. A closer look at the articulation that signified this turn is instructive about the place of ethnicity within the governmentality of the time. In the memo, Fessopoulos had asked the authorities of the elementary minority school in the village of Aratos, to replace the sign outside their school, which presented it as a 'Muslim' school, so that it be thenceforth described as 'Turkish'. The proper presentation of Turkish ethnicity was therefore a matter of instruction – Fessopoulos instructing the school authorities as he, in turn, had been instructed by the dictates of the 'Greco-Turkish friendship' doctrine. His conduct of population as a technology of the nation-state is placed within the realm of realpolitik of the Cold War system. Andreades' criticism, on the other hand, which argues that religion, and not ethnicity, is the proper descriptor for the minority, articulates religion as an index of the law (Lausanne Peace Treaty), which in turn points to the international system as a system of law-abiding states. Both Fessopoulos and Andreades then, are referring to what may be called, *pace* Stoler, 'imperial governmentalities', whereby concerns at hand are couched and legitimated on the basis of a 'global order' perspective. The difference between the two is that Fessopoulos understands this global order as premised on the separation between (western) democracy and communism, while Andreades understands it as premised on the separation between (legal) justice and barbarism. The former separation yields ethnicity as its index of operation (turning 'Muslim' into 'Turkish'), the latter replaces it with religion (insisting on the legal definition of the minority), but both take the premise of genealogy (the minority's ethnic otherness) for granted.

Pomaks were not the target then, but these imperial orders manoeuvred them into a position as the bulwark against Turkishness within the minority, a position previously (and arguably still) held by religious Muslims. In the Greece of 1955, still reeling from the divisions of the Civil War, and mired by governmental instability, with inhospitable islands still functioning as places of exile for communists even though the constitution had been restored (Panourgiá 2009: 29), 'democracy' did not preclude the military and police state, in which Fessopoulos and Andreades had invested their careers. Apart from the exile islands, this was a state that cordoned off part of the Rhodoppe mountains in order to stave off the communist threat, and in doing so, placed the majority of the Pomak population under military control. Pomak internment, it would seem, was dictated by a global order that drew its political boundaries on their doorstep. At the same time, Kyriakides was advancing his Achaean civilization mission thesis, Hellenizing modern 'Greek' Thracians into noble westerners and Pomaks (although not mentioned by name) into the remnants of ancient 'Thracian tribes' that welcomed that civilization.

By the late 1990s discussions of Pomakness still reverberated with this sense of their being 'remnants', or 'imperial debris' (Stoler 2008) of the post-Cold War period. The legacy of the Bulgarian Axis occupation of eastern Macedonia and most of western Thrace (except for the district of Evros) during 1941–1944 was a reference point for a number of people questioned on the meaning and treatment of Pomakness. Equally, the discourse of democracy and human rights was also supplanting vexed questions of origins and naming through a de-politicized reading of 'multiculturalism' where Pomak culture was celebrated as 'a piece of the mosaic' (see chapter three). It soon became clear to me that the qualified answers elicited by the question 'who are Pomaks?' were effectively answers to the questions 'who are Turks?' and 'who are Greeks?' The difficulty in articulating these qualifications was verbalized by Selim, when I once asked him over dinner the seemingly ignorant question about 'who Pomaks are':

> You see, during the war, when the Bulgarians were here, people were very scared. In the mountains it was even worse. They had no option but to learn the language if they wanted to communicate with the soldiers and bargain for their survival. But they don't speak it nowadays. 'Pomak' is not really something that people use to describe themselves. If anything, they would feel insulted to be called that.

The Bulgarians had of course also been there in the Balkan and First World Wars, but Selim was referring here to the Bulgarian occupation during the Second World War, which was quickly followed by the Civil War, fought mainly in northern Greece until 1949. What had struck me in that first response from Selim was the historical proximity in which he located Pomak identity (linguistically defined as the adoption of Bulgarian) which clearly collapses under historical scrutiny (Pomak has existed as a Slavic idiom long before). What I heard Selim articulating in this 'falsity' was an account of the relationship with those across the border, which was strained not only by the techniques of the Bulgarian occupation, which included massacre and expulsion of Greeks and settlement of Bulgarians (Miller 1975: 128), but also by the difference that his language marks between him and his Turkish friends. Selim's historical account was not about the past, but about the present. And it was not about language, but about the rejection of the genealogical reading that Pomakness has been subjected to.

In the many definitions of Pomakness that abound in the academic literature, genealogy figures prominently. Theses are presented and critiqued that define Pomaks as 'Islamicized Slavs', descendants of Turkic tribes, or Thracian races that can be traced back to Alexander the Great (Hüseyinoğlu 1972; Memisoğlu 1991; Zenginis 2001; Çavuşoğlu 1993; Foteas 1997; Todorova 1998; Brunnbauer 1999). These definitions are political not only because they allude to the national ideals of the states that espouse them (respectively Bulgaria, Turkey, and Greece), but also because they allude to the possibilities of empowerment and disempowerment of those with access to Pomak identity claims. These definitions elevate the event of religious conversion into an originary myth (Pomakness begins at the point of Islamicization), so that it is no longer the immutability of identity (e.g. blood) that maintains 'ethnicity', but the mutability of religion. In doing so, the questions of who the Pomaks were before the conversion, and of who the Pomaks could have been had the conversion not happened, are opened up and left unanswered (or answered at will, as the case may be). Thus effectively, 'Pomakness' is set up as an aporia, not a definition. It is this use of genealogy, which makes Pomakness problematic, that Selim's explanation counter-conducts. If Pomakness cannot exist, it is not problematic; the problem starts when it is foisted on someone, like an insult.

But what makes Pomakness insulting? Although Kyriakides may have Hellenized the Pomaks obliquely as ancient Thracian tribes, more recent academic studies have drawn the connections of racialism forcefully and bluntly, turning to anthropometric methods to prove the claim of Pomakic Greekness. Here, the racial difference that Kyriakides would have drawn between Thracian races and the Achaeans is eclipsed by a concern to completely identify Pomaks as Greeks. The first of these studies compared skull types throughout Greece, concluding that there is 'a racial unity of the people of Greece throughout History' and that the Thracian skull type (exemplified by Pomaks) resembles types found in Thessaly (Poulianos 1968, cited in Mylonas 1990: 38). The second, and most controversial, has proven the same thesis by comparing Pomak bloodtypes to those of 'pure' Greeks (Xirotiris 1971). Combining these findings in his memoirs as a doctor working in the mountain region of the Xanthi prefecture in the 1960s, a member of the team that carried out a pre-study to the second investigation argues that the Greek descent of the Pomaks is indisputable. Refuting a possible argument of difference based on language use, he emphasizes that 'skulls are harder than vowels and consonants' (Mylonas 1990: 43). Together, these studies are held as proof of a widely articulated claim that modern-day Pomaks are descendants of a fighting corps in the army of Alexander the Great called *Aghriánes*.

The controversy around these claims is not confined to their racist underpinnings, however, but extends to the ethics of research. According to local journalists, the data for the second study was largely based on experiments conducted on blood samples collected from the villages under the guise of vaccination (the involvement of Mylonas in his professional capacity as a doctor in the pre-study would render this plausible). The theory caused great uproar among the minority population and increased the suspicion of villagers towards outsiders to the extent that subsequently villagers refused to attend any medical examinations when Greek doctors visited the villages for fear of similar political repercussions. Yet the results of the study appear to have provided a factual foundation to at least some Pomak claims to Greekness (Imam and Tsakiride 2003: 68). The same insider account of the Pomak experience of marginality which upholds the findings of the research (celebrating their Greek descent) also criticizes the state's oppressive practices as having 'left the unfortunate Pomak people to their fate, their blood to be sucked literally and metaphorically' (Imam and Tsakiride 2003: 55, 68). If the concern with genealogy has thus placed Selim on one side and Imam and Tsakiride on the opposite side of the border drawn by the definition of Pomakness (a denigrated aspect of Turkishness for the first, and a traumatized version of Greekness for the second), what they both address and counter-conduct are the racial politics of this genealogy as a biopolitical technique of subjection.

This also held for Turkey, where genealogical concerns over Pomakness were also used to advance Turkish policy oriented towards proving the lack of Greece's protection of the minority. To this end, Pomak migration to Turkey was rendered easier than that of the Roma; although Turkey also claimed a Turkish ethnicity for the latter (Troubeta 2001: 184), the Turkishness of Pomaks was considered 'obvious'. What is considered problematic is the extent to which religion is thought to be practiced by Pomaks, which runs against the Turkish nationalist tenet of secularism. In post-1923 local history, some Pomak villages have been seen as the strongholds of religious propagandists expelled from the Turkish Republic following the fall of the Caliphate, and their inhabitants are to this day considered highly devout. This renders them 'backward', in the view of Gümülcinelis, but not necessarily un-Turkish. Pomakness is thus claimed as a subcategory of Turkishness as the politics of genealogy merge with the state politics of sovereignty. The difference that Pomakness represents is displaced from 'ethnicity' onto the plane of 'culture'. This 'culture' becomes read on the interpersonal level as a spatiotemporal difference, whereby Pomaks are seen as backward mountain people. Thus, even within the logic of genealogical unity, a difference (represented as 'cultural'), inscribes its own exclusions in the everyday.

Emplacing Ethnicity

Selim was born in 1975 in one of the mountain villages in the *balkan kolu* (the higher range of the mountain) of the Rhodoppe district. He grew up in the village and attended elementary school there. Because of the small number of students, the school only had one teacher, who hailed from the minority, and was not qualified to teach Greek. Selim was thus forced, on his own initiative, to study Greek by himself. When he finished elementary school, he took the minority high school exams and was accepted at Hayriye, the religious high school in Komotini. He lived in the school's boarding house for the first year, until his family joined him in Komotini. When I met him in 1998 he lived in one of the Pomak mahalles in a house that the family built largely by themselves and without proper building permits. His Gümülcineli friends often teased him about his Pomak identity, making comments about his intellectual capacities and purported bestial habits, in response to which he invariably laughed and seldom complained. His village origins, his current residential location, the religious studies he had undertaken in Komotini, as well as his later studies in the special training college for teachers of the minority known as EPATh in Thessaloniki, these were all blended into this teasing; however, the same was not true of his language, which he was so keen to deconstruct. His fair complexion and blue eyes, on the other hand, were taken as the 'ultimate' proof of his Pomak identity, yet curiously by 'Turkish' friends who were also fair and blue-eyed. He did not point this out to them, partly because of the power dynamics in the group, and partly because those other factors that were taken as indicative of Pomakness did not apply to them. Race was an epiphenomenon of the biopolitical regime he had been subjected to up to then. This regime has employed space (mountains, villages, mahalles) to first confine (through the set-up of military zones) and then locate Pomakness (as the identity formerly confined by these zones).

In the late 1990s, whereas valley villages were thought to be exclusively inhabited by Turks, Greeks and Roma, mountain villages were divided into two groups: the low villages of the *yakka* (the lower part of the mountain, the foothills); and the higher villages of the mountain (*balkan*). Gümülcinelis considered *yakka* villages Turkish and *balkan* villages Pomak. As is the case with any categorization scheme, such hard and fast distinctions did not of course hold up to scrutiny. When asked, many *balkan* villagers located Pomaks as coming 'from the next village up', or explained that their village had both Turks and Pomaks (they invariably failed to include themselves in the latter category). In the academic literature and public discourse, Pomaks are invariably defined as 'people of the mountain'. This connection to the mountains persists even after 'Pomaks' leave the mountain so that people living in the Pomak mahalles on the outskirts of Komotini are not seen as properly 'emplaced': on the legal plane they remain out of place, their dwelling places unauthorized (lacking building permits). In the view of the central town-dwellers they remain people who should normally be on the mountain. This spatial 'abnormality' is by implication transposed on the temporal plane rendering them 'backward'. This presupposition of emplaced normality is also echoed by Greek authors of various persuasions who often employ the term 'mountain-dwelling Pomaks' (*oresívii Pomáki*) to differentiate between migrant and non-migrant Pomak populations. These accounts are generally focused on descriptions of change in Pomak culture, either within a frame of lamenting abandoned traditions (Mylonas 1990) or celebrating the visibility of Pomak women in the labour structure (Troubeta 2001: 95–111). What they occlude, in either case, are former migration movements, the ethnic component of which has faded (recall for example the 'rumour' of Pomak presence among the ancestors of family storytellers in chapter two). They also occlude the technologies of repression that has emplaced Pomaks on the mountain during consecutive periods of dictatorship and wars.

Consider the example of Ramadan, in his late sixties in 1998. In the 1940s, he was pushed out of his village by force of circumstance. This was a mountain village, and he was born and grew up there at a time when the Bulgarian border had receded to its previous location after the four-year occupation of Thrace during the Second World War (1941–1944). This was the time, he explained, of the Greek Civil War (1945–1949) known as *andártiko* in Greek, and which he described through the rendering of the Greek word in Turkish as *andartlık*. The *andártes* (the

Greek communist guerrillas fighting government forces) – *andartlar* in his account in Turkish – had taken control of the mountain area while the Greek army, supported by the British against the danger of Communism, was fighting to push them further north. Ramadan's village had supplied the *andartlar* with all they needed during the first three years of their fight. When it seemed that they were losing the war, the army moved into the village and forced all the inhabitants out. They looted and burnt every single house so that the *andartlar* could no longer find supplies there. The villagers were forced to relocate towards the coast. Ramadan was one of many children, some of whom the family could not feed after relocation. By this time Ramadan was old enough to take care of younger siblings, so his father sent him to a big village nearby to make his own living and provide for some of the children. Ramadan began to study the Koran and raised them on very little, apart from his own creativity. He burnt his hand once, trying to handle a frying pan he had made out of tin. He then moved to another village, just outside Komotini, where he met his wife. He became an *içgüvey* (an in-married groom, moving into his wife's house instead of offering her his own), an identity that sets him apart from the 'norm' of the village and wider community. He has since made his living by growing tobacco. His children have both studied in Turkey but only his son has returned and helps his father with the chicken, cherry trees, and occasionally tobacco, while also having a day-time job in the town. A few years ago, when the village imam died, Ramadan was asked to replace him, because he was 'the only villager who knew the *ezan* (call to prayer)', he joked.

In Ramadan's story, Pomak identity was never mentioned, although it might be surmised by reference to the village where he came from. His subsequent marriage to a Turkish woman in a Turkish village has rendered his mountain origins of little significance to his children as a location for their 'origins'. In one interpretation, Ramadan might be taken as an example of the process whereby Greek government policy, driven by a fear of the communist threat during the Cold War, resulted in the assimilation of Pomaks into the Turkish minority. In conversations with villagers higher up the mountain, the experience of the Civil War was recounted as involving a relocation by the army in the years between 1944 and 1948, when their villages had fallen behind the battle line with the *andartlar* and inhabitants were evacuated into either Komotini or lower villages, then were moved up again. This unsettlement and resettlement, as well as its legacy for the ways in which 'mountain people' experienced the plains, Turkishness, and the Greek state, seldom feature in accounts of Pomakness. Ramadan's story is thus relevant in showing how geography, class, gender, politics, and religion are all components not only of the construction of Pomak identity, but also of the changes to which it has been subjected. It is in reference to this nexus that Pomaks today appear or disappear as national and/or minority subjects.

One of those villagers who had remained behind enemy lines in the Civil War explained in a matter of fact way that 'when the Bulgarians came, I fought with them. Then the *andartlar* came, I fought with them too. Then the army came and I fought with them as well.' This quotation brings into relief the fact that at the intersection of these differences lie structures of domination that in the Pomak case are intimately connected to the ordering of space presented in the previous chapter. The Pomak case therefore highlights the spatial aspect of intersectionality.[1] The connection of Pomaks with the mountains might have historical roots. However, their emplacement there, i.e. the strategy of ordering people into place, was undoubtedly effected through the repressive power of military violence.

Throughout the Cold War era (in fact since the time of the Metaxas dictatorship, in 1936) and up to the mid-1990s, the 'Pomak villages' (*Pomakohórya*) in the mountain ranges of Xanthi and Rhodoppe were enclosed within a restricted zone of military surveillance known as *epitiroúmeni zóni*. The fear of a possible Pomak state emerging resulted in stricter surveillance of Pomak villages. Thus, whereas 'restricted areas' governed by special military legislation were to be found along the whole length of the northern Greek border, the policy was especially enforced in Thrace (Labrianidis 1997: 40; 1999: 82). When people in both Komotini and the mountains were asked about this period during fieldwork, they referred to the zone as a 'border', indistinguishable from a 'national border' (*sınır*). Note that on the other side of the border, the national one with Bulgaria, the closure that followed the Second World War separated villages that had previously intermarried (Tsibiridou 1994: 14), and might have been more relevant to daily life than the internal border within Greece. This restriction was in force until 1996, when, following the collapse of communism, the zone disappeared and villagers were allowed to move and settle freely elsewhere within Greece, with many moving to the urban centres of Komotini and Xanthi as well as surrounding villages (Troubeta 2001: 58; Imam and Tsakiride 2003: 77). The relaxation of this legislation took place over a period of time and was differentially enforced in different areas. Thus, Lambrianidis shows that in the mountain area of Xanthi there has been differential development between the eastern region (inhabited by Pomaks) and the western (inhabited by Greeks) (Lambrianidis 1999: 85–90).

These processes paint a wider picture of place-making in Thrace. The installation of the military zone in the *balkan kolu* has thus effectively solidified the distinctions between the three geographical regions in western Thrace: the mountains (*balkan*), the foothills (*yakka*), and the valley (*ova*). In rendering them spaces of particular cultural significance within the Greek state, it has transformed them into places of ethnicity, the first one associated with Pomakness, the second with Turkishness and the last with mixed Turkish-Greek cohabitation. These associations persisted after the lifting of military surveillance and have come to permeate the way in which people define themselves and others, not only when they are 'in place', but outside of their conceptually 'assigned' places as well.

Constructing Pomak Morality

Military surveillance was the most extreme policy of genealogical governmentality. With the change in Greco-Turkish relations after the eruption of the Cyprus conflict, and the concomitant focus of Greek minority policy on differentiations within the minority, new policies came into being, or revised older ones, targeting ethnic differentiation overtly or covertly. This was the time immediately following Fessopoulos' memo and Andreades' publication. The latter's preface provides a sense of this context in arguing that since it is now proven that the rights of the western Thracian minority are respected in Greece, 'all fears about the fate of the Muslims of Cyprus, when the great island (*meğalónisos*) is re-united with Greece' can be dispelled (1956: 60).

If Andreades' efforts targeted domestic and international audiences who needed to be educated about Greece's minority protection practices, later governments, and specifically the junta regime installed in 1967, saw the need to educate the minority itself into genealogical governmentality. Set up in 1969, the Special Educational Academy of Thessaloniki (*Idhikí Pedhağoyikí Akadhimía Thessaloníkis*, known by the acronym EPATh) spearheaded this attempt, producing a number of minority school teachers until its closure in 2011, when this goal was incorporated into the 'minority unit' set up within the Primary Education Department at the Aristotle University of Thessaloniki. During fieldwork, schooling at EPATh was indicative of the process through which Pomaks were subjectified into a Greek population through being taught to reject claims to Turkishness. This subjectification operated largely in the mode of morality. When I visited EPATh in 2000, teachers informed me that the majority of the sixty or so students were Pomak, and that most came from the Xanthi prefecture. According to the Academy's mission statement, its goals were not simply to educate students, but to 'cultivate their personalities [so as to allow them] to become responsible and active members of the social group'.[2]

The teachers' interpretation of this goal was clear in 2000. Students' competence in the Greek language ranked highest in their priorities, alongside their 'modernization'. The teachers commented on how 'traditional' first-year students were: girls arrived in their headscarves and *fereces* (black, full-length gowns), both of which they 'take off (*vğázoun*) by the final year', they proudly claimed. Some of these girls had occasionally had relations with 'Christian' boys, I was informed, and the reverse also happened with the 'Muslim' boys dating 'Christian' girls. 'You should see the difference between how they arrive and how they leave . . . we are like parents to them, helping them in whatever way we can – supporting them morally, academically, financially', they said. Selim had spoken of his time in Thessaloniki as a happy, memorable period, primarily emphasizing the social aspects of living in a big city, where one could go out as much as one wanted.

What had struck me in 2000 was the low level of employment within the minority educational sector that the students actually achieved. In that year, there were about ninety academy graduates on the special list of the teachers awaiting appointments (*epetirídha*). This list secures employment in the public sector through appointment in minority schools, but the time one has to wait for this appointment is difficult to predict. However, the numbers of unemployed teachers, which rises every year that EPATh graduates exceed the number of appointments made, was a criticism rarely levelled against the Academy. Instead, one of the formal minority demands from the state has for many years been the closure of EPATh, together with Hayriye high school. The problem was not that EPATh did not offer transferable skills that would have secured employment elsewhere in the educational or even the wider public sector. It was that it existed at all.

Celal had once commented passionately that 'no other school closes on Friday (the Muslim holy day) any more, only Hayriye. They take these children and pollute their brains with backwardness. They teach them Arabic and the Koran, while Greek children learn technology and the Internet, and then they make them teachers and the decay seeps throughout the minority.' On another occasion, Emin, who was not yet married, told me that when he has children, it would be very difficult to decide to send them to school – 'I would rather keep them at home and teach them myself. All these graduates from Thessaloniki, they come back and you see them drinking in bars all the time – how can I entrust my child to them?' Teachers who drank in bars also included progressive Greeks who taught either in majority or minority schools – and some together with Emin and Celal. The moral point here was not the drinking per se, but what it signified about those who had been subjected to 'special', institutionalized, and confined 'minority education'.

Anti-Turkish propaganda was correctly perceived as part and parcel of this subjectification process. One of the Academy's main concerns was with Turkey's influence over the minority. EPATh teachers explained that having Turkey-trained local and Turkish teachers, the latter stipulated in the Cultural Agreement of 1951 between the Republic of Turkey and the Kingdom of Greece, was Ankara's way of keeping control over the minority (not entirely false). They then added that 'teachers from Turkey do not teach anything apart from the Koran, no matter what subject the timetable says they should be teaching, because they want to keep the minority illiterate, so that Turkey can have a better hold over it'. To them, the education that EPATh offered was about helping students to realise their true selves – being Pomak, that is, as opposed to Turkish. Pomaks, they claimed, 'are obviously not devout Muslims . . . they are actually crypto-Christians. They have a rock in the mountains of Xanthi, from where Pomak women fell to their death when the Ottomans came, to escape conversion.'[3] An essay exemplifying the good work produced at the school described marital rituals in the villages around Xanthi, borrowing heavily from Mylonas' book. The most critical comments in the essay concerned backwardness on gender issues e.g. women wearing the *ferece*, the lack of freedom as regards sexual relations and female spatial confinement. 'Modernity', as identified with the Greek state, was projected as the answer to such backwardness. Its emphasis on Xanthi villages resembled the tendency of many Greeks (scholars, politicians, and others) to present aspects of the minority problem through this area.

The moral point exemplified here was, in short, that modernity can only be achieved if the minority is freed from the pressure exerted on it by Ankara and is left to enjoy the benefits provided by the Greek state. An important precondition for this, however, is to recognize that most of this 'pressure' is geared towards insisting on Turkish naming. In this sense, the insistence of many Gümülcinelis that Xanthiotes are all 'Pomaks and untrustworthy', whereas at the same time they are 'more modern, richer, better educated and know more Greek', can be understood with respect to their perceived assimilation. Indeed, all these comments often went hand-in-hand with comments about the Xanthiotes' 'bad Turkish' and their loose morals. Thus, in a rather paradoxical fashion, both the Greek assertion that Ankara is keeping the minority backward and the Turkish assertion that Greece has a scheme to assimilate the minority were confirmed through reference to the Pomaks, who are presented as powerless victims swayed by cynical policies.

These morally charged viewpoints are, in both the Greek and Turkish cases, informed by a strong gender dimension. Women, in the view of EPATh teachers and Gümülcinelis, are thought to demonstrate Pomak 'backwardness', a backwardness that inheres in the *ferece* they wear.

Mylonas' book presents women as 'the obvious but unsung hero of their society . . . she does not speak back because on top of her hangs the threat of ostracism from the family . . . from the austerity of the paternal home she leaps into the nihilism of her husband's roof without complaint' (Mylonas 1990: 57–58). The book, the cover of which is appropriately graced by the image of a *ferece*-wearing (Pomak) woman, ends with the words of a female patient, examined on the doctor's return twenty-four years after he had left the village:

> 'Doctor . . . I know, I and all the women of this place, that our illnesses begin from the way in which we live, eat, and dress . . . It is terrible that this continues to happen. But they do not let us throw away these clothes, and then all the rest . . . the old people . . . Tell me, what should we do doctor? We also want to live like human beings . . .' I answered in one word: REVOLUTION. . . . In this direction we can also help; the presence of our own women, as permanent inhabitants of the region. We have to catch up to 'neighbours' who have already begun doing so (Mylonas 1990: 146, my translation).

The 'neighbour' the author is talking about is of course Turkey, which is vilified in this passage for seeking to modernize Pomak society for 'illegitimate' political reasons. Thus, the ultimate point of this highly orientalist passage inheres in the use of women as emblematic of the ailing Pomak condition of backwardness. The inhibition that is seen as the source of Selim's 'sexual deviance', in the words of his teasing Gümülcineli friends, is similarly premised, implicitly, on a view of Pomak women as 'closed up', sexually inactive, and therefore the root cause of male deviance. The stake in taking the *ferece* off, therefore, is no less than the modernization of Pomak society, responsibility for which is seen to lie not with Pomak women (or even men in fact) but their protector state. Women are in both accounts subject to domination, even when their emancipation is purportedly what is being sought.[4]

Lives on the Border

Kâmil points to a hollow and narrow ditch on the ground that stretches as far as we can see. 'This is the border', he says with a smirk. He had driven me and my partner a few miles north from his village in his truck, after I had asked him exactly where the border with Bulgaria lay, and whether one could cross. There are no fences, wire, or surveillance, as far as we can discern. 'So if I step across I am in Bulgaria?' I ask. He confirms that this is so. He points to a shepherd nearby, on 'this' side of the border, tending a flock we cannot see – it is probably grazing on the 'other' side, and he would probably follow them later on to bring them back. We are

Figure 5.1 The Greco-Bulgarian border

standing underneath the metal structure of a deserted military post. Until
a couple of years ago, Kâmil explains, it was manned (Figure 5.1). Now
it has moved down the mountain. Crossing was not as laughable then. In
other border villages, military surveillance seemed to still exist in 1999.
Villagers would ask if we had shown passports to get to their villages. In
one village, we were advised to leave by the wife of a man who asked us to
excuse her because she suffered from '*sinir hastası*' (nervous illness). His
father, sharing his bench with us in the empty village square further down,
had a different explanation: '*asker var, be!* [there are soldiers, man!]', he
told my partner in a tone that was both worried and paternal.

The three years after the abolition of the surveillance zone, military presence was still palpable for some of these villagers, if not visible to us. The
border, which at that point was being crossed by Bulgarians looking for
jobs in Greece, as another villager informed us, was policed in a different

mode and for a different category of 'outsiders' – not the Bulgarians of the red peril but the Bulgarians of the (then) non-EU job market. Iraqi crossers were also mentioned by someone else, long before the United States' invasion of their country. Within this new neoliberal order, of European emphasis on rights and border abolition within the EU and restrictions and border fortification without, remnants of the old order of the Cold War surveillance zone obviously existed in the minds of people and in their nerves. But perceptions about where illness, foreignness, the army, or the border itself lay were equally constructive of this existence. The border was subject to caprice: cynicism, ridicule, fear, and illness – and their second-order reading as metonyms for militarism, surveillance, or hopes for prosperity as well. This is what rendered 'Pomakness' subject to perception.

If this shift in the governmentality of borders is seen in the global contexts of the Cold War and EU expansion, then Stoler's analysis of imperial configurations is instructive: 'blurred genres of rule were not marginal manifestations of imperial authority. Nor were these blurred genres signs of states in distress; rather, they were the conditions of possibility for the precarious conditions of peoples subject to them' (2010: xix). The subjection of Pomak villages to military surveillance did not produce victims of propaganda, Greek or Turkish. It produced people who understood that their daily survival depended on navigating the fine balance between their state-sponsored carers (doctors, teachers, soldiers) and the strategies of incorporation they had to offer (racialism, emplacement, education), most of the time presented as their own 'free' choice (naming, genealogy, care). It is on this basis, then, that those bordered subjects engaged with the capitalist 'outside' of tobacco wholesalers that seemed to perpetually negotiate survival-rate prices (chapter one). Most of the time, these prices kept those family units and fields in place, while the rest of the village was experiencing migration lower down and into Komotini for the few who could make it. The intermittent menial jobs that Selim, having made it to the town, was taking up while waiting for his appointment to come, were a sobering example.

Another decade on from that time, as Greece is plunging deeper into financial crisis in 2012, the border with Bulgaria (now an EU state) is being crossed, according to reports, in the other direction, by Greeks seeking jobs there. With all institutions being affected by the crisis, the closure of EPATh and the offer of more streamlined education at the Aristotle University, which would have been hailed as a step closer to 'equality before the law and the state' (*isonomía – isopolitía*), hangs in the balance. According to University officials overseeing the transition, 'the state has enabled the opening of the special programme targeting students from the minority but has forgotten to fund it'. As economic rationality might perhaps point to Turkey or Bulgaria as a destination for study or settlement, the new logic of governmentality seems to be changing little in the subjectification of minority. What placement will such choices of education abroad entail for future national subjects from the 'minority within the minority' (as Pomaks have been called) in a future, post-crisis order? What the story has shown us so far is that the shifting governmentalities that have emplaced Pomaks on the mountain have delegitimized them as historical and political subjects. Emerging discourses on Pomaks as the subjects of minority rights within the EU cannot be seen as separate from this delegitimization. Such rights are primarily linguistic and cultural, not political or economic. The implications of this legacy for the current condition of the minority as a whole are taken up in the next chapter, when 'state care' is examined with reference to land policies.

Notes

1. Within geography, interconnections between space and other forms of gendered domination have been addressed (Valentine 2007; Wright 2009; Pratt and Rosner 2006). However, any attempt to draw wider connections also stumbles on the problem that 'intersectionality' is interpreted primarily as a women's studies' issue. As I show later, gender is also implicated in the power structures I describe here, but the issue is by no means specific to women.
2. Translated from http://www.epath.edu.gr/Sxolh/index-sxolh.htm, accessed on 29 November 2009.
3. This relates to a legend about the Greek women of Zálongo who performed the same courageous 'dance' in order to escape their imminent capture by the Ottomans, which seems to strengthen the 'Pomaks are Greek' theory through recourse to the Islamicization thesis.
4. Obvious parallels with Islamophobic discourses beyond Greece should be mentioned here; one needs only be reminded of the arguments that have based the 'integration' of immigrants on Islamic female dress – from France to Britain – not to mention the staking of pro-war arguments in the era of the War on Terror on the liberation of Afghan women.

CHAPTER 6

GROUNDS OF STATE CARE

Land Out of Place

As naming and genealogy were folded into the state's efforts to 'own' the minority (as part of its claims to sovereignty), a third modality of conducting the minority population came to focus on the more material aspects of ownership. This was the ownership of land, administered on the level of private individuals. The biopolitical import of this technology was no longer on the level of subjecting individuals to the categorizations of 'minority', e.g. the 'multitude' populating dead-end Turkish mahalles and Hellenized streets and villages, or the 'multitude' populating the mountains since the time of Alexander. Its main thrust was to configure 'minority' so that individual life choices, like where one lives or what fields one cultivates and develops, would be unequivocally enclosed within this 'minority'. As with previous processes of minoritization put into motion with the Lausanne Peace Treaty, law was the primary domain through which this conduct of population was enforced. But here I speak not only of formal legislation, but also of orders, administrative decisions, policy guidelines and the like. I speak therefore of law as a discourse, which, in contrast to the practices I have outlined in previous chapters, where much of the practice it induced (e.g. debates amongst treaty writers over legal formulation) is now 'buried', has left traces of the governmentality that engendered it in the form of decisions published, minutes certified and deeds notarized. What happened as land ownership entered the domain of minority policy was that the conduct of population was entrusted to private citizens who were subjected into becoming conduits of state conduct. This process is the focus of the present chapter. In this way, the care of the state, the third modality on the basis of which the conduct of population took shape, came to form the social contract that bound individuals as citizen-subjects: no longer the objects of the law (as war-end treaties would have them), no longer asides to the law (as inhabitants of urban-planned areas), but subjects with a choice, a choice that was nevertheless circumscribed by the law.

In his analysis of land rights in the dispute over state sovereignty in Cyprus, Erdal Ilıcan (2011) argues that property was the means through which the 'great transformation' from (Ottoman) imperial ordering to the neoliberal ordering of post-colonial nation-states was effected. My own trajectory in examining land rights in western Thrace is slightly different in that it arose from observations over a much shorter period of time of claims about the progressive disempowerment of the minority. The policy of discouraging the sale of land from Greeks to Turks from the junta period (1967–1974) and up to the mid-1990s was mentioned to me on several occasions by friends and informants from the majority and minority alike, and has for many years ranked high on the minority's list of grievances against the Greek state. How and to what extent this policy was instituted were the primary questions that led me to the Komotini land registry during fieldwork – I found that this discouragement actually originated much before 1967. The analysis of what was collected in the land registry speaks further to the question of locating subjectification in the junctures that Erdal Ilıcan explores, between state and private sovereignty, political and economic re-orderings in capitalism and neoliberalism, and between marginal citizenship and liberal 'free choice' (ibid.). Earlier, I have juxtaposed the state's efforts to spatially govern Thracian space and Komotini in particular into a place that would be Greek above all, with minority responses to such governmentality. That chapter ended with a vision of how neoliberal market logics have been operating since the early 2000s to institute other forms of governmentality, predicated on minority individuals' consent and free choice to sell their plots to companies in exchange for apartments in the blocks subsequently built. This argument exposed the need to engage seriously with the economy of governing space (including land exchanges), which I undertake here.

This chapter thus turns to policies specifically designed to deal with lands considered 'out of place'. I use this term to refer to lands which the Greek state categorized as 'problematic' because they belonged to minority members. Having in mind Douglas's celebrated definition of 'dirt' as 'matter out of place' (Douglas 1966), and its applications to political strategies of cleansing and purification (Eriksen 1993; Malkki 1995; Appadurai 1998; Hayden 1996), the lands examined in this chapter under this prism are lands that for reasons of ownership have not properly been incorporated into 'Greek space' under the strategies of Hellenization outlined in chapter four. In this chapter therefore, 'political philology' of Hellenizing Thracian place is supplemented by a focus on the materiality of land ownership. The land registry data I present relates to the question of how the 'new' neoliberal market logic has in fact been developed on the back of earlier, repressive measures against the minority regarding land and property. I thus want to add a caveat to the argument about the 'newness' of this form of governmentality: neoliberalism may have opened up the production of governmentality to the field of private enterprise, but this was only achieved after the state's authoritarian practices of purifying the landscape began to yield results. At the centre of these practices were policies that rendered certain kinds of property transactions (those involving minority subjects) illicit.

The Grain-less Archive

What I locate in the land registry of Komotini is one form of the materiality of sovereignty that Navaro-Yashin (2010) talks about in framing a call for anthropological attention to the political work of place-making. From this perspective, the enmeshment of naming and genealogy within the governmentality that frames place-making in western Thrace is starkly exhibited in the records that the land registry holds. As techniques that have divided space into a Pomak mountain region and a Greek–Turkish valley-and-foothills, the archives examined emphasize the exclusion of the first from the political economy that has organized the second into a space of contestation. The innumerable files that formalize ownership of land and other forms of immovable (and sometimes moveable) property that are stored in the land registry testify to a bifurcation of the social contract, which establishes state sovereignty, into a myriad of contracts of sale that entrust that sovereignty to private individuals.

In these files, the mountain region is almost completely absent (there are two out of a sample total of 1,782 transactions recorded). As an area that encloses the constructed Pomak population then, its absence also deletes this population from the property exchanges that found the social contract. Behind this absence may lie the presence of the military zone, the low value of the land and absence of demand, the subsistence economy of the region, or a combination of these and other factors. But whatever the reasons may be, the absence of such sales lends material form to the effacement of 'Pomaks' as actors from the literal and figurative landscape of state-making (which is implied in the educational policies and genealogical discourse reviewed in chapter five). The mountain region's inaccessibility was not merely an outcome of natural geography or cultural mentality, as the previous chapter has shown. It was an outcome of a specific state view that rendered the region a security issue and kept it without proper road networks, water, or electricity supply for many years (unlike mountainous areas elsewhere). It was also a view that resulted in the discounting of the region's inhabitants as citizens, at the extreme end of which a number of them lost their citizenship through arbitrary bureaucratic decisions (postscript). I mention this as a reminder of the power structures that inhere in record-keeping and record-produc-tion, that are discernible not only in what is shown by the records, but also in what is absent from them.

The notarized and stamped papers that I found in the thick string-tagged folders that line the basement of the land registry, sitting on wall-to-wall and floor-to-ceiling shelves, are not the palimpsests of gov-ernmental authority in its making that Stoler (2009) describes. They are not 'entangled documents that have been "scratched over" and crossed-out many times' (ibid.: 52), but rather the opposite. They are cleanly written records of negotiations already completed, testifying to the agree-ment reached but obliterating the difficulties overcome in order to reach it. They do not invite a 'reading against the grain' in the way that govern-ment policy archives might. What they allow is a reading of numbers as the only available 'truth' of those agreements. A critical reading of those numbers, then, cannot be located in the legal discourse that repeats itself formulaically from sale contract to sale contract. The affective modes in which the operation of government enters the personal (the need of one to sell land in order to make ends meet, the rise of another through the class structure that allows the building of a summer house or entry into property development, the indifference to inherited property of a person who has migrated, the determination of another to make a new start in a different place at the end of war, etc.) are rarely recorded. Yet here too, as much as in ministerial memos and committee minutes, which are nor-mally the point of focus of anthropological 'reading against the grain', there are the materialities of sovereignty to contend with.

To read my archive critically then, is to transpose and counterpose its numbers to the experiences of the subjects these numbers construct: the seller, the buyer, the land, and its location. This subjectification of land and people that the archive constructs is on one level indicative of the entanglement of people and things that actor-network theory has brought to the foreground of anthropological analysis. Green's (2005: 174–217) analysis of how official statistics construct and reconfirm Pogoni's marginal location within Greece has urged us to look beyond the embodiment of politics in statistical wars, to other senses of embodi-ment that statistical discourse reveals (even through omission). In her case this included the omitted category 'basic land use', which became apparent only through 'learning to see' the landscape in the way her informants saw it (ibid.: 176). In my case, such entanglements can be made visible: one can discern 'use' through the description of the prop-erty itself (field, plot, house, vine, shop, mill) and the comparison of such use to the unit price of the land (an unused field will have a lower unit price than a cultivated one being sold in the same year). To make these visible, as Green also finds, the 'reader' also becomes entangled in these relations. This is why I speak of 'my' archive: not because I was the one to collect the sample, but because it is my compilations of the information found on the sale contracts that I analyse. Compared to Green, it was not official tables of numbers that I found, but documents that I translated into those numbers. One trace of this translation was in the conversion of the land unit *strémmata*, used in some sales, to square metres, used in other cases, by a factor of one thousand – done in the name of consistency and with a mind to an audience schooled in English measurement. These entanglements however, are conditioned by the political context in which they arise. Hence my reading of them, as a means of exploring the minority condition, is framed by the analytic of governmentality instead of an ethnographic concern to document local perspectives on the entanglement of people with land. Thus, what I read in the archive are the ways in which governmentality operates in the materiality of people's relations to property, and how this operation becomes the effect of the technology of 'state care'.

Such a reading is mostly akin to Tarlo's ethnography of the emergency period in India, where archives of sterilization operations carried out to enable access to property rights are analysed in their biopolitical import, 'as a detailed account of personal experiences that lend insight into the texture of social and political relations at the local level' (Tarlo 2003: 225). What Tarlo speaks of are not human–thing entanglements, but entanglements of narratives; not a grainy texture of the archive, but a texture of social and political relations. The statistical information thus gains 'texture' against the stories provided by minority members regarding land and other things that I present throughout the book rather than in the ambivalences that may have prefigured the shaping of policies. Das's meta-reading of Tarlo makes clear that the larger point shown through these records of sterilization is that once those policies were set, 'the political regime of the national Emergency was able to draw different sections of the people through fear and greed into its implementation' (Das 2007: 174).

The Emergency then, as a period of 'problematisation . . . [allows the] greatest insight into the mechanisms of government and the means used to resist them' (Legg 2005: 140). In a call for incorporating Foucault's notion of population across qualitative and quantitative approaches to population geography, Legg points out that such periods are particularly instructive for critical incorporation of Foucault's 'governmentality work . . . not just as an impressive means of archaeological investigation of population policies, but also as a genealogy that seeks to explain the present and open up that present to change' (ibid.: 151). That Tarlo's data speaks of an era of emergency, and that my route into the land registry began with claims about the suspension of rights under authoritarian regimes in Greece, is not coincidental. The point that I sought to elicit from the archive was exactly about the operation of the law within that region of the licit and illicit. It was about making visible the effects of a policy that was still then (at the time of fieldwork) under dispute – that Turks were barred from purchasing land over a period of several decades was known, but its officialization as policy carrying the 'paraphernalia of recording' (Das 2007: 174) and of the law was uncertain for many of my inform-ants. If not the law as such (which did not explicitly prohibit purchases by minority members), its ultimate objective, the upholding of demo-cratic rights, was what was in question. What I found in the land registry spoke of this governmentality in the grey area of democracy and its lack, but also within a larger context of consecutive 'emergency periods' and Greek–Turkish relations.

Laws of Care

State attempts to control the private ownership of land inevitably begin, as they do in many regions around the world, with the formation of the state itself. Attached to the 1923 Treaty of Lausanne is a 'Declaration regarding Moslem properties in Greece', known as 'Declaration IX', which concerns 'rights to property of Moslem persons, who are not subject to the terms of the Convention respecting the Exchange of Populations . . . who have left Greece . . . before the 18th October, 1912, or who have always resided outside Greece' (§1). On the face of it, the subjects of the declaration are neither exchangees nor *établis*. They do, however, include western Thracian Muslims who were excluded from the *établis* category by virtue of having left the area prior to 1912, but who still held property there. Secondly, the Declaration affected *établis* indirectly, by precipitating tensions between Greece and Turkey when the former applied the declaration only to territories in 'old Greece' and expropriated Muslim properties in newly acquired northern Greece to settle exchangees (Psomiades 1968: 77–78). This in turn had possibly encouraged the 'hard-pressed refugees from eastern Thrace [to] freely requisitio[n] the property of many non-exchangeable Muslims in western Thrace, and construc[t] villages on the lands belonging to the latter' (ibid.: 77). To what extent such requisition was encouraged by the state, or otherwise related to the expropriations happening elsewhere in northern Greece is not known. But the resolution of the friction caused by that interpretation of Declaration IX was mitigated by the Ankara Convention of 1930, which agreed the expropriation of lands subject to Declaration IX, amidst much debate in the Turkish parliament (Demirözü 2008). The Ankara Convention was signed within the context of inaugurating a rapprochement effort, interpreted as having been necessitated by American concerns to 'restor[e] peace in the Balkans' (Aktar 2003: 80). The interpretation of land ownership therefore, had been tied to ethnicity since 1923, and hence implicated in the same understandings of state sovereignty as 'ownership' of population on which ethnicity was premised. It was this combination of genealogical governmentality and concerns over sovereignty that informed the conduct of 'state care' over the decades – a conduct that Andreades (1956: 26–44) locates almost exclusively on the issue of land and land-related benefits.

This ethnicizing component of land policy became obvious in Law No. 1366 of 1938, providing that a license from the (then government-appointed) district officer (nomarch) was needed for any land sales or purchases concluded in the country's 'border regions' (*paramethórious periohás*), which included western Thrace alongside regions on the northern border and islands along the eastern sea border. The law in fact stipulated that a general ban (*apağórefsi*) was to apply on land sales in these regions as well as to other forms of exercising ownership rights on such properties (e.g. modifying existing structures), and it was to lift this ban (*ársi*) that one applied to the district authorities. Law 1366/1938 was passed by the Metaxas dictatorship (1936–1941), notorious for its suppression of the left through techniques of indoctrination, confinement, persecution and infiltration (also Panourgiá 2009: 39–53) on the eve of the onset of Nazism and the Second World War. A Helsinki Watch Report (1990) cites this law as the first impediment to minority ownership of land and houses, confirming the additional oft-repeated minority grievance, that during the years of the law's application, licenses to even repair or refurbish one's own house were difficult to secure.

Minority members were not simply inadvertent victims of the persecution of the left; the fascism that the Metaxas regime mitigated on Greek citizenry was predicated on assumptions of ethnic purity that they would have never been able to fulfil. It is indicative that the only example of 'administrative arbitrariness' (*aftheresía tis dhiikíseos*) that Andreades concedes on the issue of land is attributed to the Metaxas regime (*'epí epohís tis dhiktatorías tis 4is Avğoústou'* [during the era of the 4th August dictatorship]) and concerns the occupation of grazing land in the village of Akarpos by landless refugees who turned it into a citrus plantation (Andreades 1956: 29). In this sense, Law 1366/1938 is an instance of capricious governmentality where the targeting of one population (communists) opened up avenues for repressing others too (the minority). The law remained in operation and was implemented with varying levels of ferocity in western Thrace until 1990, when it was replaced by Law 1892, after a European Court of Justice ruling against Greece in a case relating to the difficulties encountered by a foreign national buying land on the coast (Oran 2003: 107). This law rendered state control even more thorough (if less arbitrary), providing for a six-person interministerial committee (including the ministries of Defence and Foreign Affairs) to approve the exemption from the ban. However, it is interesting to note that with the implementation of this new law, sales to minority members began to rise, indicating perhaps that the problem did not lie with how many officials oversaw minority property sales but with the prioritization of state policy. Once 'civic and legal equality' took precedence over legal formulation a larger committee proved curiously more efficient than a high-level official acting alone. What had changed was the definition of 'state care' as a modality of governing population.

At the time Andreades was writing, this was a vastly different definition. By then, the communist danger had escalated into the Civil War and in its aftermath 'state care' came to focus on the 'restitution of the victims of [Axis] occupation and the brigand [i.e. Civil] war' (*apokatástasis pliyéndon epí katohís ke simmoritopolémou*) (1956: 32). The detailed account of this restitution that Andreades provides, references the inclusion of land as only one category of property that constitutes state care towards the minority. The many statistical tables that make up the restitution section register another category of property: they range from ox, cattle, donkeys, goats and sheep, to beehives, spades, saws, ploughs, animal fodder, seeds, fertilizer, building materials and cash. In the tabulated comparisons of this aid distributed among Christians and Muslims, the former seem to have received more cash compensation and less in-kind than the latter (although notably not so for building materials). To this, Andreades adds the comparative numbers of children receiving benefits from 1950 to 1955, the numbers of medicines of various types (iron tablets, vitamins, penicillin, etc.) provided to Pomak villagers, and the numbers of patients treated in hospitals and state clinics in Rhodoppe between 1952 and 1954 (ibid.: 38–43). Finally, comparisons of the amounts of agricultural credit are provided for the Xanthi branch of the Agricultural Bank, showing higher levels of credit provided to Muslims. To mitigate the anticipated readers' surprise at this, Andreades emphasizes that 'these numbers [relating to credit] are provided even though they may be taken as an attempt to elicit awe towards the Greek administration' (ibid.: 43). Other branches of the bank, the reader is informed, do not reference credit sums allocated to minority members 'because it is a known fact that generally all farmers, indiscriminately of race [*ánef filetikís dhiakríseos*] receive credit in the same way by the Agricultural Bank of Greece' (ibid.: 44). The biopolitical contours of 'state care' are thus plainly sketched out, and against an image of the citizen worthy of that care as a racially and politically defined subject (one who is Christian, Muslim or Pomak, and one who is the victim of communist brigands). The way in which this subject is cared for begins with land, extends to livelihood and health, and ends with debt and credit. Minority subjects are included because the exclusion of communists takes precedence.

That image of the subject of care was to change radically. Ten years after Andreades's celebration of the Agricultural Bank's record in the care of the minority, and this time on the eve of the military junta takeover, a different role was assigned to the bank. In November 1966, together with the Central Bank, the Agricultural Bank inaugurated a loan scheme favouring 'Greek citizens of Christian religion for the purpose of buying Muslim properties' (*Ios* magazine, 2006). The terms of the 20-year loans set repayment at 2 per cent interest. The policy was reinforced during the junta years. It was conceived by the 'Coordination Council for Thrace' (*Sindonistikó Simvoúlio Thrákis*), a body that came into existence in 1959 on which local administrators, minority educators, as well as police and secret service representatives sat (Iliadis 2004: 22). Its aim was to develop a coordinated policy towards the minority that would be implemented across government and local authority departments. Framing this aim within the logic of reciprocity (of minority 'care' between Greece and Turkey) in a meeting of the council in 1962, its president is recorded as saying that 'our interest is not the Muslim minority of Thrace per se but the Greeks of Istanbul' and that 'the [policy] line has to be the minimization of the minority in Thrace because Turkey harbours territorial aspirations regarding W[estern] Thrace' (ibid.: 33). Over the following four years, the contours of the council's policy towards the minority shifted between twin policies of 'raising the minority's life standard and strengthening the Greek element', and cultivating in 'the soul of the Muslims of Thrace feelings of gratitude towards the state of which they are citizens' (ibid.: 33–35). The 'care of the state' was framed at this top administrative level within a benevolent discourse, even if it was understood that this was a duplicitous effort aspiring to keep the Greeks in Istanbul. As that community dwindled in the years following the Istanbul pogroms of 1955, the council's policy reversed the 'favourable' treatment of the minority, with its chairman stating in a 1967 meeting that 'the Turks will leave when, through any means possible, we buy their lands' (ibid.: 35).

It was in implementation of this policy (being explained to the council a few months after its inauguration) that the loan scheme materialized. Initially targeting the buying of farmland in rural areas, but discouraging the buying of large tracts of land (*çiftliks*) lest it encouraged further business development of the big minority landowners (by raising the value of those lands still held by minority members), the scheme was extended to urban areas in 1972. As a result, land prices in the area began to increase, while minority sellers opted to invest or keep their cash in Turkey, fearing losses in case of a worsening of bilateral relations. At the same time, many prospective minority sellers opted not to sell their properties through official channels but instead to 'donate' or 'mortgage' them in shady deals that often carried financial rewards for the contracting lawyers but eventually left the minority parties without their properties (*Ios* magazine, 2006).

From the early 1970s, large tracts of minority lands were also expropriated for the building of state institutions like the local university departments (Oran 2003). During fieldwork, many informants referred to the university area as the former site of huge expanses of cherry tree cultivation. Similar expropriations took place for the purposes of developing the industrial zone and housing repatriates from the former Soviet Union (Helsinki Watch 1990). In some areas, such expropriations were challenged by the minority in both the legal sphere and through social protests, with some, if limited, results – the case of Evlalo village in the Xanthi district is one notable example (Oran 1984). Other measures included policies related to land consolidation that also targeted minority-owned lands. According to Oran, the cumulative effect of these policies was the shrinkage of minority land ownership from 84 per cent in 1922 to 20–40 per cent in the early 2000s (Oran 2003: 106; also cited in Human Rights Watch 1999). Even if potentially exaggerated (it has become a point of much debate in the literature), this claim of targeted divestment provides the frame in which the following data must be contextualized.

Counting Care

The archives of the land registry, known as the *ipothikofilákio* (the mortgage registry), in Komotini contain contracts for sales of land within the prefecture of Rhodoppe from the time the region became part of the Greek state. During this time, the boundaries of the prefecture have slightly shifted along the boundary with the Evros prefecture to the east, while Rhodoppe was divided into two prefectures with the creation of Xanthi prefecture to the west after the end of Axis occupation in 1944. The Komotini land registry keeps archives of sale records concluded for areas within the jurisdiction of the two municipalities currently in Rhodoppe, Komotini and Sappes.

In these contracts, information is recorded relating to the sale, including the names of buyer and seller, the amount of land being sold, and the amount of money it was sold for. Where foreign citizens are involved in the transaction (e.g. Bulgarians appear as sellers in two cases in the

sample) their citizenship is also recorded. In addition, some of these contracts also provide clues as to the reasons for the sale. For example, a 1951
sale from a Jew to a Greek clarifies that relatives of the seller had perished
in concentration camps (rendering the seller an heir to the property). In
other cases, the contracts were preceded by *brigosímfona*, marriage contracts agreed between the families of the bride and groom detailing the
dowry the bride would be entering the marriage with (and detailing both
moveables like pots and pans and immoveables like fields and houses).
These agreements only relate to weddings between Christians. Similar
agreements on dower values concluded for Muslim weddings are archived
in the office of the religious administration (*müftülük*) and are examined
in chapter eight.

As a record of institutional logic that guides local property exchanges
then, the archive of the land registry attests to the ethno-religious divisions that pervade the conceptualization of 'property' in general. Where
women are part of the property being exchanged (in marriage), the
exchange is classified first and foremost in terms of religious belonging,
and the agreements are filed respectively in a governmental, seemingly
secular office (the land registry, for Orthodox Greeks) and the Muslim
religious office (for the minority). Property exchanges are recorded on
two planes: that of moveable property agreed in the majority of *brigosímfona*, which may include furniture and equipment, and that of immove-
able property, where land and house sales are recorded. The agreements
concluded in the first case (*brigosímfona*) appear to lack the legal rigour
of the second set, but are strikingly similar in form to marital agreements
archived in the *müftülük*. At this level, however, there is a temporal distinction between the two, in the sense that *brigosímfona* ceased sometime
in the early 1980s (when they were abolished by law in 1983) but the
equivalent Muslim agreements continued at least until fieldwork. In other
words, the governmentality that appears to permeate the land sales record
is one where ethnic, religious and cultural differences find legal expres-
sion. It is in this context that the differences registered in contracts that
are otherwise similar (land sales, where the only differentiation between
majority and minority agents are the names being recorded), gains
salience, marking out the land registry archive as a biopolitical record.

The glimpse of this record that I provide corresponds to roughly 2 per
cent of the whole archive. To collect this, the totality of contracts was
recorded for an arbitrarily selected month (March) in every four years,
beginning in 1924, where the archive starts (i.e. sampling one month in
every 48). At a glance, the data collected detailed a total of 1,782 transactions, for which the ethnicity of sellers and buyers was recorded (deduced
by their names), together with the type of property exchanged, its location, its area, the transaction amount, and an explanation as to whether

the location of the property was in the town or a village. Based on this information, I broke down the transactions on the basis of the location of the property: in the valley, foothills or town. The totals obtained for these categories are provided in Tables 6.1–6.3 (relating to town, valley and foothills transactions respectively, and excluding the two cases of mountain land sales).

This categorization of areas was based on the realization during field-work that villages were recognized as 'Greek', 'minority/Turkish' or 'mixed', and that while *yakka* (foothills) villages were considered mostly minority/Turkish, valley villages presented a more mixed distribution. Historically, Greek refugees were settled in the more accessible valley areas in 1920s. Subsequent development also concentrated in this region, leaving the mountainous regions inaccessible and isolated. The valley, by comparison, became increasingly identified as 'Greek' space, with new settlements being erected to house refugees and at least some settling of refugees in Turkish villages. In the 1990s, there were few mixed villages in the valley, and most of the area south of the Egnatia highway (leading from Komotini to the main towns of Alexandroupoli to the east and Xanthi to the west) comprised Greek villages, with clusters of minority villages in the south-east. Most minority villages were located north of the highway, in the yakka region.

In the sample, the yakka stands out as the region with the lowest concentration of transactions – here, only Turkish-to-Turkish transactions occur consistently in double-digit numbers, even when hilly areas on the southern coast, identified as 'Greek', are included in the sample (this was my attempt to normalize the sample bias by interpreting 'foothills' in terms of altitude and not ethnicity). This suggests a diachronic pattern to the yakka area being progressively marked out as 'minority space'. In this process, the economics of lower land fertility and tourist interest fed into and perpetuated policies of marginalization that de-prioritized the development of yakka regions. Large portions of field lands were bought in this region by Greeks in 1979 and 1987, the first coinciding with a general peak in sales by Turks and the second including fields in Maronya and Xilagani (the two Greek villages in the hills near the southern coast). If the absence of the mountain area from the register of 'consumable' (tradable, desirable) land attests to its disappearance from the national topos, or its alienation from the sociability of the market, the picture presented by the yakka transactions is a reminder that 'appearance' comes with variable price tags. State policies here might have been several degrees less severe than those on the mountain, with military presence sparse and without access controls, but neglect in the form of old road systems and the maintenance of unprofitable tobacco cultivation rendered yakka lands tradable and desirable only to people similarly neglected and marginalized. By

Table 6.1 Land sales in the town
Seller-Buyer name (with indicative values of size in 1,000s square metres and price in 1,000 Greek drachma shown as x/y)

Year	Greek-Greek	Greek-Turkish	Turkish-Greek	Turkish-Turkish	Other	Total (rounded)
1924	1 (1/10)	0	1 (0.5/60)	0	5 (5/102)	7 (7/170)
1927	3 (5/135)	0	2 (4/8)	1 (1.5/1.5)	1 (1/6)	7 (12/150)
1931	1 (2/7)	1 (1/34)	7 (4/48)	14 (44/85)	1 (0.25/15)	24 (51/190)
1935	2 (2.5/18)	2 (6/5)	1 (0.2/5)	33 (84/233)	6 (6.5/300)	44 (99.2/560)
1939	5 (2/236)	1 (1.5/6.6)	4 (3.4/24)	9 (10.3/91.5)	0	19 (17/360)
1945	0	0	0	6 (51.7/308)	1 (0.5/140)	7 (52/450)
1947	3 (3.5/3,300)	0	5 (9.5/20,850)	13 (17.2/7,034)	3 (10/4,150)	24 (40/35,330)
1951	5 (8/22,500)	0	26 (94/146,600)	28 (75/66,850)	5 (20/45,000)	64 (197/280,950)
1955	10 (7/82,500)	3 (7.3/14,500)	14 (30/76,800)	18 (24/125,050)	2 (1.5/34,500)	47 (70/333,350)
1959	21 (30/216)	0	5 (15.5/42)	17 (59.5/85.8)	0	43 (105/340)
1963	25 (88.2/858)	3 (2.8/16.5)	5 (6.1/34)	22 (30.2/145)	0	55 (127/1,050)
1967	19 (40.6/580)	0	4 (3/65)	4 (1.5/49)	0	27 (45/690)
1971	10 (10/755)	0	6 (7.9/169)	0	0	16 (18/920)
1975	10 (2.5/2,990)	0	10 (13.2/1,253)	0	0	20 (16/4,240)
1979	39 (19/23,995)	0	19 (26/8,404)	1 (0.3/365)	0	59 (45/32,760)
1983	14 (24/16,870)	0	4 (12.7/1,750)	0	1 (5.1/60)	19 (42/18,680)
1987	34 (11/47,324)	0	5 (1.9/661)	0	0	39 (13/47,990)
1991	15 (5.7/50,412)	0	1 (1/1,900)	0	0	16 (7/52,310)
1995	14 (45.3/96,284)	1 (8.4/1000)	0	3 (4.1/7,255)	0	18 (58/104,540)
1999	41 (26/379,345)	1 (1/500)	0	2 (3.9/5,765)	1 (0.5/5,000)	45 (31/390,610)

Table 6.2 Land sales in the valley
Seller-Buyer name (with indicative values of size in 1,000s square metres and price in 1,000 Greek drachma shown as x/y)

Year	Greek-Greek	Greek-Turkish	Turkish-Greek	Turkish-Turkish	Other	Total (rounded)
1924	0	0	0	0	0	0
1927	1 (1.5/3)	0	2 (16/16.4)	3 (555/106.4)	1 (0.2/2)	7 (573/130)
1931	2 (9/4)	0	7 (58/32)	17 (640/163.8)	0	26 (707/200)
1935	2 (10/6.3)	2 (5.3/4.8)	12 (219/128.3)	22 (108.3/76.6)	4 (333/207.5)	42 (676/420)
1939	5 (34/64.5)	1 (0.5/3.5)	110 (2,201/1,422)	18 (119/169)	3 (184/150)	137 (2,539/1,810)
1945	0	0	0	1 (14/186)	0	1 (14/190)
1947	0	0	3 (17.3/3,500)	2 (5.5/1,300)	0	5 (23/4,800)
1951	3 (23/4,800)	0	30 (684/330,700)	30 (358/113,250)	0	63 (1,065/448,750)
1955	3 (21/9,500)	0	18 (113/79,800)	23 (245/105,850)	0	44 (379/195,150)
1959	2 (17.5/19)	0	9 (101/80)	27 (134/145.4)	0	38 (253/240)
1963	12 (86.6/122)	2 (6.5/12)	3 (19.5/28.5)	11 (150/135)	0	28 (263/300)
1967	29 (374/1,121)	0	9 (141/231.6)	5 (4/74.5)	0	43 (519/1,430)
1971	12 (138/489)	0	7 (258/774)	0	0	19 (396/1,260)
1975	9 (7/530)	0	18 (150.4/1,094)	0	0	27 (157/1,620)
1979	37 (448/20,044)	0	34 (542/12,055)	0	0	71 (990/32,100)
1983	19 (176.6/5,156)	0	1 (6.7/505)	0	0	20 (183/5,660)
1987	54 (445/19,439)	0	38 (212/17,864)	0	0	92 (657/37,300)
1991	22 (117/21,439)	0	0	0	0	22 (117/21,440)
1995	31 (504/53,855)	14 (93.2/12,646)	2 (20.2/2,050)	3 (13.5/3,100)	0	50 (631/71,650)
1999	31 (239/37,947)	3 (14.3/636)	1 (5/500)	14 (27.8/7,245)	0	49 (286/46,330)

Table 6.3 Land sales in the *yakka*
Seller-Buyer name (with indicative values of size in 1,000s square metres and price in 1,000 Greek drachma shown as x/y)

Year	Greek-Greek	Greek-Turkish	Turkish-Greek	Turkish-Turkish	Other	Total (rounded)
1924	0	0	0	0	0	0
1927	1 (0.25/30)	0	1 (2.5/7)	0	0	2 (3/40)
1931	1 (2.5/3)	0	1 (2.5/25)	12 (67/48.6)	1 (16/8)	15 (88/90)
1935	4 (31.8/13.5)	4 (33/40)	6 (35/23.2)	26 (115/92.6)	1 (12/12)	41 (227/180)
1939	2 (7/11.5)	1 (6.3/15)	6 (18.7/45.5)	20 (121/203)	0	29 (153/280)
1945	0	0	0	1 (7/20)	0	1 (7/20)
1947	0	0	2 (8/1,480)	5 (61.8/10,950)	0	7 (70/12,430)
1951	1 (12/3,000)	0	8 (23.5/8,800)	19 (161.3/60,800)	0	28 (197/72,600)
1955	3 (19.5/9,000)	0	5 (31.7/53,000)	47 (437/248,100)	0	55 (488/310,100)
1959	8 (11.8/35.8)	1 (2/2)	7 (26/24.5)	44 (127.5/216)	0	60 (167/280)
1963	5 (32/44)	2 (1.2/4.5)	0	6 (35/71)	0	13 (68/120)
1967	7 (18.8/42)	1 (1/4)	1 (0.3/3)	4 (9.3/65)	0	13 (29/110)
1971	6 (8.6/99)	0	5 (103.6/644)	0	0	11 (112/740)
1975	2 (7.5/70)	0	6 (25.5/173)	0	0	8 (33/240)
1979	6 (76.8/1,104)	0	13 (164/4,299)	0	0	19 (241/5,400)
1983	9 (43.5/1,176)	0	0	0	0	9 (43.5/1,180)
1987	19 (93.4/2,303)	0	10 (81.9/12,772)	0	0	29 (175/15,080)
1991	8 (28/3,510)	0	0	2 (5.5/400)	0	10 (34/3,910)
1995	15 (81.4/20,822)	6 (31.5/4,295)	2 (15.3/970)	2 (0.7/1,500)	0	25 (129/27,590)
1999	8 (69/10,080)	7 (28.4/5,500)	1 (2/50)	5 (7/11,365)	0	21 (106/27,000)

comparison, valley land exhibits the opposite pattern. Having progressively become a fertile region of cotton cultivation, and with a coast popular amongst the local population and beyond, its land has been bought and sold throughout the century in much higher numbers across the categories examined. Greeks have cumulatively been the most numerous buyers, whereas Turkish-to-Greek sales have topped intra-ethnic transactions. Unit prices of yakka land are considerably lower throughout the sample than unit prices of valley and town properties.

At a glance, most of the property sales have been executed between individuals with names recognized as Greek (651 cases, or 36.5 per cent of the sample). On the contrary, sales from individuals with Greek names to individuals with Turkish names (shorthanded as 'Greeks' and 'Turks' henceforth) have been exceptionally low (56, or 3.14 per cent of the sample). In between, Turkish-to-Turkish transactions were the second highest (542, or 30.4 per cent), and Turkish-to-Greek the third (497, or 27.8 per cent). Sales involving 'others' (Jews, Armenians, Bulgarians) totaled 36, or 2.02 per cent (I have discounted these in the analysis that follows). This reading, which employs the logic of ethnicizing names, shows the effects of the ethnicization of property in individuals' practices as national-cum-market subjects. Over the course of the period reviewed (1924–1999), the most dramatic differences concerned cross-ethnic sales (Figure 6.1). There, Greek-to-Turkish sales have been consistently low, ranging from zero (over a number of years) to eight (in 1935), and rising only in 1995 and 1999, while Turkish-to-Greek sales have been fluctuating, and peaked in 1951 (after the Civil War) and 1979 (after the war in Cyprus). Sales between Greeks and between Turks show different trends (Figure 6.2). Between Greeks, the sales begin to rise significantly in the 1960s, just as sales within the minority dwindle (and eventually cease in the 1970s and 1980s), with earlier troughs noted for 1945 and 1947.

This suggests that Law 1366/1938 had an initial effect of containing sales altogether, since most sales were taking place amongst minority members at that time (the increase in Turkish-to-Greek sales was relatively incremental). During the Second World War and Civil War, sales remained low (in fact no archive existed for 1943, which is why 1945 was counted instead), picking up in the immediate post-war period, with the majority of transactions performed between minority members. The 1966 loan policy then almost obliterated minority buyers: in the sample there were seventeen cases during this period, of which only one concerned buying from a Greek. Following the lifting of these restrictions, minority buyers increased dramatically. In 1995 and 1999 alone, there were more Greek-to-Turkish property transactions (thirty-two) than there had been in all previous years for the sample examined (a total of twenty-three). Greek-to-Greek transactions picked up in the second half

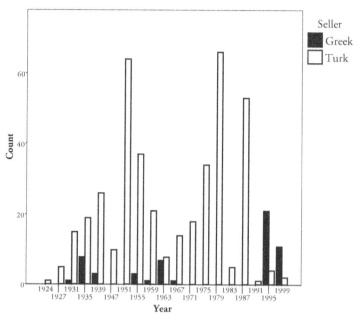

Figure 6.1 Cross-ethnic sales over time

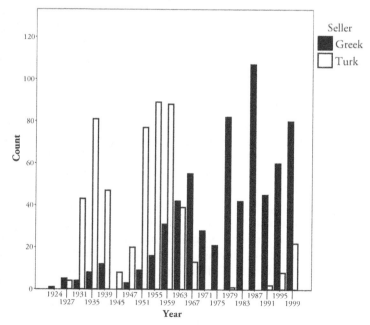

Figure 6.2 Intra-ethnic sales over time

of the century, indicating that in this period, Greeks in the region became increasingly interested in land as property, and came to acquire enough of it to exchange it amongst themselves following the initial period of receiving land from the state. The process whereby this population were transformed into Greek citizens included the cultivation of their relationship to the new lands they were settled in. After the state's humanitarian intervention of securing their livelihood by giving them land, capitalism transformed this relationship to the land by turning the settled Greeks into active participants in the buying and selling of land. As more land came under Greek ownership, the numbers of transactions also increased.

The quality of the property transacted is another indication of the cumulative effect of governmental policy. Classified by type, the property sold by Greeks included more plots, flats, offices and shops than that sold by Turks, which in turn included more fields, houses, vines and gardens. Greek sellers engaged in more transactions of property that required government-administrative labour (securing permissions to turn fields into plots, plots into flats, flats into offices), and which was probably also of higher value for this reason (Figure 6.3). A comparison of unit prices (the amount paid divided by the size of the property bought) shows that the highest-priced properties were sold by Greeks from the 1970s onwards (Figure 6.4). This also indicates comparative possibilities of property development, as the highest-valued properties in the 1990s spikes correspond chiefly to town flats, houses and plots. The neoliberal capitalist phase of development of town properties (through schemes like that of *andiparohí* mentioned in chapter four) was thus developed on the back of earlier policies of restricting sales on the basis of ethnicity.

These policies have also divided the wider Rhodoppe area into a largely Turkish yakka area and a mixed valley region. This is indicated in area-specific sales. The sizes of land transacted in the Turkish-to-Greek direction are significantly larger for valley areas than they are for either town or yakka ones (Figure 6.5). A Turkish-to-Turkish distribution, by comparison, indicates large sizes for both valley and yakka, and significantly lower ones for town properties (Figure 6.6). Larger yakka properties had been sold to Turkish buyers up to the 1960s, after which Greek buyers have been buying smaller units and the number of Turkish buyers has been dwindling, whereas valley properties have been sold on a large scale to Greek buyers throughout (Figure 6.7). This comparison could be taken as a rough schematic indication of the transformation of Rhodoppean space from Turkish to Greek ownership as it passed through private transactions. The qualification that these numbers indicate only transactions between individuals is significant, as it fails to account for alternative methods of land transfer, not mediated by the market. Lands that may have been abandoned by individuals 'choosing' to migrate post-1923

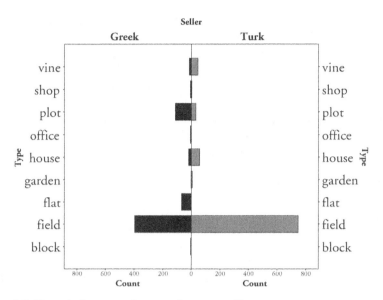

Figure 6.3 Cumulative counts by types of property sold

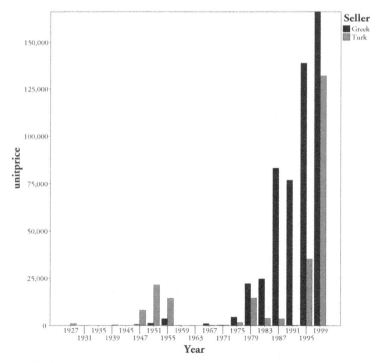

Figure 6.4 Unit price ranges over time

(to whatever extent this might be considered 'free choice') or that may otherwise have been expropriated and used to house refugees or state structures (or later build and widen roads) would be an additional factor in this process of Hellenizing Rhodoppean space.

Of direct relevance to this point is the sharp peak in Turkish-to-Greek transactions in the valley in 1939, which shoots numbers off the chart in figure 6.5 and which has been scaled down to make lower values visible in figure 6.7. This 'abnormality' is due to a single bulk sale in the area of Shoinia, a village halfway between Komotini and the coast (it has been excluded from figure 6.1 to 'normalize' the trends). The village appears on a 1935 map of the region, but not on current maps, which only show the neighbouring village Pagouria. This sale consisted of 94 transactions, registered one after the other and detailing the sale of fields of similar size (c. 22,000 m² each) for similar prices (around 13,600 Greek drachma). These sales were concluded between the same six Turkish-named individuals on the sellers' side and various Greek-named persons on the buyers' side. These indications suggest that the sellers may have been heirs to a large *çiftlik* estate, owned by an absentee landlord and worked by those who eventually became the buyers.

According to Troubeta (2001: 37), such large *çiftlik* owners chose to emigrate to Turkey after 1923, selling their lands or, if the Shoinia case is indeed within this category, some choosing to keep them until their heirs found it more expedient to sever the links. Shoinia in fact features in Andreades's examples of 'state care', as an estate (*aǧróktima*) belonging 'partly to Christian landowners [presumably some of them buyers in 1939] and partly to the Muslim Haji Ahmet oglu Hasan', covering an area of 8,637 *strémmata*, out of which 3,900 (a mere guess would be that they mostly fell under the latter's ownership) were expropriated under Law 2185/1952 and distributed to villagers of surrounding settlements, of which 147 families were Christian and 20 Muslim (Andreades 1956: 31). A further 2,500 *strémmata* 'belonging mostly to the Greek public' (perhaps through earlier expropriation or similar practice, the fear of which might have induced the 1939 sales) were given for cultivation to Muslim villagers of Kehros, and 800 'were finally assigned (*dhietéthisan oristikós*) for grazing to Pagouria villagers' (ibid.). Altogether, this would mean that at least 600 *strémmata* from the sale of 1939 became part of this redistribution.

The reason for this redistribution are unclear. Perhaps this was indeed expropriation that was ethnically indiscriminate. Perhaps though, it was related to legal disputes involving the 1939 sales, which would explain Andreades's choice of the word 'finally' to describe the assignment of the last portion to the Pagouria villagers. Note that the Kehros community, which benefited from the largest portion of the estate, would

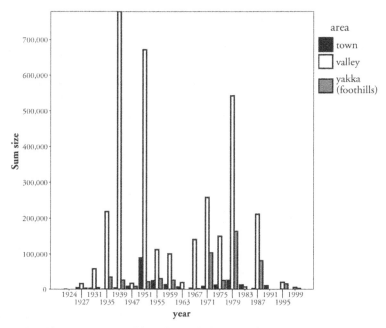

Figure 6.5 Sizes of property sold in the Turkish-to-Greek direction, by area over time

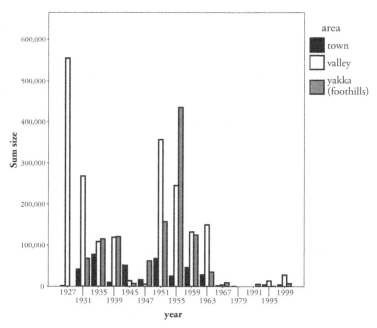

Figure 6.6 Sizes of property sold amongst Turks by area over time

probably have found it difficult to make use of their grazing rights, since the village lies at a distance of about eighty kilometres, in the mountains. As an 'exception', then, the Shoinia sale can be considered indicative of other exceptional processes, like expropriation, or large-scale takeover of lands, which took place in later years but were not recorded as part of the sample (perhaps having occurred in months or years not examined). For the Xanthi prefecture, Andreades provides examples of eleven such expropriations of estates, one of which appears to have had Christian owners. Might the 1939 sales have been induced by the coming into force of Law 1366/1938, and the transaction hurriedly concluded? Might 'the Muslim Haji Ahmet oglu Hasan' have been a local claimant bypassed in the decisions of other heirs? Or might the original owner not have been an absentee landlord at all, but a member of another category that called law and policy into question? Shoinia is, in other words, an example of how the grey area between the law and the illegal (if, for example, the 1939 sales were indeed disputed) might have been brought under the realm of the former through special legal measures (expropriation) which themselves bore the taint of illicit (discriminatory) practices of 'state care'.

Shoinia might also be normalized within wider political abnormalities, like the Second World War, on the eve of which the 1939 sale was concluded. The peaks of transaction numbers and property sizes sold by Turks over time (Figure 6.8) show the relevance of political context in shaping an individual's 'free' market behaviour, which renders the latter instances of biopolitical behaviour. After the near-freezing of the market in the war period (including the Civil War) sales spiked in 1951, when unit prices also increased due to hyperinflation. At this point the corresponding values for Greek sellers were minimal, indicating perhaps greater impoverishment of the minority community. There followed a gradual decrease in sales by Turks until 1971. At this point the Cyprus dispute was unfolding, its repercussions felt elsewhere from the start, when it induced the 1955 Istanbul pogroms. From 1955 to 1967 the numbers of sales were consistently higher than land sizes, indicating that higher numbers of individuals were selling smaller pieces of land. In 1979 there was another rise, in both numbers and sizes, reflecting the insecurity felt through the worsening of Greco-Turkish relations in the aftermath of the war in Cyprus (1974).

These economic reactions to the political environment show that the Hellenization of space described earlier was not only about naming topography. It also called upon a genealogical logic that ethnicized properties along with people, and mapped these on the landscape (through differentiated development and concomitant access to the market). And it also elicited techniques of 'state care' that subjected land, as an extension

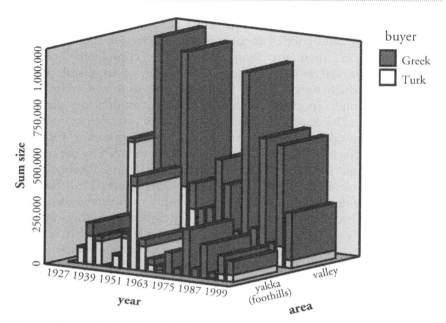

Figure 6.7 Cumulative sizes of yakka and valley properties bought over time

of the people who owned it, to this ethnicized mapping: expropriation, prohibition of sale, administrative arbitrariness, exclusion from loan schemes, and differential land redistribution. This governmentality of 'state care' set the stage for the differentiated development opportunities that opened up under neoliberal policies once the trend of discrimination was halted in the era of 'legal and civic equality' of the 1990s.

Stories of Place and Property

Speaking of her family's claims to being modern and progressive, Selda often described her grandmother's pride in living in a house her husband had built himself, away from parents' houses (as is 'traditionally' the norm). The story invariably ended with expressions of relief that her grandmother died before receiving the notice from the local council that it was to be torn down to make space for a wider street. The house was in an old Turkish neighbourhood south of the river, and was the last one in the mahalle to survive similar evictions for planning projects. In Andreas's sketches (chapter three) this mahalle appears in one of the two mixed areas in 1975, and as homogenously Greek by 1999. The flat where I lived in 1998–99 was also near an old Turkish mahalle. The only Turkish

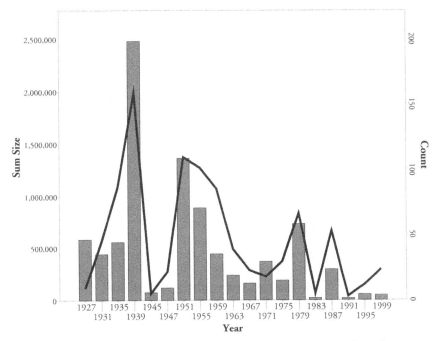

Figure 6.8 Number of sales and cumulative property sizes in transactions of
Turkish sellers over time

houses in the area that were still inhabited were located next to a disused
mosque and seemed an oddity in the midst of multistorey grey concrete
structures that now house Greek-owned shops and Greek middle-class
families. Such concrete blocks had usually been erected by wealthy Greek
locals, and the flats rented by students or bought by families who could
not afford to build their own house. Empty plots often separated these
blocks (presumably indicating the locations of Turkish houses that had
been torn down), and on the sidewalls dead-end street labels were visible
(apparently designated for removal since the plots opened to the streets
behind and connecting paths were already being laid out and prepared
for asphalt paving).

The newest of the blocks in my area gave reason for friends to recol-
lect the former state of these sites, including their former Turkish owners,
who had sold them either as houses or as plots of land for a variety of
reasons. Despite these differences in circumstance, these sales seemed
symptomatic of the onset of neoliberal development on the restrictions
imposed by Law 1366/1938 and the loan scheme policy of the junta
period (1967–1974). Vague references to this 'ban on property investment' were made by minority individuals at every occasion when land,

discrimination or state relations were discussed. Selda now seldom passes the spot where her grandmother's house used to be. One of the few times that her mother returned to her old neighbourhood was to offer condolences to a Greek neighbour's daughter on the passing away of her mother. This fading of visits and thinning of relations emphasizes even more the totalizing quality of the removal of mahalles – the vanishing presence of particular people from particular locations. It is in this sense that the incomplete process of opening up dead-ends testified to this 'becoming of space' and the power inherent in it.

Consider another example of this power: when Esra recalled her childhood years in Germany, she noted that the move was prefigured by the destruction of her father's shop in the town centre following a flood in the 1960s. The reason for the drastic decision of emigration as a response to what she claimed was a fairly minor natural disaster can only be understood in the frame of the restrictive policy framework of the time. 'It was too much of a hassle to apply for all the permits needed to fix the place and he just decided not to bother', she explained when I asked why her father did not refurbish the shop instead. In the context of the drop in sales presented above during this period, her point gains poignancy.

As the effects of a policy geared towards 'driving Turks out of Thrace', the patterns of land transfer glimpsed in this chapter show the extent to which biopolitical regimes of power have successfully rendered Rhodoppean space Greek. Their connection to current practices of sale further illustrates the interrelations between strategies of domination, driven by nationalist ideology, and neoliberal market strategies, geared towards profit-making in a world that is seemingly ordered by individual freedom to choose and the existence of win-win relations (seller–buyer). It illustrates that this freedom is in fact predicated on previous forms of governmentality that have been marred by inequality, racism and oppression. The biopolitical strategies evidenced here were not confined to property transfer but have also extended to the domain of population management, where, spurred by a concern about the perceived 'lack of response' of the Turkish population to the land policies, the Coordination Council for Thrace proceeded, in 1967, to initiate a policy of granting financial incentives to Greek families bearing children. In a chilling parallel to the private initiative of creating Pomak dictionaries in the 1990s, the head of the council is recorded as having anticipated minority reactions to the demographic policy under consideration, and to have suggested pre-empting them by channelling the financial incentives through a private donor (*Ios*, 17 April 2005). Viewed against the backdrop of evidence in previous chapters, the management of space, ethnicity and demography is marked out as a continuum of governing minority life in the widest possible sense.

Widening the perspective, we might ponder, through the example of western Thrace, about the wider configurations of capital movement in the neoliberal age. Harvey (2003: 94–124), amongst others, identifies these configurations as being chiefly about the ability of capital to migrate from spaces of production to spaces of consumption through large-scale infrastructural projects and other investment. The Olympic Games facilities are one example he cites, which can then be left to degenerate as capital moves on – in a process he calls the 'molecular processes of capital accumulation'. I would argue that this movement, of which property is an integral part, is predicated on previous shifts established through oppression in the nation-state and Cold War period.

The ruins of 2004 Olympic facilities in Athens bear testament to this process. Erected on land bought by the state from a monastery on Mount Athos in a scandalous deal that exchanged the monastery's Ottoman-era rights over a lake in the Thracian valley (Hellenic Parliament 2010), the ruins mark not only the whimsical flight of capital, but also the intricate links across time and space between imperial orders and their shifts. And if the 'scandal of Vatopedi', as it has become known in Greece since its eruption in 2008, has been unrelated to the minority, the fact that it has taken place on the minority's doorstep gives cause for considering the larger context in which western Thracian land continues to be coincidental to the workings of the neoliberal state under a governmentality that has been guided by steering the law in closed meetings, and divesting citizens (in my examples the minority, in the Vatopedi scandal the taxpayers) of rights and prosperity, belying the definition of 'state care'.

CHAPTER 7

THE SELF-EXCLUDING COMMUNITY

Bordering the Religious Community

In January 1955, two weeks after Fessopoulos instructed in his memo that the sign 'Muslim school' discovered in the village of Aratos should be 'replaced immediately' with one that refers to the school as 'Turkish', the president and finance officer of the school signed an affidavit (*ipéfthi-nos dhílosis*) describing a meeting they had with the Turkish consul in Komotini. Their statement was presumably made to the police authorities since one year later it found a place in Andreades' appendix. According to the statement, the meeting concerned a teacher from Turkey who was insisting on moving the school's rest day from Friday to Sunday, and his allegation that should this not take effect, he was bound by the consulate to resign his post. This was a different yet related matter to the naming of the school, on which the two men had already complied with Fessopoulos' directive, signing their *dhílosis* as officials of the 'Turkish school of Aratos'. According to the statement, the consul confirmed this allegation, and threatened that should the school authorities not comply with the rest day change, he would take the matter to Commander Fessopoulos, who would in turn order a gendarme to forcibly close the school on Sundays. He further threatened, the statement continues, that

> 4) . . . he would place us on the black list, so that we cannot travel to Turkey.
> 5) He labelled us retrogressive (*opisthodhromikoús*) and the enemies of twenty million Turks.
> 6) We declared that between us and Turkey stand the Greek borders (*apó tin Tourkía mas horízoun ta elliniká sínora*) and that we cannot comply with this, adhering to our ancestral traditions (*ta pátria*). (Andreades 1956: 77)

The statement is provided by Andreades as proof of the Turkish Consulate's meddling in minority affairs. It has been a diachronic argument in Greece that the frictions between the minority and the Greek state are instigated by Turkey and therefore minority claims that turn against the state are illegitimate. This claim does not take into account the fact that the Turkish and Greek consulates in Komotini and Istanbul respectively were assigned a central role in overseeing matters of minority education in the Protocol of the Greco-Turkish Cultural Commission signed in 1969. This protocol still guides the organization of minority education in the two countries. In protesting against this meddling in 1956, yet failing to rectify it in the Protocol signed thirteen years later, the statement evidences part of the capriciousness of borders as devices of cynical (and sinister, perhaps) governmentality. As evidenced earlier, it is a governmentality that produces clashing discourses over naming (Turkish/Muslim) and contested policies of care (who is responsible for the minority and how such 'care', here in the form of education, should be administered) based on an uncertain politics of genealogy (who is a kin state and what form of behaviour is legitimate to pursue in that capacity). This wavering and uncertainty over discourse and practice has rendered the matters debated by Andreades issues of diachronic debate stretching to the current day, as has previously been shown. This may not only evidence the inability of Greece and Turkey to maintain a resolute (or reconciliatory, it could easily also be said) stance in the agreements that stemmed from the Lausanne Peace Treaty (in such a case, the consulates might have been relieved of their role in minority education). It may also in fact evidence a deliberate attempt to render state 'care' a contested terrain so that minority governmentality would be able, in its whimsicality, to manoeuvre the changing dynamics of Greco-Turkish relations.

Does this capriciousness leave room for counter-conduct? The affidavit suggests that it does. Against the Turkish consul's claim (that the two petitioners are the enemies of twenty million Turks), which attempts to conduct a population of 'retrogressives' into submission, this population of two (a seemingly ridiculous exaggeration of the demographic balance of the minority, vis-à-vis Turkey), is counter-conducting the border as the limit of protection and ancestral respect. There is a noteworthy irony here that inflects capriciousness: the phrase '*ta pátria*' is not followed by '*edháphi*', which would render it the widely used phrase to refer to 'ancestral/native lands' and ultimately 'the fatherland' (as reference to Greece). Instead, the phrase is left gesturing to the Ephebic oath of ancient Athenian soldiers (who were vowing to protect their traditions with the ultimate goal of protecting the land). While doing that, it leaves the object of the two signatories' adherence vague: not to Greece as fatherland but to ancestral traditions, which might be those of ancient Greece, but also those of the ancestors that have been upholding Muslim traditions (of which the Friday rest day is one). The border thus emerges

as an instrument for protecting these traditions against their self-declared
'enemies' (the consul and the Turks he represents).

And yet, even this reading is put into question: is the location of the
border between the signatories and Turkey purely a defensive strategy
in their conflict with the consul? Might this statement ('between us and
Turkey stand the Greek borders') also be read as regretful of the location
of Turkey on the other side (where perhaps had this not been the case,
had this been Turkey, would it not have been a different Turkey, and they
not considered the enemies of Turks)? There is undoubtedly counter-
conduct here, but its subjects are not the Muslim Greek citizens that
Andreades would like to present. They are minority subjects navigating
the sovereignties of Greece and Turkey, and the multiple ways through
which they materialize: Fessopoulos' memo (they, after all, signed off as
the authorities of the 'Turkish school of Aratos'); the consul's threats; the
requests of teachers from Turkey; the Greek gendarmerie (who are the
addressees of the statement); the Greek witnesses who signed the statement; and the black list. The border plays a key role in this navigation
exactly because it is capricious: it bars them as outcasts on the one hand
('enemies'), but embraces their traditions on the other (enables them to
defend '*ta pátria*'). It is also used as a tool for fending off their subjectification into a 'Greek' or 'Turkish' population, putting into question the
seemingly straightforward meanings of '*pátria*' – as that which the border
separating them from Turkey protects or as the regrettable cause of their
'inability' to comply with the consul's order.

At the time of the incident, religion had been the key issue of debate
regarding the minority. Andreades's study is strewn with references to
religion, both in the main text and in the numerous appendices. In the
text, he confronts the 'most violent polemics' appearing in the Turkish
press that 'Greece is failing to crush Islamism and tolerates the actions
of old Turks' (*dhen sinthlívi ton mousoulmanismón ke . . . anéhete . . .
tas ipér tou mousoulmanizmoú praxis ton paleotoúrkon*), using language
that leaves no doubt as to where force and tolerance lie on the divide
between the stances of Greece and Turkey. The appendices build on this
dichotomy to show that the former's stance is actually guided by minority needs. They include twenty-three documents meant to present the
minority perspective (letters, affidavits, village council decisions, notes
to the government of minority organizations) on a number of issues,
the most pressing of which is religion (Andreades 1956: 47–51; 67–97).
These documents, of which the affidavit above is an example, speak
firstly to the context of secular Ataturkist reforms in Turkey which pitted
the 'new/young Turks' [*neótourki*] faction within the minority against
the pious 'old Turks'. Secondly, it speaks to the Greek context of anti-
communism and stress on ethnic purity. I have earlier (chapter five) given

the example of the 'Muslim Union of Greece' arguing for the establishment of a *medrese* that would function 'properly' (in comparison to the then recently-established Hayriye) to avert the communist-atheist threat. In the same petition, reportedly signed by two thousand individuals, this new *medrese* is envisioned as a vehicle for 'ensur[ing] the assimilation of pure Muslims within the state' (*exasfalízete i pros to krátos afomíosis ton akrefnón Mousoulmánon*) as well as 'the gratitude and commitment of the law-abiding class of Muslims' (ibid.: 74). In these pronouncements, a minority Muslim subject emerges who is the willing subject of assimilation (supposedly into a racially pure, since obviously not religiously homogeneous, nation) and of 'state care' (for which gratitude is the proper affect to exhibit). This subject is not, however, the unreflexive subservient victim of nationalist propaganda.

It is a reflexive subject who can be presented under the category of 'victim' in so far as their rights to equality are to be sought vis-à-vis the deleterious effects of the practices of 'new Turks'. Against these Turks, 'pure Muslims' level complaints regarding the switch to the Latin script, the gradual abolition of women's veiling and men's traditional head garments, and attempts to control the boards administering Muslim religious property. 'If the followers of the new Turkey had suffered 1/10 of what we have suffered', one passage reads, 'they would have all left for Turkey. But they enjoy every privilege and service. Had we been offered only five per cent of what [the state] offers the new Turks, we would be grateful' (ibid.: 72). This rights-claiming subject is aware of the script of national priorities and the frames of naming, genealogy, and 'state care' within which the state has configured its minority policy as a matter of national priority. Such awareness is evident in self-ascriptions used in other statements that include the designation 'Muslims by race living in Greece' (*en Elládhi Mousoulmáni to yénos*), and in pronouncements about 'the known superiority and pride of the Greek race' (*tin eğnozménin anoterótita allá ke iperifánian tis Ellinikís filís*) (ibid.: 87; 69). These are phrases that gesture to naming and genealogy as the bases for claims to particular forms of state care. Within these frames, even threats against the state can be levelled: 'in the case that the Latin script is violently imposed', another passage reads, the two thousand signatories of the earlier memorandum 'will protest honestly, but also with due respect, that the Greek government has offended our religious sentiments and that therefore our right to remain in beautiful Greece has lapsed' (*tha dhiadhilósomen ilikrinós, allá me ton prosígonda sevazmón, óti i Ellinikí kivérnisis mas éthixen is ta thriskeftiká mas esthímata ke óti élixe pléon to dhikéoma paramonís imón en ti oréa Elládhi*) (ibid.: 76). Even when threatening, these statements are carefully worded to navigate the pitfalls of counter-conducting capricious distinctions between 'beautiful' homelands and policing 'kin' states.

This is a time when the institution of the *dhílosis* as a repressive measure against the left was well established. I have glossed this as 'affi-davit' above, but Panourgiá historicizes its more sinister form of *dhílosis metánias* (declaration of repentance [for having joined the Communist Party]), as a legal platform, instituted since the Metaxas regime, geared towards profiling citizens and propping up governmental technologies of terror, torture and infiltration (Panourgiá 2009: 42–53; 94–103). In the year prior to the publication of these communications between the minority and the state, the pogroms against the Greeks of Istanbul ren-dered the minority's position in Thrace precarious as potential 'enemies of the state' through the logic of reciprocity that tied the two minorities together. The pogroms elicited a number of letters and *ipéfthines dhilósis* (declarations under oath) denouncing the violence and expressing grati-tude to the Greek state for the good relations existing in Thrace between 'Greeks and Turks' or 'Greeks and Muslims'. These statements constitute another large part of Andreades's appendix.

Within this frame, the statements can be read as a particular form of counter-conduct that inheres in the awareness that their signatories appear to possess of the governmentality that subjectifies them. The anal-ysis of this form of counter-conduct therefore calls attention to the modes in which this 'awareness' is communicated and their implication in the formation of political subjectivity. In this chapter, I concentrate on the issue of religion as a platform where the fissures of community come to be interpreted as a technology of government that seeks to divide the minority into that population that can be ordered productively as 'proper' Greek citizens (Muslims) and another population that needs to be sub-jected through more repressive measures or otherwise excluded (Turks). An aspect of this was also the genealogical modality that brought Pomaks (in their classification as 'Muslims' and 'non-Turks') under the fold of Greekness, and the ordering of state care that used disenfranchisement of land rights as a means to drive Turks off the land. Religion is a platform where counter-conduct elicits a questioning of the primacy between the communal and the individual.

Religion and Care

The split between 'old' Muslims/Turks (terms used interchangeably) and 'new' Muslims/Turks, was a key concern of policy makers, much before the issue flared in the 1950s. After the abolition of the Caliphate in Turkey (1924), the sphere of religion fell completely under the control of the state through the establishment of a Directorate for Religious Affairs (*Diyanet İşleri Bakanlığı*) (Davison 1998). Objectors to this brand of secularism, including the last Caliph, Abdülmecit II, his relatives and possible successors, were exiled under (Turkish) Law 431 of 1924 (Özoğlu 2011: 28). Further to these expulsions, a group of 150 individuals who were thought to have remained loyal to the Ottoman regime and to be constituting a threat to the security of the Turkish state were excluded from amnesty by a special protocol attached to the Declaration of Amnesty in the Treaty of Lausanne and were duly expelled in June 1924, once their names had been decided from an initial list of 600 (Decree 544 of 1924) (ibid.: 30). In 1926, fourteen of these '150ers' (*yüzellilikler*) found their way to western Thrace (Alexandris 1983: 92) and settled there as teachers, religious representatives, and newspaper publishers. These activities have been widely interpreted as having galvanized religious resistance to Ataturkist reforms in the late 1920s, before the expulsion of the group from Greece in 1931 following a request from Turkey presented in the context of the 1930 rapprochement. This was mirrored by the requested expulsion of Papa Efthim from Turkey. Papa Efthim was a Turkish-speaking Orthodox Christian who, following the 1923 war, proposed the replacement of the Greek Patriarchate in Istanbul with one that would promote a Turkish Orthodox Christian faith and would be disconnected from the church in Greece. Andreades (1956: 48), and the Muslim Union he quotes, declare that Turkey did not in fact expel Papa Efthim, despite the removal of the '150ers' from Greece.

Nearly three decades later, in Fessopoulos' own account of the failures and prospects of policy making, published in 1957 and based chiefly on his experiences in Thrace, a short chapter referring to the minority mentions the religious split as a key characteristic of social dynamics. Alongside it is an acknowledgment of Pomaks' deep religiosity, a Hellenic Islamicized population, he notes, about which the issue is 'very serious and delicate and should not be the subject of public discussion' (*to théma íne polí sovarón ke leptó, dhen dhínate na sizitíte dhimósia*) (Fessopoulos 1957: 151). In this publication, Fessopoulos finds fault with the subservient stance of Greece which has followed friendship pacts with Turkey to the letter. Turkey, on the other hand, he laments, has proven insincere in their application, allowing, among other things, 'the Consul to terrorize the population [in their majority law-abiding and simple] ... [whom] for the sake of pleasing post-war chauvinist Turkey, we have wanted to push towards the new Turks, and we have disappointed them' (*en ti politikí mas na efharistísomen tin metapolemikín sovinistikín Tourkían, ithelísamen na ton [aghathón, nomotayí plithismón] othísomen pros tous Neotoúrkous ke ton estenohorísamen*) (ibid.: 152).

That two years earlier Fessopoulos' name was used by the consul to scare Aratos' school staff into compliance with secular reforms is of course not mentioned (nor is any other part of Andreades's publication) – but tellingly, he advocates a policy of continuing to seek amicable relations with Turkey in the hope of a future turn in Turkey's stance (ibid.: 154). The religious split, in Fessopoulos' 'public' (as his cautionary comment on the Pomaks reminds us) view, is being used against Greece by 'two foreign powers, the first trying from its inception to achieve the removal of the Ecumenical Patriarchate from Constantinople, the second doing so of late because of a wish to divert attention from the Cyprus issue' (ibid.: 151–52). He is speaking of Turkey and Britain of course. The religious split thus becomes the platform on which complicated Cold War manoeuvres are made in order to socially engineer a 'simple' population into enemies of Greece.

In his analysis of the archive of the Coordination Council for Thrace, Christos Iliadis presents a different facet of the involvement of Greece in the split. In December 1955 (a few months after the Istanbul pogroms and almost a year after Fessopoulos' memo), the inspector of minority schools, who would become one of the leading figures in the council four years later, argued for a policy that would make use of the religious split between 'old Muslims' and 'Turks' already existing within the minority. '[T]he deeper and greater this division is, so much the better, and a need furthermore imposes itself upon us to foster it, indirectly, and undercover', he says (Iliadis 2004: 32). During a meeting of the Council in January 1967, the president of the council referred to this split again to predict that 'the future undoubtedly belongs to the modernists (*neoteristés*) . . . the view that the modernists are Greek-haters while the old Muslims are Greek-lovers ['philhellenes'] is wrong. They are both Turks. The difference is that the first have ethnic fanaticism and the second religious' (ibid.: 37). Read via a historical analysis, as Iliadis does, the significance of these quotes obviously inheres in the exposition of sinister technologies of government. Read through an anthropological perspective, however, it calls forth additional questions of subjectivization through resistance and complicity (something which Fessopoulos seems to understand, albeit in the limited sense of a passing acknowledgment of popular 'disappointment'), as well as other possible counter-conducts that reveal the workings of the law and its grey areas on the everyday. It is these forms of counter-conduct that I now turn to.

Representing Community, Exempting the Self

Not far from Aratos, in one of the villages of the yakka, midday prayer is being called. An old man enters the mosque, dressed in traditional *potur* trousers and thick black-rimmed glasses. The mosque is a square concrete

Figure 7.1 Man posing next to minaret structure adorned with Greek flag before prayer

structure of simple architectural design. Its function as an Islamic house of prayer is evidenced by the minaret that has been erected, quite evidently not concurrently with the main building. The minaret is in fact located not on the roof of the mosque but inside the concrete-paved yard, which contains the fountain for pre-prayer ablution. This minaret is a curious structure: it consists of a four-faced pyramidal body made of tin that sits on four short tin stilts. On top of it protrudes a tin crescent, while on the stilts flies a Greek flag. On a visit to this village in 1999 with minority friends who hail from the neighbouring village, my attention was pointed to the structure and the man in the traditional dress and I was urged to 'take a picture' (Figure 7.1).

'This was tradition', I was told, in full view, and needed to be immortalized. The 'tradition' that was being indexed in this visual composition was not the positively connoted tradition that bears discursive links to 'heritage' – as 'the broken minaret' might be (chapter two), or the phrase *ta patria* might imply. It was 'tradition' that had been vilified, a 'tradition' that had been used on many occasions before our visit to signify 'backwardness', low status, resistance to progress and modernity, ignorance – or retrogression, as the Turkish Consul would have put it in 1955. And here, it was being displayed through the indexes of culture (dress) and religion (the activity in progress). The architecture that framed this picture was noted as befitting the ridiculousness of religion that the mosque professed. But if the 'tradition' on display was being pointed to as yet a signifier in itself, a signifier for the 'minority condition', this architecture bore marks of the politics that attend this condition.

The minaret, I was informed in jest, was as ridiculous as it could architecturally possibly be, resulting from the 'height dispute'. The designation referred to the concern of Greek authorities about the appropriate height of minarets in western Thrace, which had been the focus of intense discussion in 1999 (but an issue of controversy from much earlier) and which had remained current until at least 2008. In that year, the Minister of Education and Religions, who hailed from Evros, rejected an application for the minarets in three mosques under construction to be exempted from the urban planning regulation, which capped this height at seven-and-a-half metres. The General Building Code contained in Law 1577 of 1985 defines the structures that may be erected on top of buildings (Article 16) as well as the provisions under which exceptional permits may be granted for the building of structures outside the code's regulations (Article 21). Minarets are not mentioned in these stipulations, despite the broad range of structures being covered by the said articles (including church bell-towers, chimneys, billboards, flower pots, and water tanks). This silence seems to echo an official unwillingness to acknowledge mosques, and especially functioning mosques, as legitimate structures within the national landscape in line with the logic of Hellenization that has guided space-making strategies, an unwillingness that is chiefly evidenced by the ferocious objections to the prospect of erecting a mosque in Athens (Antoniou 2011). Minarets are therefore pushed to the margins not only of the main construction law, but also of its 'exception' clauses, as structures regulated by exceptions that fail to name them.

Over the years there have been repeated denials to erect minarets of 'unacceptable' height (in some cases 'limits of the acceptable' having been interpreted by reference to the height of church bell-towers), just as there has also been permit-less erection and subsequent demolition. This mechanism of permit granting and denial through an opaque bureaucratic process effectively renders the minaret dispute part of the afterlife of now revoked policies of restricting building permits for the minority population that were mentioned in the previous chapter. Through this linkage, religion is effectively incorporated into the sphere of domination strategies that regulate the minority's everyday. In a comparative frame, the 2009 referendum in Switzerland supporting a ban on the building of minarets (arising from an initial request by a Turkish cultural association to build a minaret in 2005) might be mentioned as a similar attempt to regularize, through law, a religious exception. By another comparison, objections to the building of a complex near New York's Ground Zero in 2010, on the basis that it would have included a mosque, as well as the eventual completion of the project are indicative of a slightly different politics of legitimacy, where neoliberal strategies override the technologies of governing exception.

In the Greek case, even though from the perspective of the Greek state the minority is emphatically claimed as 'Muslim' above all, this religious identity is rendered problematic the moment it begins to become conspicuous (in the materiality of minarets) and is therefore at that moment subjected to legal restrictions (and legal silence). The framing of the problematique of height within the norms applying to churches in this sense parallels the concerns presented in the previous chapter over local demographics that are framed in terms of a competition between the Muslim and Christian populations. They also parallel the concerns of educators about the *ferece*-wearing practices of Muslim women, which cast religion as a field allowing domination by Turkey (chapter five). As an operation of governmentality then, religion is not simply a technology of differentiating docile minority subjects from unruly ones. Local and national press articles published in 2008 covering the latest phase of the minaret dispute refer to the existence of 280 mosques in the area, and point a finger at the Turkish Consulate in Komotini and even Saudi Arabia as the funders behind the new dispute-flaring mosques (Eleftherotypia, 1 June 2008; Hronos, 17 May 2008). This possibility of 'excessive' religiosity thus indicates the limits of 'normality', whereby religious identity is benign when it conforms to Greek 'cultural values', one of which is Christian Orthodoxy (and its attendant bell tower norms). The notion of excess, articulated as 'fanaticism' in the discussions of the Coordination Council, works to bind religion and nationalism within the adversarial discourse of the Greek-Turkish binary. Religion thus emerges as another dimension on which the fissures of community, which would complicate this binary, are played out and formulated into the problem of management of the minority population.

In the explication of these fissures, counter-conduct becomes the condition of possibility of this management (conduct). Against this conduct
of 'population' being shaped on the assumption of a minority unity, the
instance I describe speaks to another view of community. In being asked
to take a picture of this man (who smiles, in acknowledgment) as a 'representation' of 'the minority community', my attention is drawn to the
double gesture of 'pointing a finger' at this community: pointing it out
(in representation) and undermining it through the castigation of the
falsity of that representation. For my interlocutors, the man represents
'their' community, but it is a community from which, at the very same
time, they exclude themselves. Elif and her husband, Taner, were hosting
me in their house in the village for the day and had driven to a nearby
village to give me a sense of the place. At home, the children were left to
do their schoolwork and play video games, under the supervision of their
grandmother, who lived next door, in a house attached to Taner's. Elif
and Taner did not go to the mosque, were not religious, worked in the
town, and spoke Greek well. This enabled them to speak of 'the minority'
in the third person of objectivity (the 'they' I introduced in chapter two),
but also in an inclusive sense of inside knowledge. Both thus spoken in
the 'we' and the 'they', the minority community that they sought to represent to me became a community of differences that did not, however,
defy representation.

The man in the thick glasses, the children at home, the mosque and the
work environments in which I met Elif on other occasions were a simultaneously singular and plural community, unified and fractured. This was
not an isolated instance, but the general mode in which Gümülcinelis
spoke to me about their community and the 'minority condition' – the
backwardness, the ethnic divisions, the impoverishment, the nationalist rhetoric, and so on. These were discourses of criticism that often ran
counter to state representations of community (those of Greece as much
as those of Turkey). This 'community', against which the self stood in a
simultaneously included and self-exempted position, was, it would seem,
the key form in which counter-conduct was conceptualized.

This community, that bears so fundamentally on the anthropological
project, in the sense that it features in all analytic discussions we have
with our informants, and which has often been captured through the
notion of reflexivity, still seems to be slipping through divisions of inside
and outside. In the constitution of such a community, Nancy (2000) has
drawn our attention to the coexistence of singular plurality. Critically
reading Heidegger's notion of 'Being', he states that:

> [o]ne cannot affirm that the meaning of Being must express itself starting from
> everydayness and then begin by neglecting the general differentiation of the

everyday, its constantly renewed rupture, its intimate discord, its polymorphy and its polyphony, its relief and its variety . . . 'people', or rather 'peoples', given the irreducible strangeness that constitutes them as such, are themselves primarily the exposing of the singularity according to which existence exists, irreducibly and primarily – and an exposition of singularity that experience claims to communicate with, in the sense of 'to' and 'along with', the totality of beings (ibid.: 9).

It is this community that the spectacled and spectacularized man and his mosque enunciate. As the self co-emerges with the community, the divisions that pluralize the latter and expose its singularity call attention to a different political register than the inter-state. This is the biopolitical register of comportment, positioning and imposition (say of a camera foisting 'communal representation' on a man on his merry way to prayer); of the 'domestic' that is similarly inaugurated in the singular-plural co-emergence (internal disputes and divisions, the domesticity of religious practice, the ways in which the religious dispute has entered households in Thrace). And it is ultimately a discussion of borders, yet again, where the space of the border (when it can no longer be conceived as a line) is the space that inaugurates this singular plurality.

Commenting on the generational gap between herself and her mother, Esra described her mother as 'partly illiterate'. This was because her mother had difficulty writing in the Latin script, and used the Arabic one instead, in which she had been educated in the elementary school she had attended in the 1950s. Osmaniye, her school, was the last elementary school to implement the conversion from Ottoman to new (Latinized) Turkish, as the Ataturkist reforms were being fought over in different villages and neighbourhoods in Thrace through the course of the first half of the twentieth century. 'I sometimes get phone messages I cannot read!' Esra exclaimed, laughingly. Her father, who does write 'proper' Turkish, had nevertheless embarrassed himself when he tried to use 'old' Arabic words that he had learnt at school and through subsequent reading, to impress distant relatives visiting from Turkey. The visiting couple eventually asked for a translation, politely explaining that 'people in Turkey do not use such words any more'. These manifestations of the communal split emerging in the 1990s were the remnants of the rifts that the Aratos school authorities' *dhílosis* of 1955 articulated.

For 70-year-old İlhan, an ardent secularist, the *Cumacılar/Pazarcılar* split (between adherents of the Friday and Sunday rest days respectively, which elicited the visit of the school principal to the Turkish Consul in 1955) was indicative of the minority's backwardness vis-à-vis Turkey – discounting, of course, the wider politics through which a Christian rest-day has entered the global calendar of 'modernity', while the Muslim one has been relegated to 'tradition'. Thus, whereas following the reforms in Turkey, the *Pazarcılar* (Sunday observers) campaigned for its application to shops and schools, the *Cumacılar* (Friday observers) vehemently refused. Speaking of a nearby village, İlhan exclaimed that 'half the village closed their shops on Friday and the other half on Sunday; and this was just near here, right next to the town, going on in the 1960s!' When I asked, 'what happened next?' he simply said, 'then the junta came, and such differences didn't matter'. İlhan's answer pointed to Greek intervention as the primary factor shaping the progress of these debates, and thus to an awareness of an ultimate sovereign over community matters. For both İlhan and Esra (yet in different ways) communal splits could be analytically articulated in the 'they' only via the co-emergence of a 'we'.

Their difference, in this light, brings the domesticity that renders religion a biopolitical issue into perspective. Esra's comment speaks of the ramifications of the split on familial communication. İlhan's emphasizes the absurdity of dividing up economic time and with it the astonishment at the public exhibitions of this internal dispute. Both of them ultimately point to the emergence of community through differences that matter and differences that do not, as Green would have it (2005: 128–58). In doing so, they show that 'what matters' is a question of gradation, whereby an absolute answer is decided on criteria determined by the wider political environment. For both, the emergence of community happens not only with respect to the self (bringing out differences that ultimately, when the junta comes, do not matter), but also with respect to Greek community (bringing out the significance of their not mattering). The different language that Esra's mother writes in, and her father speaks, alienates her through temporality (it is pre-modern, backward, 'illiterate') in a parallel way that 'the minority condition', linguistic and cultural, might alienate majority Greeks. And what İlhan finds objectionable is similarly the obstinacy of *Cumacılar* to modernize and assimilate into the only culture possible: that of unified market time (and 'Greek' no less, as the time of the state that orders that market).

This co-emergence appeared on other occasions as well. When visiting the mountain villages in the summer, in short-sleeved tops and trousers, some of the women commented to me that '*bizim kızlar da böyle çıplak gezinii* (our girls too go around naked like this)' – a reference to a shared comportment of secular modernity from which they exempted themselves, but also a reference to a common habitation between 'Greek' and 'Turkish', or 'Christian' and 'Muslim' modernity that they refused to be part of, but which was becoming nevertheless 'theirs' through 'their' girls. What I am suggesting in reading this through Nancy's singular-plural is something beyond inter-subjectivity. I am suggesting an orientation of the self towards community that at once sets up and deconstructs an inside-outside opposition. If it counts as counter-conduct, it does so through the countering of the positioning of 'minority' as a pre-existing category of bounded differences, internal disputes, and familial similarity. Yet this counter-conduct exists as a repercussion of minoritization processes and, in turn, those processes are enabled by it.

The Religious Population

This co-emergence of community, which is also the co-emergence of conduct and counter-conduct, runs directly counter to liberal notions of co-existence that partake in popular representations of the minority. Yeni Cami, one of the two large mosques in Komotini, is a staple feature of such representations. Above its dome rise its minaret and the town's clock tower. The clock tower, on top of which flies the Greek flag, rises as high as the minaret, which was not always so. Photographs of the 1930s show a dome apex, since replaced by a right-angled neo-classical cube that sometimes accommodates a soldier guard, armed with gun and binoculars. The conversion was undertaken during the military junta period, like many other infrastructural and aesthetic projects – and like them, it has endured. As one of Komotini's landmarks, the clock tower appears in most postcards next to Yeni Cami's minaret, signifying the co-existence of the two communities – a success story about a 'mosaic' form of multiculturalism. On the few occasions that I watched nationally broadcast documentaries about Komotini with my Gümülcineli friends, they mockingly predicted that the first shot would be of the clock–minaret pair, and they were invariably right. Their objections were not only directed at the banality of that 'first shot', but also its illusionary qualities; and not only regarding the success of co-existence, but also the representation of themselves in the lop-sided minaret crescent.

The only time Selda had seen the inside of the *müftülük* (the office of the religious leader of the minority), which is attached to Yeni Cami, was when she got married. She had to do this, she explained, because there was no other option. Minority religious affairs (of which marriage is one) is a matter for the müftülük, civic affairs a matter for the state. According to the appointed müftü of Rhodoppe, Meçço Cemali, whom I interviewed in 1999, the responsibilities of the müftülük covered two of the life spheres designated in the Koran, those of *muamelât* and *ibadet*. The first (literally meaning 'transactions') governs family law, inheritance, religious property, and other such matters. The second ('religious service') regulates religious observance (e.g. instruction on fasting and charity). The third sphere of Islamic practice, he noted, *ukubât* ('retribution', regulating criminal law), is not under the müftülük's jurisdiction in

Greece, but under that of the state courts. As the müftü put it, 'the *sheriat* is followed as long as it does not contradict the laws of Greece. When it does so, as in the case of polygamy, Greek law prevails.'

Selda's brief encounter with *muamelât* had interpellated her into a religious subjectivity that seemed to matter little to her everyday, but which legitimated the governmental organization of a particular community as a rights-bearing minority within a democratic state. This organization was of course part and parcel of the governmentality we have seen earlier, where 'state care' (here in the form of access to *muamelât*) is directly tied to naming (subjectifies the community as 'Muslim'), and as Fessopoulos' account and the minutes of the Coordination Council make clear, in an undercover way to genealogy too (religion being viewed in conjunction with Pomakness). This awareness was the main reason for Selda's dismissal of that interpellation as inconsequential to daily life. Yet it is a dismissal that is belied by experiences of lesser orders of 'normality', when the subjection to *muamelât* takes the form of a biopolitical constraint: for example when the müftü's decisions over a divorce, or over inheritance, bear the brunt of injustice (whether 'perceived' or 'real' is of little consequence here) and elicit decisions to avoid the mechanism of müftülük arbitration altogether.

Such exceptional situations have been the matter of critical studies of the institution of the müftü in Greece, which point out that the ability of the state courts to override the müftü's decisions is limited to examining the process rather than the substance of the decisions, and that in practice the courts rarely scrutinize such decisions in depth (Kotzabassi 2001; Ktistakis 2006). Indeed, there have been reports by human rights NGOs which have brought to light cases in which polygamy, underage marriage and forced marriages have taken place – all of which would be strictly prohibited in the müftü's account of the separation of powers given above (Greek Helsinki Monitor [GHM] and Minority Rights Group – Greece [MRG-G], 2002: 3; GHM and MRG-G, 2005: 2). Greek legal and other scholars have thus argued for the need for the Greek state to thoroughly revise the institution of the müftü, because the way in which it currently functions makes Greece 'the only European country in which Muslim religious law is applied', which is 'anachronistic and contrary to the principle of gender equality' (Kotzabassi 2001: 4, 7). Similar claims are made by Boussiakou (2008: 3), who also cites Anagnostou (1997: 5), Stavros (1995: 23), and Ktistakis (2006). As with much of the debate on women's rights in Islam, this position is prone to orientalist assumptions (Howard 1995: 118–20), not least because it equates practice with religious law and precludes alternative, including feminist, interpretations. As Mashhour (2005) shows, such interpretations can be accessed through the notion of *ijtihad* (independent juristic reasoning) and a serious unpacking of the application of scriptures that separates theological from patriarchal injunction. I would however add that such interpretation might equally lead to ultra-conservative Christian positions, such as the ones promoted by Islamist feminists whose work was celebrated by the Bush administration (e.g. Manji 2003).

Instead, in the case of Greece, research is premised on the exemplification of actual human rights violations against minority women and children who experience the potential arbitrariness of müftü decisions. The maintenance of the *sheriat* is thus viewed as potentially discriminatory, and legal justifications for keeping it as part of domestic law on the basis of bilateral agreements (the Lausanne Peace Treaty) are rejected as contravening international instruments ratified by Greece, which should take precedence (Ktistakis 2006). This approach maintains a legal–political distinction that is untenable in practice and which limits the space for criticism, by privileging a criticism of an inadequate legal system (the legal failures of the Greek state with respect to the issue). This privileging precludes a critical assessment of both law as such (e.g. in the possibility of serious engagement with the *sheriat*) and of the politics of legal enforcement and argumentation (e.g. criticizing specific failures of application). Thus, for example, the problem of human rights violations to which the müftü decisions may give rise is not identified in the potential for arbitrariness but is rather approached as a failure stemming from the very existence of the institution. Had this potential been the focus of concern instead, more radical suggestions about how to counter such arbitrariness, which might also go to the heart of the debate about his role, could have been envisioned. Such suggestions might have included the formation of alternative structures to counter arbitrariness, including through incorporating minority women's voices in institutional reform. Instead it is a strictly legal affair and as such the problem is identified in the judicial powers enjoyed by the müftü. This view underplays the political dimension in two important ways: it fails to scrutinize state politics (and its possible involvement in a potential reform that would radically take gender into account) and it reduces the scope of empowerment (because such inclusion of women's voices is foreclosed). Instead, for women (and men) like Selda, what is at issue is not the legal standing of the müftülük, but its role in representing 'community'.

Selda's marriage in the müftülük thus displaces the question of the law by reintegrating 'the ordinary' into the question of representation – not so much a question of 'who decides' any longer (the müftü or Greek courts, this müftü or another one), but of what is represented in the müftülük. Selda's marriage is an instance of her subjectification as a Muslim person under the laws of Greece, of her 'choice-less' complicity in becoming interpellated into a subjectivity she would have otherwise rejected, as well as her complicity in upholding an institution she would have otherwise despised. At the same time, this is not to be read as a form of victimization. Selda does not regret having got married there. She recounts it as an awkward part of her relationship with the religious leadership and the biopolitical governance of minority life. Her lack of choice is factually inaccurate, because the option of civil weddings is open to minority members (even if few of them, to date, have taken it up). But it is not something she considered, simply because as a minority woman, she took it for granted that she would follow 'custom'.

The example may sound facile; almost all of our informants exhibit at some point a reflexive attitude towards 'tradition', and anthropology has done it since its inception. But what I want to point to is something that still seems to elide analysis when the limits of that awareness that informants exhibit are to be explained. For what I see being articulated in that 'awkwardness' of marrying in the müftülük is the 'interruption of myth' (Nancy 1991: 43–70). By this, I mean the acknowledgment that the specific form of institutionalizing this ritual works in tandem with the making of a specific community, and that to comply with that message knowing this, inaugurates something else than the 'traditional' under-standings of community. As Nancy puts it, 'the interruption has a voice, and its schema imprints itself in the rustling of the community exposed to its own dispersion' (ibid.: 62). It is this 'rustling' and this 'dispersion' that anthropological analysis can pay more attention to.

The Finger of Legitimacy

A political way to read this dispersion is in the contest over the office of the müftü itself, which has been the main cause of friction between Greece and Turkey on issues regarding minority religious affairs since 1985, when the death of the müftü of Rodopi opened a succession debate (see also Tsitselikis 2004a; 2004b; 2006). A new müftü was ini-tially appointed by the state, but minority political leaders argued on the basis of the Treaty of Athens (1913) that 'the muftis, each within his own community, sh[ould] be elected by Mussulman electors' (Article 11).[1] In 1990, when the second of the three müftüs in Thrace, responsible for the prefecture of Xanthi, also died, another appointment was made, and rati-fied through Law 1920/1991. Following this development, communal elections were called, during which two other individuals were elected in the position of müftü in the two towns. Since then there have been two müftüs in each of the two towns, one elected and one appointed. The elected ones were recognized as the religious leaders of the community by the Turkish government, while the appointed ones were recognized by the Greek state. Each government in turn refused to recognize the other müftü as a legitimate representative. The appointed müftüs have been involved in the administration of the minority's religious affairs as explained above, while the elected müftüs have been managing the minority's religious politics – by lobbying for their right to be recognized as müftüs and more generally for the restoration of the rights of the minority (which include the rights to be ethnically identified as Turks, the right to better regulation of the education establishments, and self-administration of the *vakıf* properties). However, these activities have at various points been received with hostility by the Greek government and local nationalists, who see them as attempts to incite the minority's anti-Greek sentiments (see also, Tsibiridou 2007).

In other words, the two müftüs are in charge of different biopolitical spheres: that of family matters in the case of the appointed one, and that of political rhetoric in the case of the elected one. But while a private–public terminology may also seem applicable to this differentiation, this would overshadow the fact that family matters affect the whole of the minority in that they regulate *bios* (marriage, death, inheritance, divorce), and in doing so bring it under the regime of religious politics. Similarly, the 'public' domain of political rhetoric, which may appear restricted to politically impassioned individuals, bears direct links to wide-ranging life processes such as communal rituals (circumcision, memorials), which the elected müftüs are often called upon to perform. It is no coincidence that Ahmet Sadik's rise to power was catalysed by his role as a *sünnetçi* (circumcision expert) around the Rhodoppe villages. The battle over religious representation is thus a battle 'over hearts and minds' as well as bodies, where those immediately concerned (the minority 'population') have little at stake apart from the formalities of cultural life. This 'cultural life', I would suggest, is a variant of 'bare life' (*zoé*) because it misses the higher scope of 'political life' (in the sense of an involvement in governmental practices that would reconfigure sovereignty). Thus, the biopolitical regimes on offer by the two types of religious representation (elected and appointed) are essentially the same. And it is from this recognition of the irrelevance of this religious political contest to what is actually at stake in the everyday of the minority as a political community that other kinds of 'community' begin to emerge. The irrelevance of the müftülük in Selda's everyday, as articulated by the memory of her wedding day, exhibits an enmeshment of the self-excluding community in the religious contest of representation I have just outlined.

On another occasion, I had been talking with Bilge about my work in the müftülük marriage archive, where I had spent a month over the summer of 1999, and she happened to mention the elected müftü – at which point Celal joined the conversation. Having missed the beginning of her sentence, he asked for clarification about which müftü we were talking: 'You are talking about the finger müftü, right?' he asked. This designation surprised me because I had never encountered it outside the müftülük office, where supporters of the appointed müftü had explained to me that the elected müftü is called the 'finger müftü' (*parmak müftüsü*). It is a mocking designation that refers to the process of his election. 'When the Consulate decided on him for the post,' the appointed müftü's supporters said, 'people gathered in the mosque. They were asked whether they wanted him as müftü, and told to raise their hands. They counted fingers [hands] and by virtue of that called him a müftü.' This was a clearly political statement, which exposed the mechanics of the process by which the elected müftü claims political legitimacy, and undermined that process on the premise that the electorate had not been representative of 'the community' at the same time as it evacuated those claims through humour.

My secularist friends, who had in previous conversations insisted on the right of the minority to elect its religious representatives, were now invoking the same detachment from the issue when referring in jest to the '*parmak müftüsü*'. They seemed to be using this designation with glee, in all its sexually derogatory connotations that I found difficult to detect in the much older and more propriety-concerned supporters of the appointed müftü. Without reading this as an idealized form of resistance, what could be asked of such attempts to ridicule the processes of election and appointment is which finger is being referred to in the designation 'finger müftü': are they 'showing the finger' to the debates taking place on a level far removed from their daily experience of marginalization, or pointing out the 'sore thumb' that belies the attempts of both the Greek and Turkish states to deal with questions of secularism and religious pluralism?

Either option would indicate a countering of the conduct of population shaping up in the very same instant that this population is being conducted – the latter does not precede the former. And this is the analytic question that I have posed in my interpretation of Nancy's singular plurality. Nancy's own commitment to an ethical standpoint in the development of the concept is clear in his choice of historical moments of violence and war as introductions to the problem of the alienation from community and the need for a singular plural world (Nancy 2000: xii–xiii). While recognizing this, what I have tried to suggest is that there is an anthropological analytic point here as well. The co-emergence of community is not necessarily the Derridean 'democracy to come' (Derrida 1997; and on the relation of the two projects see Secomb 2006) but a practice of the ordinary, in Das's (2007) sense of the unsublimated 'everyday'. This allows people to comply with interpellations, negotiate differences, reinvest commonality with different meanings, disagree with interpretations, laugh them off, and employ them at the same time – it allows them, in short, to negotiate and reappropriate some of the capriciousness of the borders that surround them. This capriciousness runs right through the communal and the personal in framing the biopolitics of the domestic domain, to which the next chapter turns.

Note

1. It should be noted that the Treaty of Athens is much more comprehensive on delineating the rights of Muslims in Greece than the Lausanne Peace Treaty, with extensive injunctions on the treatment of Muslim property (*vakıf*), religious representation, and the organization of religious rights. One of the points that is striking in the current conjuncture is the stipulation about the construction 'of a mosque in the capital . . . where need is felt therefor' (Protocol III, §4). This seems to have gone unnoticed in the debate over the Athens mosque. While it is true that Law 1920 of 1991, detailing a new procedure for appointment of müftüs, has been interpreted as having declared the supersession of the Treaty of Athens by the Lausanne Peace Treaty, the finality of this declaration still remains a theoretical point of argumentation. More to the (practical) point is the reminder of the place of law vis-à-vis political sovereignty: the Treaty of Athens is a bilateral document that pertains to Greece and Turkey, the first as the state holding sovereignty over the territory where such a mosque is to be erected (which is still the case), the second as the state with the responsibility for protecting its 'own' (i.e. ethnically Turkish) Muslims within Greece (which is not the constituency 'needing' such a mosque in twenty-first century Athens, following the evacuation of 'Turkish' Muslims post-1923).

CHAPTER 8

THE POLITICAL LIFE OF MARRIAGE

Creating the Married Population

Meral's experience of the müftülük is similar to Selda's: it is embodied in a single document she keeps locked away in a drawer – her marriage certificate, issued by the müftü when she got married. It is a document that is both fascinating and meaningless, as neither she, nor her husband, can read it; it is written in Arabic script (Figure 8.1). This document symbolizes the chasm between the role of the müftülük as the arbiter of biopolitical relations within the minority (as it is the authority responsible for ordering the sphere of family law [*muamelât*]), and the legitimacy of this role in the form of objections, by large sections of the community, to Islamic religion as a key identity marker. It is also a document that represents the imbrication of different biopolitical regimes that order the gendered lives of minority members: citizenhood, minoritization, religious law, and 'community'. Each of these regimes projects particular gender subjectivities that intersect but may also contradict each other. Their negotiation and its implication in informing aspects of counter-conduct are the subject of this chapter.

In bringing forth these aspects of subjectivity, Meral's marriage certificate, neatly filed in her drawer, interpellates her as a Greek citizen who is also a gendered subject of the minority community. It fulfils the function of the Althusserian policeman's hail in including her within the fold of the community that is being policed. In this sense, it resembles the state documents that Navaro-Yashin examines in their power to interpellate their Turkish-Cypriot owners into subjects of the British state (Navaro-Yashin 2007). And on reflection – when Meral draws it out to show to me, for example – it also reminds her that she is part of a particular population conducted on the precepts of religion and gender: the married minority population. But it is not on reflection that she experiences the

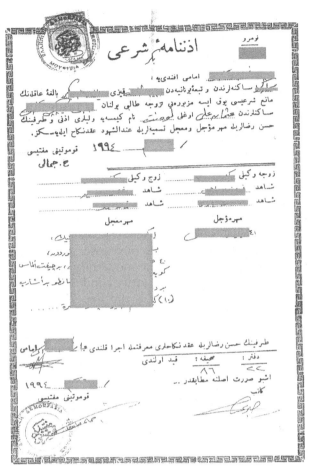

Figure 8.1 Marriage certificate from 1994

ramifications of the conduct of this population – she does so in her ordinary domestic and public life: the relations with in-laws, the organization of chores, the interactions with her son, the worries and quarrels and negotiations of married life.

Talking of her wedding, Meral often commented that she had married 'the modern way', for love: she had dated Enver for years before the wedding, and unlike traditional weddings, the two families had little involvement in the arrangements. She had not cared about the dower and had not entered into negotiations for it. It was thus set fairly low, by common agreement with her husband. 'It was like a Gypsy marriage in that respect', she joked in recounting the event. For Meral the comic aspect of the story was that her marriage agreement represented a different cultural reality to what she had intended it to be. As a lifestyle choice, her wedding had been a mark of her 'modernity', which set her apart from Gümülcinelis who were 'traditional' and stuck to the old rules: married young, had an arranged marriage whereby their partner was chosen by their parents, had extravagant dowers agreed upon, settled into marriages where the husband would be the breadwinner and the wife the child-carer.

To Meral, these marriages were also, because of their 'traditionality', often loveless, and many of the women she knew who participated in them were coping with oppression they were or not aware of (infidelity, lack of financial autonomy, dependence on husbands to approve choices of dress, entertainment, and work). Such inequalities of course also existed amongst 'modern' couples, and conversely there also existed 'traditional' women who surprised Meral by their entrepreneurial skills when they set up their own small-scale businesses, and by their 'courage' when they decided to divorce. But the modernity/traditionality distinction maintained the image of the 'minority condition' she was excluding herself from, in a similar fashion that it did for Elif and Taner (chapter seven). Thus, Meral had not cared about doing things the 'proper' way (i.e. sticking to all the wedding customs). She recalled her wedding day with amusement, describing the customs that had been followed (such as the groom's family putting money in the bride's shoes) more for the way her friends had poked fun at her than for the cultural logic that lay behind them. It was in this context that they had decided to set a low dower, signalling the modernity of their love marriage.

The certificate she keeps but cannot read states the details of the couple, as well as the date of the wedding and the dower agreed. She showed it to me as an anachronistic document that recorded a religious ceremony for a couple who were vehemently secularist. Filed alongside other similar documents in the müftülük's records, it misplaced Meral not only in time but in terms of ethnicity as well: in stating the low dower agreed, it resembled the marriage contracts drawn up for the Romani individuals marrying in the müftülük. Thus, while Meral had otherwise striven to establish a 'modern' marriage, the trace that she had been left with had categorized her as part of the 'wrong' population – temporally (traditional), religiously (a believer) and ethnically (Roma). In enunciating these categorizations, Meral's marriage certificate keeps her locked into a specific kind of Greek citizenship – a minority one, which in the formal terms of civic documentation cannot be calibrated or transgressed; it is a digital-binary operation. She is unequivocally married, without qualification as to the 'how' of that marriage (which was the major point she would like articulated), just as she is unequivocally a minority member, without qualification as to the kind of membership that is. And the minority identity that produced that certificate is now proof of it.

In other words, the marriage certificate indexes an apparatus in the governmentality of gender within the minority. This apparatus works to maintain the key distinction between majority and minority by interpellating the latter into the fold of this distinction. In this chapter I will examine some of the discourses that make up this apparatus in their interpellative and categorizing import. In this way, the sphere of gender relations is opened up as an aspect of the emergence of 'community', where conduct and counter-conduct can be clearly seen to sustain each other. What I am particularly interested in are the operations of 'divorce', 'intermarriage' and the dower system, through which minority practices become indicative of 'community', or 'minority culture', defined both from the inside and the outside. As *dispositifs* then, i.e. institutional structures based on a particular knowledge system, divorce, dower, and intermarriage become instruments in the process that I would call the minoritization of gender. This minoritization is based on the institutional setup of wedding contracts, and the conceptual frame that organizes understandings of tradition and modernity. It is therefore from these that I begin.

The Minoritization of Gender

The revocation of dowry documents (*brigosímfona*) listed, until the 1980s in the land registry as chapter six explained, resulted from the revisions in Greek family law that introduced civil marriage (Law 1329/1983). This introduction limited the role of the church in regulating certain aspects of family law and placed them under the control of the state (e.g. divorce arrangements) (Tsaoussis 2003). In doing so, however, it rendered minority family law a matter of double jurisdiction, whereby the müftülük, not being the church, retained control over decisions (registering dower, settling divorces) that would otherwise, for the Greek majority population, have involved only judicial officers. Minority members can thus conduct civil weddings if they make a point of choosing against müftülük weddings, and their divorces are decided on by the müftü in the first case and endorsed by relevant civil servants. This keeps dower agreements firmly within the legal marriage process that Muslim minority members undergo, despite the fact that the secularization of (Christian) Greek society has banished such agreements from both the (Orthodox) religious and the (majority) legal spheres.[1]

This prism of jurisdictional ambiguity in the regulation of gender relations punctuates the biopolitics of marriage within the minority. The material conditions, which rendered the minority a community divested of a range of rights and opportunities, have also had an impact on gender relations. The müftülük, as the authority responsible for issuing marriage certificates and annulling them, holds records that index material, practical and legal inequalities within the minority and in the sphere of nuptial relations. I turn in later sections to these records to look more closely at the subjectivization of the minority through the institutions of marriage and the müftülük as they emulate and reproduce the state's governmentality. What is important here is that the cipher of this record (the minority condition) is coded in the discourse of development, articulated as the distinction between 'tradition' and 'modernity'.

As the quintessential aspect of 'traditionality' that religion was held to be amongst my minority friends in 1999, it represented a particularly salient factor in the process of minoritization. This political way in which the purportedly unified and singular population was produced as 'minority' entailed its subjectification under Islamic family law, regardless of religious persuasion (thus including individuals who rejected the ascription 'Muslim' as definitional of their community in a collective sense, but also of themselves individually). This subjectification also entails a pathology whereby 'minority' subjects in religious, official, domestic and other spheres are seen to be plagued by the ills of traditionality and conservativism. As Davis shows in her analysis of the culturalization of mental illness by Alexandroupoli hospital staff treating minority patients, this minoritization produces at the extreme wives, daughters-in-law and mothers who are ill because they are minority (Davis 2012: 117–87). This 'minority condition', largely created and reproduced in the home, is what the institutionalization of religious subjectification, as symbolized in the müftülük, underscores.

The documents issued that subjectify individuals into this 'community' also alienate them from it. In analysing the process through which community and the married population coincide as political techniques of interpellation, it becomes pertinent to ask, along with Butler, 'how the sphere of reproduction that guarantees the place of "gender" within political economy is circumscribed by sexual regulation, that is, through what mandatory exclusions the sphere of reproduction becomes delineated and naturalised' (Butler 2008: 52). The marriage archive indicates the effects of this naturalization, but it is the understanding of 'development' that maintains these exclusions as part of 'the minority condition'.

This became clear to me on a night out with Elif and Taner. During the course of our dinner, Taner asked me to look around the room and point out the Greek tables from the Turkish. 'The Greeks come here with their wives and they sit in mixed groups, while the Turks are sitting in all-male tables', he then explained. Indeed, the mixed tables next to us were speaking in Greek, while the minority individuals we knew were in all-male, segregated groups and speaking in somewhat softer tones in Turkish. Our table stood out immediately as an exception, mixed in terms of both gender and ethnicity. As if reflecting on this, Taner qualified his categorization scheme by adding a temporal dimension: 'minority people still go by the old rules – the women must stay at home and only the men can go out and have fun'.

The distinctions that Taner was using to classify himself through his behaviour were based on ethnicity (Greek/Turkish) and perceptions of development (tradition/modernity). According to this schema, his own behaviour would most probably be described as resembling Greekness. Taner's comment reveals, in this sense, the paradoxes minority members face when subscribing to hegemonic understandings of their 'otherness', whereby 'culture' is mapped onto 'ethnicity' and then onto social power relations. Thus, whereas the gender dynamics of our table could indicate a 'modernity' that Taner would proudly claim, this modernity is also an indication of 'Greekness', an identity that he would not claim. This exemplifies how gender relations are ultimately ordered by political relations and by the conceptual underpinnings of politics. In earlier chapters, I have shown that these underpinnings, based on the minority-majority difference, have been produced through the governmental modalities of naming, genealogy and state care. It is on this premise that gender difference maintains and reproduces 'community', as analysed earlier. In initially inviting me to her house, Elif had described their family situation with Taner as 'traditional'. Although they lived next to Taner's parents, Elif explained to me, each house kept 'separate accounts' (*xehoristá portofólya*, literally meaning 'separate wallets') and this is what kept their relations (primarily with in-laws) healthy. In describing the 'traditionality' of her domestic life, Elif had smirked at the separation between 'tradition' and 'modernity' she had just vocalized. The meaning of both seemed confused in her case – the distinction inappropriate in reference to her lifestyle.

In countering the seemingly clear contours of this distinction, Elif's articulation also complicated the dichotomies it is often mapped onto: urban–rural and lower–upper class. Elif and Taner both come from villages in the valley and they now live there, although they both work in the town. Agriculture is the main occupation of Elif's in-laws, and although the couple often provide help with work in the fields, they are both white-collar workers during weekly working hours. Elif's description of her home situation speaks to both the 'success' and 'compromises' the couple have made: they are financially independent and thus enjoy autonomy of decisions from in-laws, but they also live in close proximity to them and contribute, and receive, labour and (assumedly) emotional support.

Aspects of the gender roles that Taner and Elif adopt (division of labour
in the home, roles relating to patrilocal residence) are naturalized within
'cultural' frames. Elif does the housework according to a 'norm' common
to both Greek and minority culture, and they reside patrilocally according to the minority cultural 'norm'. In recognizing the latter pattern as
'cultural' but failing to notice the former, gender inequalities that pertain
to Greek majority culture are normalized while minority norms become
the subject of critical assessment. This limits the scope of questioning
inequality to those issues where minority differs from majority – mixed
tables might thus be mentioned as an example to emulate, but Taner
could not imagine an all-female table or a women's 'night out' (at least
not in 1999). Gender equality becomes relative, in this way, with respect
to majority culture, not evaluated within the universe of possible gender
roles. This is how 'tradition' and 'modernity' become the conceptual
instruments for minoritizing gender.

I have, elsewhere (Demetriou 2006), shown how aspects of 'development' in globalization, in the form of migration and the expansion of the
sex industry in the region, were becoming inserted, in the late 1990s,
within this patriarchal frame of development. In this frame, minority men
and women were repositioned at the bottom of the economic and 'devel-
opmental' scale, as a corollary of their own 'free', yet bad, choices arising
from 'cultural backwardness'. Here, I want to shift the focus of that
analysis on the ways in which one particular aspect of gender relations,
inaugurated by wedding and finalized in divorce, interpellates individuals
as citizens inhabiting particular legal statuses (minority married adults)
that are punctuated by class positioning. I am speaking of marriage not in
its everyday inter-subjective reproduction through affect (conjugal relations), but at the moments of its inauguration and dissolution which offi-
cialize it as a technique of governance of population. At these moments,
such governance is bifurcated: minority members are subjected to the law
of the state but also to the (religious) law of their 'community' in ways
that leave little room to counter-conduct their alienation from both. It
is this foreclosure that illegible marriage certificates signify – when they
exist, that is, in the drawers of individuals who have conscribed into
this 'married population'. Still other battles remain for those who, in
not marrying, have not conscribed to this population and who face the
castigation of being unmarried adults.

This connection between law and 'the conjugal institution of the heterosexual family' is precisely where Cornell (1999: 101–2) locates patriarchy: 'the word patriarchy', she says, 'indicates the manner in which
a woman's legal identity remains bound up with her ties to the state
as wife and mother within the traditional heterosexual family'. What of
the situation, I thus ask, where women are not citizens because they are

mothers in the general, but are particular kinds of citizens because they are Muslim mothers? In Cornell's analysis, the counter-conduct of 'community' is directly related to social recognition, since '[c]rucial to allowing women the moral space to contest the interpretations of their "sex" imposed by religious and cultural traditions is a challenge to their external cohesion [within the minoritized community, for example], and thus the cognizability of their existence as a group' (ibid.: 173).

The workings of hetero-normativity as a technique of governance are here amplified in the double circumscription of the conjugal family in law (of both majority and minority). Amongst the minority, references to homosexual relations are absent from public discourse except for the constant use of '*ibne*' (faggot) as a swear-word amongst men. Considering this, I would argue that in fact people do not seem much more able to escape the heterosexuality prescribed to them than they would be to escape their race or class. This calls for a reconsideration of Fraser's classification of gender as a matter of recognition on the assumption that 'homosexuals are distributed throughout the entire class structure of capitalist society' (Fraser 2008: 21). If homosexuals are 'distributed' across the majorities and minorities of Greece, the manifestation of homosexuality is clearly not. For while in the Greek majority population, as in the United States, of which Fraser speaks, queer subjectivity is framed in law (which has decriminalized, but otherwise refuses to acknowledge it), for the minority, this legal subjectification is also nested in a religious one (through which the legal first passes). And this religio-judicial circumscription around 'community' encloses a presumed and naturalized heterosexuality that characterizes the minority subject. Other forms of sexuality are not 'tolerated', vilified, or ridiculed, as would be the case for the majority. They are instead unseen, unacknowledged and rendered inexistent; their 'distribution' is not simply covert, but effaced. In this respect, the Lausanne Peace Treaty enunciates not merely a minority population, but also a population gendered and sexed in particular ways (as heterosexual and married). And in the process of its reproduction, the wedding record suggests, this population also becomes circumscribed by concerns of ethnicity and class. And if marriage is where this population is enunciated, divorce is the mechanism through which the distinction between majority and minority is underscored.

The Archive of Marriage and Divorce

Following on the trail of insights from the land registry archives, which provided a view of dowry agreements as a trace of the gendered biopolitical order, the following sections examine data secured from the müftülük marriage archives between July and August 1999. The records examined covered the period between 1925 and 1999, and are dominated by two kinds of events kept in different registers: weddings and divorces. For weddings, a summary logbook was consulted which summarizes the details that marriage certificates record, as these are entered at regular intervals by müftülük officials who file the original certificates elsewhere. The logbook thus registered all the weddings performed in each year through columns that recorded the mahalles of both spouses, the dower paid (normally registered as gold coins called *reşat* and filed into separate books for the period prior to 1950), as well as the previous marital status of the bride. The groom's details were limited to 'origin', which was defined by mahalle if inside Komotini, by village if within the Rhodoppe prefecture, by town if within Greece, and by citizenship in the case of foreign nationals. The bride's details included this information, but also clarified whether she was *bakire* (virgin) or *dul* (widow or divorcée, i.e. previously married). For divorces, a more simplified logbook registered the mahalles of the bride and groom for the divorces in each year.

The contrasts to the land registry of this form of registration is telling, both ethnographically and methodologically. In the land registry, my work was confined to the basement room where archives are kept and was carried out for the large part in isolation. My research in the müftülük was made highly visible, by comparison. I was provided with a desk in the office of the müftülük clerk, in the main reception area. Permission to access the data was granted after a formal interview with the müftü, whereas a presentation of my research capacity sufficed for land registry clerks. Unlike the land registry, my research in the müftülük also required institutional investment, in the form of the assistant registrar's help in bringing the files, overseeing my work, and occasionally helping with the deciphering of Ottoman scripture. After some initial training, I was able to decipher the names of the seventeen mahalles that made up the müftülük's official mapping of the town (Figure 4.1), consulting the clerk occasionally for confirmation.

The experience of the müftülük as a 'field' brought into view the implication of the majority–minority differentiation in the power dynamics that pervade many of the encounters taking place there. Throughout the time I spent working there, a sign pasted on the door of the reception room instructing women in Turkish that they should enter the office with their heads properly covered, reminded me of the exceptionality of my presence. I was allowed, indeed expected, to appear without such head cover ('*açık*' – 'open'), so that my membership outside the minority community was evident 'at first sight'. This also applied to Greek women lawyers, who did not read Turkish and who would occasionally visit the müftü, dressed in business suits and carrying briefcases (often, I assume, to negotiate divorce agreements with the müftü). My presence, it would seem, needed to be obvious because of the 'otherness' it exuded (in this space more than anywhere else).

It is to the difference between this binary (ethnic) otherness and subtler forms of communal otherness that the marriage record speaks. The lack of head cover is in this sense similar, and in the case of Greek lawyers coincidental, to divorce as indication of otherness. The sample I concentrated on consisted of town marriages and divorces. For marriages, I overviewed all the weddings in the first of every five years for the years between 1925 (when the records began) and 1985, for spousal origin (this excluded years for which this data was unavailable, notably 1955). From 1985 onwards, I recorded data for every year between 1985 and 1997 (when logbook entries ended) to allow for a more detailed view in recent years. I also noted wedding totals in Rhodoppe for every year between 1925 and 1999 (up to the point of data collection) and the previous status of the bride appearing in the summary entries. These totals represent all the 44,688 weddings within Rhodoppe recorded up to then. The years I sampled (25 of 75) included 14,415 weddings, roughly 32 per cent of the total. Of those, I concentrated on the town weddings that totalled 2,477 (roughly 5.5 per cent of the total). For the years after 1950, I also recorded dower values. Prior to that, the summary logbooks did not register it; and all other details (apart from spousal origin) relating to the weddings were filed elsewhere and in a manner that made it impossible to trace in the time available. On divorce, I noted divorce numbers for the years between 1948 and the available part of 1999, (pre-1948 divorce data was more difficult to access due to the filing system).

At first glance, the gender-based discrepancy of record keeping (where only the wife's previous marital status is recorded) is a clear indication of the patriarchal structure pervading gender relations. The much lower numbers of divorces (4,460 out of 32,111 for the years post-1948, i.e. 13.8 per cent) and of re-marrying brides (6,096 of 44,688, equivalent to 13.6 per cent) relative to the number of weddings involving first-time brides (86.4 per cent, Table 8.1) reflects this structure. These figures are also indications of divorce rates, which can be correlated to the degree of the woman's emancipation within the patriarchal frame, but can equally indicate the context within which this structure operates. Looked at the normative way, and reflecting the figures available from 1985 to 1999, an average figure of 83 divorces per year in a population of roughly 80,000 minority members (about half of the total estimate, on the high end, of 150,000 to represent the department of Rhodoppe) would, by orthodox methods, produce a figure of 1 divorce per 1,000 (higher for more modest population estimates). In Greece as a whole, a figure of 0.8 was reported in 1985 and 1.1 in 2004 (Symeonidou 2009: 213).[2] Counted

Table 8.1   Total of recorded weddings, divorces (post-1948), and remarried
women (*dul*) by year

Year	Weddings	Dul	Divorces
1925	470	35	
1926	656	170	
1927	549	139	
1928	619	174	
1929	522	91	
1930	487	103	
1931	480	87	
1932	431	70	
1933	465	69	
1934	521	68	
1935	478	58	
1936	523	91	
1937	566	118	
1938	493	127	
1939	482	92	
1940	406	84	
1941	566	109	
1942	614	86	
1943	636	89	
1944	767	99	
1945	749	181	
1946	641	119	
1947	456	73	
1948	377	72	23
1949	660	90	1
1950	667	102	9
1951	589	93	76
1952	648	82	46
1953	627	96	70
1954	590	90	39
1955	691	83	57
1956	694	89	57
1957	684	82	59
1958	647	77	80
1959	627	100	77
1960	555	69	75
1961	578	95	78
1962	516	83	90
1963	585	86	85
1964	601	80	113
1965	668	98	114
1966	604	65	101
1967	635	80	97
1968	648	75	124

Table 8.1 *continued*

Year	Weddings	Dul	Divorces
1969	621	93	92
1970	677	67	107
1971	641	68	101
1972	665	67	94
1973	780	98	126
1974	736	92	119
1975	776	81	121
1976	805	103	126
1977	820	84	143
1978	785	91	97
1979	723	92	122
1980	723	82	94
1981	679	78	90
1982	641	65	98
1983	676	77	109
1984	617	70	112
1985	599	65	85
1986	607	47	97
1987	615	56	86
1988	602	40	82
1989	539	31	99
1990	484	33	79
1991	528	41	76
1992	511	49	86
1993	525	59	79
1994	504	44	89
1995	543	44	60
1996	541	46	94
1997	470	46	79
1998	483	44	87
1999*	304	24	60

*incomplete year

in another format, as a percentage of weddings, the minority divorce rate in Rhodoppe stood at 19.74 per cent for that part of 1999 that was recorded and at 16.13 for the decade. In a comparative context, Greece had an overall divorce rate of between 15 and 17 per cent in the 1990s (Bagavos 2000: 2), and 18 per cent in 2001 (Symeonidou 2009: 213). In 2000, Rhodoppe was cited as one of the prefectures with the lowest divorce rates overall – only 6 per cent in a census of both majority and minority populations.

As an indicator of greater oppression of women arising from religious custom (where the 'community' would be signified by the conservatism of low divorce rates), minority divorce percentages appear anomalous. If anything, the 'conservatism' of Rhodoppe seems confined to the Christian population. This belies not only perceptions about 'the minority' within Greek society, but also representations of 'the minority' by officials like the müftü, who pointed out to me that for every five hundred or so weddings performed every year, there are two to three divorces among the Turks – he also clarified that Pomaks divorce even more rarely than this, and that high divorce rates only occur amongst the Roma population. At least the latter distinction is not borne out by a scanning of the breakdown of divorces by location, where the two Roma mahalles, Kalkanca and Alankuyu, account for roughly half of the divorces in the town in any given year, but not more – they also total 862 for the years between 1948 and 1999, against 1,164 elsewhere in the town. That latter number, furthermore, averages at 22.38 divorces per year for an estimated population of roughly twenty-five thousand Gümülcinelis (the town population totalled forty thousand in the 2001 census), or 0.90 divorces per 1,000, which does not show great discrepancies from the overall rates for Greece. Excluding Kalkanca and Alan Kuyu divorces from the figures of the 1990s, the divorce rate drops to 12.85 per cent, but not lower. Divorce numbers are not per se indications of the minoritization process. What makes them seem that way though, is. And the Roma population is exemplary because of the ways in which seemingly exaggerated divorce rates provide the basis for pathologizing problematic family structures that in public perception are held to be indicative of Roma 'culture'.

In a further breakdown, the divorce figures show that the large majority (2,601 or 58.32 per cent) of divorces occurred in marriages where both spouses were from a village, while similar percentages pertained to marriages between town dwellers or between town dwellers and villagers (9.73 and 12.44 per cent respectively). By comparison, the Roma mahalle divorces, as we have seen, accounted for 19.28 per cent of the total. Considering the overall low rate of minority urbanization (as a rough indication, consider that 82.81 per cent, representing 11,938 weddings out of 14,415 in the sample, were amongst village dwellers), and the even lower population percentage within the Roma areas in Komotini, village divorces would appear low, and Roma percentages high. Yet neither of them easily bears out the rarity (in the case of village divorces) or frequency (in the case of Roma) with which they are associated in public and official perceptions. According to these perceptions, Roma divorce rates throughout Greece are taken as a cornerstone of Roma 'cultures'. They then become a prejudicial device, when they give rise to moral evaluations of Roma culture as either loose, or not family-oriented. Alternatively, minority village dwellers – exemplified by the image of 'mountain Pomaks' – are perceived, as we have seen, as confined within oppressive societies (gender- and age-wise), conservative and isolationist.

These perceptions speak less to the question of how and why divorce takes place than they do to the construction of a 'healthy normal' that represents the Greek majority, defined along these lines not as 'any' population, but one defined in political terms. This is a liberal population, that is family-oriented yet not communally isolationist, neither morally loose, nor overly oppressive. Gender, in other words, functions through these perceptions as a platform for calibrating cultural norms of excess (too many/too few divorces) against more 'normal norms' in an ultimately political exercise. Similar calibrations are also applied to Greece when it is placed on indicator scales against EU or global trends of course, in similarly political exercises (which are part and parcel of the project of empire, as innumerable feminist studies have argued). The difference is that those indicators are not about perceptions of domestic life but chiefly about state policy. In culturalizing the patterns of marriage and divorce, a neoliberal governmentality is inserted into the domestic that places responsibility on the already pathologized community. It is on this logic of minoritization that mental illness is then read and evaluated on the moral basis of individual responsibility (Davis 2012: 124–59). If the question shifts from the count of divorces to the process of divorcing, however, a different picture emerges.

According to the Islamic code followed by the müftülük, a man has easier access to divorce than his wife. The triple declaration of divorce (*talaq*) that has been widely discussed in Western literature (Wegner 1982; Shaheed 1986; Tucker 1998: 78–113; Mashhour 2005: 571–77; Ahmad 2009) is recognized as part of the written code, but the müftü was adamant that this is not enough for him to issue a divorce. He instead described his role as an arbiter, confronting the couple on the grounds of the divorce and the wishes of each spouse, and then normally granting them a reconciliation period, at the end of which it is hoped they will renege on the decision to divorce. If not, he considers the situation of each spouse, and grants material compensation accordingly. In this scheme, the man is construed as the breadwinner and divorce initiator, and the wife as the penniless victim being abandoned. Thus the dower is normally the main asset being decided on, and this is given to the wife to allow her to sustain herself after divorce.

Should she be the one to decide to divorce (a practice referred to in legal scholarship as *khul*), this may be granted (usually after the consent of the husband has been secured, or, where there are extenuating circumstances such as domestic violence, without it) on condition that she gives up her claim to the dower as compensation. Thus, the primary considerations in deciding on a divorce are firstly, which one of the partners wants to divorce, and secondly, which one is more willing to stay in the marriage. These considerations are read in conjunction for the purposes of deciding the material distribution of wealth. The net effect is that women's access to property after divorce is negatively affected, which is exacerbated by the fact that divorce grounds such as domestic violence are effectively treated as subsidiary to the husband's will (if he is unwilling to divorce, the wife who has suffered violence is granted it minus the dower payment). In such cases of *khul* requests, the grounds for divorce become 'normalized' through the set mechanism of the müftü suggesting recourse to reconciliation as a first measure in all cases.

From this frame of inequality, the post-divorce material distribution is subject to a twofold decision: (1) whether the dower is due at all and (2) whether additional assets are due. This decision is based on the considerations cited above, as well as on the existence of any children who would need to be supported (the interpretation of Islamic injunctions on custody is considered in tandem with the müftü's discretion in judging the particulars of the case). Even when decided, alimony is difficult to enforce, and in fact its enforcement falls largely beyond the scope of the müftülük's jurisdiction after the divorce is finalized (the müftü can apply moral pressure on the husband through his religious stature, but cannot impose material sanctions in the way the state might). This difficulty might in part account for the frequent visits of Greek lawyers to the müftülük.

Upon marriage and divorce, certificates issued by the müftü are merely endorsed by government officials who then issue the additional state certificates in a straight-forward bureaucratic process. The fact that the müftü's decisions are not scrutinized insulates the sphere in which minority family law is executed. This insulation leaves little room for access to civic norms of gender equality (represented for the majority population by the detailed legal clauses on divorce and alimony that have replaced the *brigosímfona*). Even though alimony and divorce still remain problematic areas in Greece from the perspective of gender equality (Cowan 1996; Pantziara 2003; Tsaoussis 2003), in the legal framework applied to the minority this is accentuated. The müftü has neither the authority (as he is not a welfare officer and cannot issue instructions to the police) to impose and effect payments, nor the expertise (since he is not a medical expert or a social worker) to intervene effectively in cases of domestic violence. Thus, both failure to pay alimony and domestic violence are treated, in a resigned manner, as 'occasional' and 'regrettable occurrences' or 'cultural ills'. These views are not as indicative of a personal stance, as they are of the wider frame (institutional, communal and national) in which minority life is culturalized. Kalkancan women were frequent visitors to the müftülük, often appearing for alimony pleas. In the nonchalance with which they were treated (their visits considered, by müftülük officials, minority friends and Greek interlocutors alike, symptomatic of a 'cultural trait') the workings of intersectional inequality was palpable. The exceptionalization of Roma 'culture' worked to normalize 'the minority condition'. In this, the institution of dower, to which I now turn, was instrumental.

Wedding Prices, Marriage Values

In the culturalization of minority conservativism, the institution of dower is seen as part and parcel of minority cultural rights, not as a vehicle of gender inequality with which the state can interfere. Hence, its consideration as an institutionalized form of prenuptial agreements, something which scholars have proposed for the United Kingdom and the United States (Spencer 2011; Zakaria 2011), has remained beyond the purview of Greek critical scholarship. Such a consideration would not necessarily improve the situation of women's rights, just as prenuptial agreements elsewhere do not (Fehlberg and Smyth 2002; Mackay 2012). But it might have created a space of civic subjectivity that might question the boundaries of the communal, as Cornell (1999) suggests, allowing minority individuals to draw them up or not, as subjects of a law that is not specific to them, but applicable to the majority as well.

The way in which dower is confined to the müftülük records, makes it thus an instrument for marking these boundaries of the 'communal'. In recording the dower as pieces of gold coins (*reşat*), which the müftü had explained represented gold British sovereigns, the contracts which authorized the marriages were not only contracts of marriage, but of divorce too. *Reşat* represents wealth due to the bride on dissolution of the marriage, not wealth transferred to her or her kin at marriage. That these gold coins are still circulated in marriage transactions is indicative of the quality Green (2010b: 15) ascribes to gold sovereigns as an index of 'kinship and belonging'. They are part of the process that creates the married population of Gümülcinelis as a minority population, different to the 'majority' that has dispensed with such technologies of community-making.

But if gold coins mark the difference of the minority that still uses them in opposition to the notional gold coins 'of the past' of the majority, that circulate only as memories of an earlier era of trade and border-crossing in the Mytilene-Ayvalık region, they also bear an uncanny political relation to those notional gold coins. In Green's case, '[t]he gold was no longer circulating, growing or being used on people's skins; it was stuck in the abandoned houses in Ayvalik' and in this (in)capacity it 'linked people, islands and places in the Aegean in a way that people felt had been destroyed after 1923' (Green 2010b: 14–15). In its circulating capacity in Komotini, however, it still referenced that originary event of 1923 that established the community of its users as heirs to the *établis* population that exceptionalized the nation-state by being subjected into a minority within it. The use of this gold referenced, to them, to the Greek state and to their majority neighbours, their 'stuck' status as a population, in traditions that Greek law and Greek society had superseded.

Describing the dower settlement for his approaching wedding in 1999, Turgut joked that the agreed 101 coins was a 'fair' settlement. Nergis's (his bride's) family had originally requested 201, his own offered much less. 'So why not settle at 81?' he had asked her (the numbers should be odd, he explained) to which she agreed saying 'OK, so 101 it is'. Turgut made it clear that nobody within the negotiating parties, much less himself and Nergis, had taken the process seriously. Yet the recounting, voiced with a sense of mock complaint, spurred substantial discussion around the table (of mainly men) about the tactics each of them and their families had used to settle 'good' prices. Metin recalled how his father presented his elder son's marriage certificate indicating a dower of 51 coins to Metin's wife's family, and declared that this is 'their' price (the family's norm) – he proceeded to present the same document, this time fortified with Metin's own certificate, to another close family member's negotiation and so on for another three weddings, prompting laughter around the table.

This ridiculing of the process, I would suggest, is part of the reflexive attempt to counter-conduct the minority condition of being 'stuck' in traditional customs. Yet it is a counter-conduct that ultimately succumbs to the state's interpellation, in the same way that Meral is interpellated by the neatly filed illegible certificate. Ultimately, the presentation of the actual coins or their monetary equivalent, which happens upon divorce, is what re-positions women, from the status of autonomous decision-makers in the prenuptial negotiation process, to subjects of the müftü's jurisdiction and their ex-husband's willingness to abide by religious injunctions. Such willingness would assumedly be lessened by the ridiculing in which the dower-setting process and the müftülük as an institution is steeped, so that 'modern' men might more easily become unwilling payers. In the meantime, these gold coins remain notional and their effect largely scriptural (noted on certificates). Through the life of marriage, more corporeal practices mark 'modernity' on women's bodies, such as the birth control methods that Halkias (2004) analyses as an unacknowledged mechanism for reproducing the nation (or not) amongst Athenian women. Such practices were similarly present and similarly silenced in Komotini in the late 1990s. It is against these considerations that a biopolitical reading of the müftülük archives emerges.

Table 8.2 Number of weddings between town-dwellers and others (expressed as bride-groom origins, locations with less than 1% totals excluded)

Year	Town-Town	Village-Town	Town-Village	Town-Kalkanca	Kalkanca-Town	Town-Iskece	Town-Turkey
1925	62	1	3	0	0	3	0
1930	68	9	16	1	0	1	0
1935	87	6	18	0	0	1	0
1940	41	8	19	0	0	0	0
1945	100	17	27	0	0	1	0
1950	59	4	11	0	0	0	0
1956	38	11	22	1	0	0	6
1960	32	18	18	1	2	1	3
1965	54	10	29	3	1	1	5
1970	39	21	25	4	3	3	17
1975	62	21	30	3	3	2	32
1980	64	27	28	5	1	5	9
1985	43	12	26	1	5	1	6
1986	50	19	33	4	2	1	8
1987	52	17	24	4	5	1	6
1988	64	13	26	3	1	0	7
1989	37	10	16	2	1	0	5
1990	38	6	22	0	3	1	7
1991	40	17	26	1	3	0	5
1992	41	10	34	1	2	0	0
1993	39	13	38	2	0	1	0
1994	32	20	33	2	1	1	1
1995	36	16	31	5	4	2	1
1996	34	10	33	2	3	2	1
1997	37	12	32	3	4	3	1
Totals:	1249	328	620	48	44	31	120

The dower not only indicates 'community' as minority vis-à-vis majority, but also qualifies this 'community' as spatially determined. In the breakdown of the town marriages sample (Table 8.2), weddings where both spouses were town dwellers were the most numerous (1,249 of 2,477), yet the rural/urban divide was noticeable. In town–village weddings, the number of village women marrying town men was noticeably less than village men marrying town women (328 against 620). In these weddings (between village brides and town grooms), the mean dower range (i.e. not the complete spectrum of the range) was significantly broader than in weddings where both spouses were from the town and significantly lower than the range relating to village men marrying town women (Figure 8.2, not showing village-village weddings, which were not part of the sample). Correlated to the tradition of patrilocal

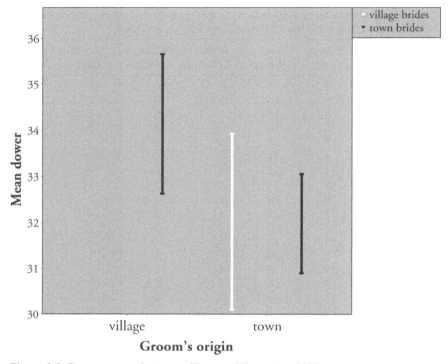

Figure 8.2 Dower ranges for town-village weddings since 1950

post-marital residence, the lower numbers of women 'moving into the town' through marriage, and for generally lower dowers, would imply that the overall effect of town–village marriages is the downward mobility of women: the higher numbers of town brides marrying village grooms could either signify women 'moving out' of the town to follow traditional patterns of residence or men moving into the wife's family home as *içgüvey*s (in-married grooms) of lower status (for which a higher dower, topping also the mean range for weddings within the town, might be seen as compensation). Neolocal residence would in this frame signify a break from these traditional norms, exposing them exactly as the two options (rural settlement of an urban bride or *içgüvey* status for a rural groom) that assign newlyweds to a class position.

In this sense, the dower works in tandem with the spatial aspects of marriage. Its value takes account of who is marrying where, and thus exposes marriage as an interrelation of groupings that are spatially and genealogically constituted. From this perspective, the spatial relations that marriage reinforces suggest a reading of 'intermarriage' as a form of governmentality that frames conjugal minority unions. This is a very different reading from the understanding of 'intermarriage' that prevails in local and wider, public and academic, perceptions, i.e. as marriages between 'Greek' and 'Turks' or 'majority' and 'minority'. The frequency of that 'intermarriage' is a staple question of many visiting journalists and its rarity has rendered it a major literary and medialized trope for presenting 'the minority' to the Greek public (through novels and a drama series, for example). Such an interpretation perpetuates the dichotomic distinction, even as it searches for 'hybridity', as the fundamental precept from which everything else follows. Instead, the kinds of intermarriages that the wedding record reveals expose the multiple distinctions on which the minoritization of gender is predicated.

Thus, considering locations of spousal origin outside the town other than rural ones, brings further differences into relief. Within Rhodoppe, town-Kalkanca weddings, which from the point of view of Gümülcinelis would be considered 'inter-ethnic', are a small fraction of the sample and equally distributed between men and women (forty-eight cases of town women marrying Kalkancan men and forty-four the other way). Although overall this is merely 3.71 per cent of the sample total, it is considerably larger than the total of thirty-one (1.25 per cent) weddings where town women have married men from Xanthi (İskeçe). In the absence of numbers for registrations of Xanthi (İskeçe) brides marrying into the town, I would presume that such weddings would be registered in Xanthi. Even so, Kalkancan grooms are more than İskeçeli grooms. Thus, in terms of 'intermarriage' beyond the urban–rural distinction, location seems to take precedence over what is normally considered 'ethnicity': Xanthi is further away in spousal choice than Kalkanca. Alternatively, this difference may also indicate the relative salience of different ethnic identities, if Xanthi is to be considered as 'inhabited by Pomaks', as prejudicial Gümülcineli discourse has it. Weddings between town dwellers and people living in mahalles considered Pomak (like Harmanlık on the outskirts of Komotini) could be used to indicate this, but the numbers were too low in 1999, as Harmanlık was a relatively recent mahalle (thirteen weddings were recorded for Harmanlık brides and only two for Harmanlık grooms). In either case, the existence of both sets of intermarriages confirms that in the politics of creating 'ethnicity' the boundaries of location and class are transgressed and maintained through marriage. Dower correlations show this (Figure 8.3): grooms from the town promise the lowest dower on average to brides hailing from Kalkanca, while 'outside' grooms from Xanthi and Turkey appear to promise the broadest mean dower ranges to town brides, by comparison to Kalkanca, village, and town grooms. Kalkancan grooms promise the second lowest dower on average, still higher than town grooms promise Kalkancan brides.

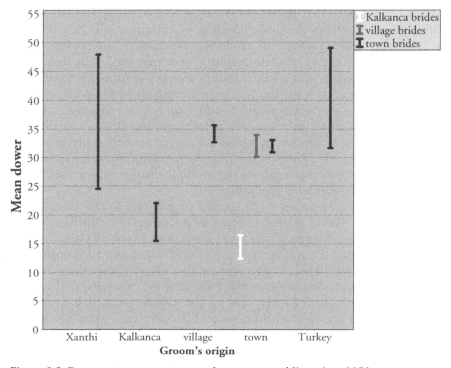

Figure 8.3 Dower ranges across town and non-town weddings since 1950

Of particular relevance to the geography of marriage is the location of Turkey, which, numbers would suggest, has a primarily political aspect. Thus, within the 'out-marriages' set (i.e. excluding town-town and town-village weddings), weddings to Turkish nationals are dominant (totalling 124), especially where these are grooms from Turkey (120 of the 124). In fact, at particular points in time, the numbers of Turkish grooms are comparable to those of village grooms (Figure 8.4). The low numbers of Turkish brides in the same period may be indicative of weddings with Turkish women being registered in Turkey. Given that the peak in weddings between Gümülcineli women and Turkish men occurs in 1975 (i.e. the year after the war of 1974 in Cyprus when, according to most accounts, minority life became extremely difficult), the registration of these weddings in Komotini may not necessarily indicate an in-migration of Turkish men but rather an out-migration of Gümülcineli women. Registering the wedding in Komotini might thus have been a ritualistic choice or a fall-back guarantee of maintaining civic ties to Greece.

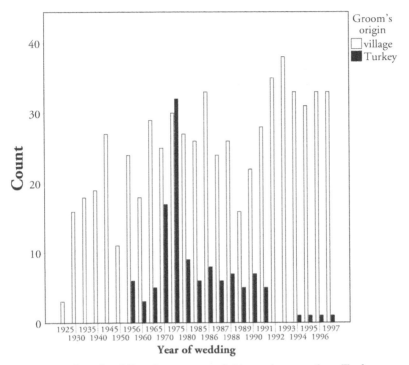

Figure 8.4 Number of weddings between town brides and grooms from Turkey and villages

In fact, for the same period, these results are dwarfed by the numbers of weddings to Turkish nationals registered throughout Rhodoppe, mostly of Rhodoppean women to Turkish men. In 1975, 113 village women married Turkish nationals (the number of town brides was 33), and in 1980 the number of village brides was 41 against 10 town brides. The number of intermarriages between village brides and Turkish grooms was in double digits throughout the period between 1970 and 1991 – the same time when land policies have been shown to have been particularly oppressive. This evidences how politics on the inter-state level enters the domain of domestic and sexual politics. The out-migration enabled through marriage that these numbers indicate cross-cuts the political and the personal, enabling such migration to be normalized as marriage choice, rather than as political flight. Contrary to the temporary migration of Esra's family to Germany in the 1960s, explicitly rationalized on political grounds (the difficulty of securing permits to renovate business premises destroyed by flood), Turgut described his uncle's migration to Turkey where he is married to a Turkish national as

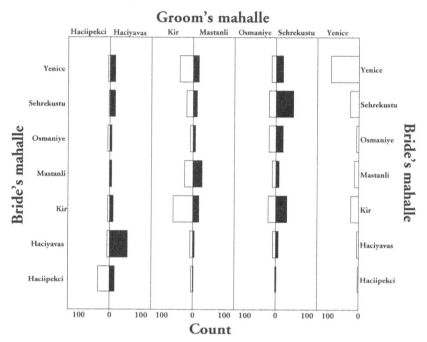

Figure 8.5 Number of town weddings by mahalle of bride and groom

a matter-of-fact event. In the climate of the latter 1970s however, such migration moves appear to have been as much 'a matter of the heart' as a matter of politics. Underscoring this was the worry that Metin often expressed in the significantly more relaxed climate of the late 1990s over his sister's relationship with a Turkish boyfriend, developed while she was studying in Turkey.

Within the town, mahalle locations also seem to be a factor in spousal choice. Of the 1,249 weddings where both spouses were Gümülcineli, 420 (33.6 per cent) were between people of the same mahalle – a proportion of 17.0 per cent of all the weddings sampled. Considering the 289 possibilities of combination between the sixteen mahalles in the town (and 'village' locations as an extra category), these are both high proportions (compared to the expected 17/289 or 5.88 per cent under a normal distribution), indicating a significant preference for same mahalle partners. In the matrix of bride–groom mahalle correlation (Figure 8.5), each of the town mahalles examined (excluding those with counts below 5 per cent) shows a majority of same-mahalle spouses in relation to spouses hailing from other town mahalles (with the exception of Osmaniye).

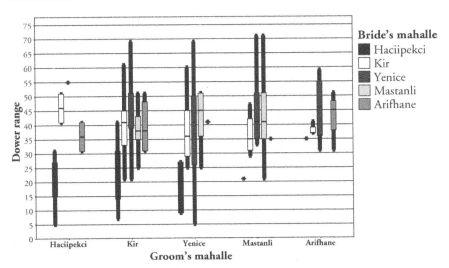

Figure 8.6 Dower ranges for selected mahalles in town weddings

This locational aspect calls for a 'social' reading of mahalle ordering, that takes account of perceived differences between mahalles. Such differences include class, race and religiosity, whereby some mahalles are associated with the higher stratum (e.g. central ones such as Cemaati, Tabakhane, Mahkeme and Aşçıhasan), others with the middle stratum (e.g. eastern mahalles like Yenice, Arifhane and Şehreküstü, and southern mahalles like Serdar and Kocanasuh), and still others with the lower stratum and with conservativism (e.g. northern mahalles like Kır, Yeni Şehreküstü, Yeni and Hacıyavaş). Some mahalles are also considered 'Gypsy' mahalles (e.g. western mahalles like Hacıpekçi and Hacıkaragöz), while others are considered more 'Pomak' (e.g. the northern mahalles of Mastanlı and Harmanlık). A class-based reading of space under this prism points to a maintenance of the class structure, with gender as the agent of it.

For the period of consecutive year sampling (1985–1997), a selection of mahalles from the different categories identified above shows some limited variation in dower ranges (Figure 8.6). Hacıpekçi mahalle has the lowest ranges overall and features insignificantly in weddings outside the lower- and middle-class mahalles. The large Kır Mahalle features highest ranges for brides marrying in from Yenice Mahalle (also a large mahalle considered higher in class terms than Kır Mahalle). In Yenice Mahalle the broadest range concerns same-mahalle brides, as is the case for Mastanlı. In Arifhane, the broadest range occurs in weddings with Yenice Mahalle brides (slightly lower in class perceptions); and while same-mahalle weddings show a relatively high dower range, weddings with Kır Mahalle brides (even lower than Yenice in class terms) are limited in dower range and size.

Overall, a 'norm' appears to emerge whereby dower is set in the region of thirty to fifty *reşat*. Significant differentiation from that 'norm' occurs generally for Hacıipekçi Mahalle on the lower end, and Yenice Mahalle on the higher end. It thus seems that the thirty to fifty *reşat* 'norm' maintains a semblance of socio-spatial equality that is punctuated by particular understandings of difference (whereby some weddings simply do not occur). The semblance of equality projected by the 'norm' is belied at every point a too low or too high dower is paid – the very point where weddings like Meral's are likened to weddings of 'others'. This semblance of equality, therefore (set by the 'norm' of dower), maintains difference by creating 'community' in custom (the dower). The negotiations over gold coins are negotiations over community boundaries first and foremost. This is brought clearly into relief when considering that the eventual *reşat* price agreed is ultimately fictive: it remains stated in the marriage certificate yet only takes material form on conclusion of a divorce, and if the divorcing wife requests it.

In contradistinction, dower also includes jewellery (heirlooms or newly bought) which exists in material form, is often part of the marriage contract as well, and is the woman's to use from the inception of the marriage. In Nergis and Turgut's wedding, this jewellery was exhibited on the sitting room table of Nergis's mother's house on *kına gecesi* ('henna night', the bridal shower on the eve of the wedding). It sat there alongside silk scarves, home accessories, and underwear, for the bride's friends to peer over and giggle. This exhibition was a reminder that the ridiculing of negotiations, as counter-conduct to the boundary drawing around communities of class, ethnicity and religion, would always lack the material underpinnings (*reşat*) that even in their fiction (scriptural form) sustained those boundaries.

Gender relations within this religio-juridical patriarchy frame (where 'custom' necessitates the objectification of women through the setting of dower values) are thus ordered by understandings of class, space and ethnicity, and punctuated by the time-specific political environment. Women, in this order, are the key bearers of distinction, where their status as 'property' reflects the dividends of 'irregular' unions (outside the mahalle). This is also important as an indication of what is perceived as 'irregular' or 'extraordinary' within a context where most discussions of marriage relating to the minority have been asking the question of 'inter-marriage' with Greeks. In the reading of their lack as 'cultural avoidance', the deep structural inequalities that plague majority–minority gender relations are overwritten. The impact of these inequalities, however, is crucial – not simply in inter-communal, but intra-communal gender dynamics as well. Thus, alongside 'divorce', this reading of 'intermarriage' and of the dower as 'cultural' curiosity de-politicizes the minoritization of gender, which is perpetuated through the interpellation of willing and unwilling individuals into 'the minority condition'.

The question that has instead concerned state institutions on the topic of gender equality has been the binary dilemma of whether the application of Islamic law to minority family matters should be continued or not (Kotzabassi, 2001). The state's implication in the perpetuation of inequality is thus rendered secondary to the problem of religion and culture. But as Das (1995: 91) shows in her discussion of the Shah Bano divorce case in India, culture has a 'double life': it has 'the potential to give radical recognition to the humanity of its subjects as well as [a] potential to keep the individual within such tightly defined bounds that the capacity to experiment with selfhood – which is also a mark of humanity – may be jeopardized'. As I have shown, the question cannot simply be to take religion out of the equation, but rather to render the possibilities of moving in and out of 'community' (religious, class, political, ethnic) more tangible.

On Equality and Community

In the local elections of 2006 the Socialist Party PASOK took a 'radical' decision to put forth a young Pomak woman as the party's candidate for one of the highest posts in prefecture level. This decision was received with scorn, and ultimately failed to win minority votes because it was interpreted as an opportunistic, shallow move aiming at 'presenting' the minority to the Greek public in a particular way. In this presentation, specific aspects of minority 'modernization' were highlighted in a prescriptive frame that ultimately orientalized the minority.

Gülbeyaz Karahasan was presented as the young Pomak woman born in a remote village, who was able to 'break the mould' of tradition and become a lawyer after finishing her studies in Athens. Her media profile was of a young professional in a business suit with flowing hair, with little to distinguish her from the Greek lawyers I saw entering the müftülük. As a symbolic gesture, then, her candidacy highlighted the 'backwardness' of Greek society represented by a 'public opinion' that criticized her selection on the basis of nationalist concerns. But in their evaluation as a substantive attempt to address the assumptions on which prejudice is built, many minority activists felt let down.

In contradistinction to this 'showcasing' of her success, there is a different gender order reality that the minority experiences in divorce, as much as in the everyday negotiations of gender roles – as I was frequently reminded by women friends. Müftülük marriages are an aspect of this – but they are not primarily a 'cultural' issue that can be solved through education only, or by taking off the *ferece*; they are chiefly a political, legal-juridical, structural and economic issue that ultimately hinges on the forms that minoritization, as a process of community-making, has so far taken. The salience of questioning that 'community' thus again appears as an urgent issue, and it is to this that the conclusion returns.

Notes

1. Muslim foreigners may also choose to marry under Islamic custom by registering their wedding at one of the müftülüks of western Thrace.
2. See also http://archive.enet.gr/online/online_text/c=112,dt=19.10.2003,id=6 4735668 (accessed January 2010) and http://www.helleniccomserve.com/ divorceperspective.html (accessed 28 March 2012).

BEING POLITICAL

Reflecting on 'Community'

We were driving back to Komotini from a nearby beach, when nine-year-old Sinan began querying his mother about what the celebration arranged for the circumcision he had just had would involve. Having been told that only women would be present and that there would be a session of Quranic readings before the noon feast, he was slightly alarmed at the absence of any prospect of entertainment. Looking out of the window, he pondered for a few seconds, then sunk back into his seat and voiced his threat: 'Well, if I get bored I'll sing the national anthem!' The reaction was what he expected: 'Sinan, listen well: you'll do no such thing!' Meltem screamed in mock horror, lifting her hand from the steering wheel momentarily and pointing her index finger at the road. Then, half laughing and half complaining, she turned to me and said: 'My God, Olga, I didn't tell you what he did to me when these ladies came to wish us well for his circumcision – listen up, you'll love this story!'

And thus, Meltem started explaining how a few days after Sinan's operation, carried out at a clinic by a doctor they trusted to avoid all the blood spilling and the pain and the mess of having it performed ceremonially by a non-medically trained practitioner, a small group of women, friends of Sinan's grandparents, had come to visit and congratulate him on his successful passage to boyhood. Meltem had patiently answered their questions about her job, the changes they had made to the house, their latest visit to Istanbul, Sinan's school, and the well-being of her parents and other family members; and she had prepared coffee to serve with the biscuits bought especially for the occasion. But as the visit lengthened, she went to the kitchen to get more sweets. The questions were then directed to Sinan, who was getting bored and frustrated. 'And then suddenly, while I was in the kitchen, out of the blue, I heard him sing the Greek national anthem! Can you believe it? I was looking for a place to hide myself! The ladies were stunned – God knows what they thought!' Her voice broke into laughter, and we joined. I turned to Sinan, who was still laughing, and asked him why he had behaved in this bizarre way: 'Well, I was bored, and they weren't leaving, so I sung the anthem', he explained in a matter-of-fact way – and then smiled mischievously.

His explanation seemed logical: he had resorted to this explicitly nationalist statement in order to arouse the feelings of discomfort among this group of elderly Turkish women for whom the Greek national anthem represented the state in which they lived, and which they viewed, following the official discourse, as the oppressor of the minority. His explanation was not only logical, it was accurate; after hurriedly tasting the sweets that Meltem had brought in from the kitchen, the visitors thanked the hosts and were on their way. On that day, singing the national anthem had become Sinan's tried-and-tested method of fighting the boredom of social visits by strangers around whom he was admonished to behave 'properly'.

Sinan's singing establishes a relationship between the nationalism symbolized by the anthem and the propriety or impropriety of specific modes of socialization. His explanation, based on this assumption, reveals a perceptive analysis on the limits of propriety in relation to a supposedly separate domain of politics in which nationalist symbols were seen to belong. It was 'reflection as resistance and insistence of community' (Nancy 1991: 42) at work. What I have tried to trace in this book is the potential of such reflection to found a counter-conduct of a minority population as it has emerged through interaction with state apparatuses morphing in various domains since 1923. The notion of 'community' that has stood at the juncture of this interaction has provided the basis upon which processes of subjectivization took shape. In these terms, this book has been about the emergence of what Jean-Luc Nancy calls 'a clinamen' (ibid.: 3–4) – what there is around an individual that makes them what they are and at the same time undoes their individuality – 'the decline of the individual within community' (ibid.: 4). The thinking on community so far, Nancy argues, has been rather idealizing of the binding force between individuals, and born out of the realization of the death of God. This means that loss is 'constitutive of "community" itself' (ibid.: 12). What is shared in community is incomplete and incompletable. And the sharing that takes place is an 'uninterrupted passage through singular ruptures' (ibid.: 35). It is in this sense that community is not a matter of operation, of work, or of a goal – it is inoperative. Calling for a rethinking of the ethics of community, he argues that 'reflection is the resistance and the insistence of community' (ibid.: 42).

Nancy is here trying to capture an essence of 'community' so far eschewed by the disillusionment with the realization (albeit questionable) of 'communism' and the horror of totalitarianism. One of the most concrete examples he uses is the man of the Nazi camp, in whose singular death he sees the ultimate resistance of community (Nancy 1991: 159). This image coincides with Agamben's *Musselman* (1998: 184–85), who exemplifies bare life. I want to suggest that at this extreme, we may be missing the mundane exemplifications of such 'community', and the biopolitical processes that are involved in it. The 'singular plural' stuff of community (Nancy 2000) in Thrace is about becoming and disappearing on an everyday level, and within unexceptional networks of power (unlike what goes on in migrant detention centres, for example). Reflection is instructive about community on this level, not only when it disappears. In these terms, my engagement with Nancy's notion of community is essentially about trying to locate the 'everywhere' of the political.

In putting 'reflection as resistance and insistence of community' into practice, Sinan was enacting a particular form of the political. He was using a specific kind of politics (that of Greek nationalism), which he was at that stage beginning to see as incompatible with the minority's sphere of sociality, as a tool for combating what he called 'boredom'. I would argue that this 'boredom' in fact entailed a specific politics of managing intergenerational difference, through which this difference was culturally interpreted. Sinan's politics of boredom was nothing less than a politics of community. Firstly, it was shared (and perhaps partly informed) by his mother, who became complicit in his behaviour through her tacit condoning of it (anger that, attended by the appreciation of the comic element of the incident, appeared only partly genuine). Secondly, in publicly exhibiting the disdain for etiquette that Sinan knows his mother shares with him in the privacy of their home, his 'inappropriate' choice of song caused the private/public separation to collapse. The public sphere, in which nationalist politics determines community, was thus brought in to puncture the private sphere, where the politics of sociality maintains the contours of that community. And this was done through the otherwise unremarkable efforts of a boy to reorder his domain of privacy, which had been upset by the intrusion of the guests. In the process, both the nationalist politics performed in this irreverent manner, and the politics of sociality under attack, were mocked and deconstructed. The performance (thus interpreted on the basis of Sinan's adoption of a Greek nationalist persona) had taken place in the domain of the private-cum-political. And in undermining the separation between the politics being adopted (nationalism) and the politics being attacked (community), it showed that in fact the political begins with the mixed feelings of horror and enjoyment, with agreement and admonition; the re-constitution of 'community' begins in the kitchen.

Typicality and the Politics of Exceptionalism

In this conceptualization of politics, the friend/enemy distinction that Schmitt used to define 'the political' is complicated. The Greek–Turkish opposition that guides nationalist ideology is appropriated in the sense that it is claimed as one's own to mock. It is appropriated in order to cast the particular enemy as such, rendering the self something it is not, while the identification with and difference to this something is suspended and held in question. The women who left in a hurry may well have got the hint, may have even seen the joke of it. But they may also have felt insulted, exactly because they read it as a strategy of antagonism. Or still, they may have left wondering whether a young Turkish boy was slowly being inculcated with Greek nationalist propaganda at school and was on the way to losing his (assumedly obvious) identity. They may have discussed these possibilities between themselves, or not, blamed his mother or both his parents, or related the experience to other acquaintances. In all these possible actions, and in Sinan's underscoring of his 'feat', power is at play, power that legitimizes the self and delegitimizes the other, power which casts the self as enduring what others inflict upon her, or him.

What interests me is that the main referent of this power is the community that comes into being concurrently with the self. Community is reproduced through the power of reflection and in the forms of resistance and insistence. The fact that Sinan belongs to the minority is undisputed. But when he mocks its representatives and its values he creates a question mark about his own place in it, which in turn becomes a question mark about what the community is becoming. Each instance of counter-conduct I have described here opens up these question marks. In order to understand the multiformity of the political relations these instances point to, it is necessary to conceptualize the self as co-emerging with the community. The issue here is that the self is always part of the community, even in those instances where counter-conduct is seen and carried out in terms of 'radicality'. The radical self is radical against something, without which the issue of radicality ceases to exist.

And this brings me to the question of method – because in exploring such radicality, we often tend to exceptionalize it, and thus set it apart as distinct from the community. In talking about my research over the years, interlocutors have often asked 'how representative' of the minority as a whole the people I had lived with were. Their bilingualism, political leanings, involvement of some in minority affairs as lawyers, journalists or sociologists, were issues at stake – they made their 'representativeness' questionable. To me this is a question that presupposes a certain view of 'typicality', 'exceptionality', 'individuality' and, ultimately, 'community'. As I hope to have shown, these definitions are far from straightforward.

They are political definitions in any event, but they are doubly so in Thrace; for 'typicality' in terms of the minority also implies victimization, disempowerment, lack of critical reflection, and so on. For Nancy, typicality would be non-community, for it precludes reflection. Anthropology would call this typicality-driven form of cultural depiction 'ethnocentrism'. Yet at the same time, it is anthropology which enacts typicality, whenever we claim that the X are, or do, Y. I think the challenge in thinking differently about 'community' lies in rejecting this notion of 'typicality' – and perhaps also in reflecting once more on the community we enact in the field, and how we become in it.

My concern with co-emergence has been focused on the question of how nationalist politics is implicated in inter-personal relationships even when, in fact especially when, it is being undermined. 'Politics' is constantly deconstructed in Thrace as it is in other thoroughly politicized environments. Nancy Scheper-Hughes (2007: 227n) comments on the 'scare quotes' around South African racial classification. Aretxaga (1997: 33) speaks of the implicit knowledge about communal identification involved in the practice of hailing a taxi in Northern Ireland. Thus, unremarkably I would claim, in Thrace, locals voice views about the other, placing themselves within or outside frames of nationalist rhetoric, within or against discursive structures that ultimately relate to the opposition between Greece and Turkey. Instead of skin or mannerisms, a person's name is always and unmistakably a pointer towards their placing within these frames. The question is how one re-reads, re-enacts, or reflects on the pointer.

When my informants in Thrace claimed to be different to 'typical' minority individuals, they set up a web of identifications which made it near-impossible for the stereotyped 'minority' to escape. Qualities were pitted against one another: bilingual vs. Turkish-speaking, religious vs. secularist, naively nationalist vs. reflectively anti-nationalist, modern vs. traditional, perhaps even identity-secure vs. not quite 'Turkish'. Yet in setting up these dichotomies, they also acknowledged the sets of questions attending them: Turkish- or Pomak- or Roma-speaking? Secularist or outright atheist? Naïve and traditional for whom? I would argue that actually, in asserting those oppositions, one was asserting power: the power of knowledge of the insider looking in from the outside.

Many of the discussions I had in Thrace sounded like anthropological analysis. Celal once described being in southern Greece, hosted by the family of one of his Greek friends, a student studying at the local university, and how he got deep into conversation with the grandmother. Not knowing his origin, she began to elaborate on how bad the Turks were after describing her soup that had gone wrong 'Turkified' (*toúrkepse*). I asked why he would enjoy this sort of conversation – had he not had enough, heard it countless times? 'I like to observe', he said, and looking at me with a smile of meaning he went on to idealize the fascination with exploring how these stereotypes worked in the head of an elderly woman. Yet I think there is an aspect to this homology between my task and his that anthropology (despite all the discussion on reflexivity which ultimately focuses on the anthropologist) has not quite addressed, and this is the power involved in making the step to the outside, across Mignolo's 'thought border' – in the exceptionalization of the self (which would require shifting the focus to the 'informant').

Much has been made recently of the politics of exceptionalizing others (Agamben 2005), following the Schmittian view of deciding on the exception as indicative of sovereignty (Schmitt 1996). Re-workings of that theory have shown that such exceptionalization does not always lead to complete disempowerment, as Agamben's arch image of the camp would imply, but rather that those exceptionalized may seek further exceptionalization as a strategy of resistance (Constantinou 2008). Building on this, I want to suggest here that such self-exceptionalization may not be only about the self; it may entail strategies of domination over others, in this case those who are cast as 'typical'. In fact, being cast as 'typical' may be exactly about delegitimizing others' positions, and the danger of having one's own delegitimized as well.

A wife who is critical of her husband's late-night drinking, absence from the house, or lack of engagement with the family is cast as 'typical' in the sense of being conservative, irrespective of other political concerns. In fact, if 'radical' in other ways, she could be said to be betraying her own values. Yet her wifely and motherly duties are a 'natural' expectation, hardly considered 'political'. In other words, what is constructed as 'political' stems precisely from the power relations that its discourse seeks to undermine. It is in this sense that the political begins in the kitchen – the kitchen no longer as the starting point of the domestic and private in its opposition to the public and political, but rather the site of the struggle over differing definitions of the 'political'. And even though this struggle may often be the woman's to wage, it is a feminist struggle in a wider sense of claiming the exception for one's self, of announcing reflective work, of claiming community and risking one's own disappearance in it.

Reconsidering 'Friends' and 'Enemies'

In the public spaces of entertainment venues in Komotini, political affiliations are expressed in terms of inter-ethnic relations of 'friendship'. During my fieldwork, youngsters from the minority and students from all parts of Greece used to sit together at mixed tables and socialize – drinking, eating, singing. This kind of sociality was seen as a political statement in a context where nationalism had reached a peak leading up to, and following, the Öcalan affair. 'Friendship' was a particular mode of socialization that endowed the social with political connotations. In these settings, Schmitt's assertion that the political concepts of 'friend' and 'enemy' can only be communal is undermined. 'A private person has no political enemies', Schmitt writes (1996: 51), and continues to assert that 'citizens of a state who declare that they personally have no enemies . . . at most say [they] would like to place [themselves] outside the political community' (ibid.), in which case 'it is a matter for the political community somehow to regulate this kind of non-public, politically disinterested existence (by privileges for aliens, internment, exterritoriality, permits of residence and concessions, laws for metics, or in some other way)' (ibid.: 51n). The declarations of friendship I am describing undermine this assertion. They are not attended by a wish to be outside the community, and consequently delegitimize the state as the unquestionable arbiter on such measures. Critiques of the 'they' cannot be divorced from the inclusion of the self in the community, and the price for being 'radical' (e.g. being gossiped about, or pressured out of full-time work to tend to the house, or refused recognition of one's activist work) draws whatever weight it may carry precisely from the recognition of this inclusion in the community. What therefore results is not a simple placement of the social self across political (enemy) lines, but rather an uncompromising confluence between the social and the political.

My relationship with people in Thrace was also part of this mode. The intimation of Sinan's 'feat' targeted my ability to 'see the joke' because the overlapping relationships between the social and the political was something we all commonly understood. In this sense Sinan and I shared similar experiences of 'enculturation' into the processes through which subjectivity in Thrace is formed, processes during which socialization and politicization are merged, processes that ultimately create community. And in this sense perhaps the incident could be seen as a celebration of Sinan's active engagement with these processes as a minority person – his successful passage to minority boyhood.

These are parallel processes: encounters of 'friendship' between youngsters involve similar dynamics of managing intergenerational difference through the power of 'disrespect' that Sinan's singing of the Greek national anthem had exhibited; the legitimation of such 'disrespect' hinges in both cases on the same system of equating 'tradition' with 'backwardness'; and in both cases this system of evaluation is shared by people whose views construct the minority no less than its members. Thinking through the possible future implications of my work towards the end of fieldwork, friends commented on the 'importance' of having a different perspective on things voiced academically (referring to the difference with nationalist accounts), and said they hoped their views would be represented instead of those of politicians. In a similar vein, they expressed the hope that Greek students from elsewhere in Greece, who studied in Komotini and sat at the same drinking tables with them, might return to their homes with changed views on what the minority is about.

Both of these articulations are anthropologically unremarkable: they follow the discourse many informants use when relating to 'learned' anthropologists, instructing them to 'note this down', or 'to tell this to the world'. They are, as a number of anthropologists have noted (Crapanzano 1980; Gupta and Ferguson 1996; Clifford and Marcus 1986; Rabinow 2007), ultimately discourses about power differences, about the inability to change one's situation, and the acknowledgement that those with the ability to do so have very little time for 'local' priorities.

But although it may supplant discourses of cynicism that ultimately preserve the structures of the state, affirming top-down power differences, as for example Navaro-Yashin (2002) has shown for Turkey, there is a questioning of them that points to the possibility that things can be different. It is between the idealism inherent in this questioning and the acknowledgement of the constraints involved that I have positioned my analysis. Most of the times when informants expressed this wish to relate their local experiences to the world at large, it was the result of being pushed to think about the 'ultimate' reasons for engaging in practices considered radical or rebellious. This is an important difference with Sinan's explanation, which hinges instead on the nonchalance of 'just being bored'. He does not wish to send a message about nationalism to the world; the most that can be claimed is that he questions what nationalism really consists of, and rejects the idea that an anthem can on its own represent the nation (and through this logic sends home those who might believe this). But the reason for his action is not the wish to change people's minds – it is to have his living room space back. In a similar way, I would propose that changing the minds of the relatives of Greek friends elsewhere in Greece, or indeed the mentality of state institutions, is not the driving force for setting up drinking tables. It is instead, 'just being', perhaps even simply 'not being bored'. Indeed, the significance of boredom in the Heideggerian constitution of *Dasein* and Agamben's reading of this constitution as a condition arising from the politics of defining the 'human' in modernity (Agamben 2004), indicates the anthropological import of such politics of boredom as constitutive of community.

This opens an analytical question of whether we could theorize coexistence without the ethical presuppositions of responsibility most frequently associated with Levinas in the sense of being-for-the-Other (Levinas 2002) and the Derridean concept of 'democracy to come' – a democratic ethics always in the making (Derrida 1997). In other words, what the example of Thrace offers, is a view into how such ethics might be reconfigured on the ground. For the power invested in deconstructing nationalism and ethnic difference because one just does so, rather than with a moral aim in mind, is guided by an ethics of otherness in which responsibility is no longer of a humanitarian nature but about 'thinking things differently', about enacting difference reflectively. I want to return to the point about the camp here, because in the Derridean exemplification of responsibility what we again have as an arch symbol is the complete divestment of rights in the form of the refugee (Derrida 2000). Based on this, accounts of how this ethics of responsibility can be put into practice have often resorted to incorporating 'local ways of thinking' (Popke 2003), which effectively typifies otherness. Yet for Levinas himself, 'responsibility' appears to cover a wide spectrum of possibilities located in the broad space of 'difference which is non-indifference' (Levinas 2002: 139). Within this space, I argue, there is much that goes on outside the limit cases of the camp or other forms of destitution. And I think that it is by bringing this into focus that those limit cases might be made more familiar as well. This is why I have throughout employed the Foucauldian notion of counter-conduct (and not resistance, radicality or rebellion) as the frame of practices that enunciates the 'inoperative community' (rather than the pre-existing, knowable, and bordered, even bored, community).

Sinan can be understood and admired because he unsettles identities, not because he calls forth some 'local', definitively 'non-Western' way of thinking. His ethics is an ethics of disrespect – for traditional rules of age hierarchy as much as for state rules of national reverence. By playing one against the other he undermines both, and calls forth an ethics of questioning. The encompassing structures of hierarchy are certainly not undone. But the community he enacts announces the loss of the myth of homogeneity (both of the nation and of the minority group), as well as the capricious decline of his own individuality in it.

BORDER LIVES

Border Citizenship

It was mid-1999 when I visited a minority MP for a chat about the political issues of the day. Across from his desk sat a man, looking old and in despair. He was told that his case was a difficult one. Phone calls were then made to the prefecture office, seeking information about the paperwork that needed to be filled in, and a pile of documents he had brought with him from the mountain village he was from were pored over, and identification numbers noted. Patiently, the MP explained which offices needed to be visited, and what papers would be needed for each one. Once this work was done, his office would be able to take the matter up again. The man was shown out with wishes of hope, the MP's face marked by an empathetic look of desperation.

This man was 'stateless' (*anithayenís*), I was told later. Born and raised in a mountain village near the Bulgarian border, he had left the country once, many years ago, for a short visit to Turkey. He had since been stripped of his Greek citizenship under Article 19 of the Greek Nationality Code which, before its abolition in 1998, provided that persons of 'other [non-Greek ethnic] origin' (*alloyenís*) who had left the country could be considered as having severed their ties to Greece and therefore could have their citizenship withdrawn. The article was introduced in 1955, replacing older legislation of denationalization that had been adopted since 1927 aiming at ethnic homogenization (Sitaropoulos 2006: 113–14). In parallel, other articles of the Nationality Code accorded special recognition, and still do, to the category of '*omoyenís*' (people of 'same' [Greek] origin), referring to migrant diaspora groups and Greek communities in the former Soviet Union and elsewhere. Minority representatives had for years campaigned against the discriminatory logic of Article 19, and had asked for its withdrawal. When it was finally scrapped, one of the 'conditions' for the state 'giving in' to minority demands was that the abolition would have no retroactive effect. The Consultative Committee of the Turkish Minority of Western Thrace (2009) estimates that around sixty thousand people have been stripped of their citizenship over the years; and the Council of Europe (2009) reported that about two hundred minority members living in Thrace continued to be stateless in 2008.

The man in the MP's office was one of the 'extreme cases' bearing the brunt of the application of this Article. Having travelled to Turkey to visit relatives, he had faced no problems on his return, and had not been informed that his citizenship had been withdrawn. He had continued to live by growing tobacco, an existence beyond the pale of state bureaucracy – until he had requested access to his pension, and was refused on the grounds of not being a Greek citizen. Like other minority members in his situation, he now had to apply for naturalization, and wait until his application was decided. As such an extreme case, however, he exemplifies the predicament of living lives on the borders – of nation-states, imaginary communities, purist aspirations, and belied homogeneities. He exemplifies the precariousness of being a subject of 'otherness', an ideological abnormality, a border(line) citizen.

Capricious Borders

This book opened with a series of questions about the subjectivization of otherness. In the course of exploring this process, governmentality and the contradictions it gives rise to have been a constant reference. Considering the ways in which Gümülcinelis make sense of their lives in this border region that constantly brings forth the question of otherness, what remains striking to me is the arbitrariness that guides the drawing of exclusionary lines. Such capricious borders, I have striven to show, result from the idiosyncrasies of nation-state priorities at particular historical junctures.

It is thus the shifting of borders, not of people, that rendered Gümülcinelis 'established' (*établis*) as an indigenous population in this particular region. Had the abandonment of Istanbul not been as disastrous for the Greek national imaginary, this region might have been 'cleansed' of minority presence as others were in 1923. Similarly, this construal as 'established' of a community largely consisting of emigrants who had themselves been forced out of other areas of border shifts, might not have been formulated in preference to those other Muslim communities that might otherwise have been exceptionalized under the Lausanne Treaty instead. The sacralization of borders that guided the

Turkish national imaginary, formulated in the Turkish parliamentary vote of 1920 on the National Pact (*misak-i milli*), constructed western Thrace as an area outside the homeland, the eventual status of which should be decided through voting by its inhabitants, at that time Muslim in majority (Featherstone et al. 2011: 2–3). Had the Greek and Turkish national imaginaries been formulated differently, the borders of this community might have been different. They would still, however, have been whimsical.

Over the decades that followed 1923, conceptualizations of the Thracian border oscillated between antagonism, belligerence and conciliation. Of this oscillation, the year of my fieldwork (1999) was the crowning example. One of its effects was the multiplicity of views about Thrace and their constant shift: an 'outpost' of Hellenism, a frontier region, Greece's backwater, an adulterated space, 'not quite Greece'. In a documentary produced at around that time for a large educational project aiming at the social integration of 'Muslim children' (*Prógramma Ekpédhevsis Mousoulmanopédhon*), that began under the directorship of George Papandreou at the Ministry of Education in the mid-1990s, a Greek Komotinian kiosk owner expresses bitterness at the fact that 'Greeks elsewhere in Greece consider us half-castes (*miğádhes*)'. Her anxiety, meant to be communicated to Greek teachers from 'elsewhere in Greece' who would then be asked to apply the integrationist educational teaching during their posting at minority schools, conveys the coincidence of racism and familiarity that frames ethnic coexistence in Komotini. The racism that she articulates is reproduced in the scaling-up of locality-state, as the local distinction between Greeks and Turks bifurcates into the national distinction between 'pure' Greeks and 'half-castes'. But it is also scaled down as it equally bifurcates amongst groups within the minority, through claims to 'pure' Turkishness and accusations of Greekness. At each level, the dialectics of difference and familiarity are at play.

These dialectics, I would claim, reveal that at the very basis of this bitterness about how outsiders perceive 'us' is an anxiety about borders and their meanings. To the majority of Greeks from 'elsewhere in Greece', the concept of 'Thrace' as location has been popularized in one of the best-known Greek rock ballads, the title of which, 'Didimoticho Blues', bears the name of a remote town in the Evros prefecture. The lyrics of the song convey the disillusionment of a young (male) army recruit transferred by accident for service on the Thracian border, where the grand ideal of protecting the homeland is transformed into the meaningless and dreary task of executing orders, rising to the morning call, and keeping watch. In the final stanza before the guitar solo, the story returns to the meaning of '*Didimóticho*' as emblematic of the nonsense that grand ideologies of Greek patriotism belie: the emptiness of the 'nation' as signifier. An imperfect translation might go something like this:

Didimóticho, its name is the cause [of my blues];
'Didimóticho blues':
a hole on the geographical map,
an empty photograph,
servicing the irrational,
stressed-out masturbation.

The 'stress' indexed here, I want to suggest, which has made the line above one of the most popular lines in the Greek music industry, refers to the same anxiety at the heart of all attempts to border-mark: what if the line does prove capricious in ways unforeseen by its painters? Like the State, it could be said, the border was, for those painters, 'the chief representative of each nation's symbolic order in the geopolitical stock exchange' (Gourgouris 1996: 14). But if on the 'natural' border of the Evros/Maritza river an electronic line is drawn mid-stream that orders communication east and west, the artificiality of borders devalues the 'stocks' of natural and national injunction. Their plunge into mere 'capriciousness' raises the spectre of a crash and, perhaps, a nation-state recession (e.g. when it spreads to fiscal borders). Sovereignty is shown to have a logic that is far from natural and far from stable. Border-marking, this book has striven to show, and the ordering that structures its afterlife, is the outcome of power structures inherent in state-making in the heart as much as in the margins of Europe. As such, a recovery can only employ neoliberal forms of repression that prop up the State unfettered by the consistencies that the national imaginary purports.

The Afterlife of the Border

The decades that followed 1923 brought about a solidification of the Greco-Turkish border in Thrace that stands in sharp contrast to the fluidity of the river boundary. In its eventual transformation into an EU and then Schengen border, the governmentality that has taken minority lives as its prime target is now giving rise to a different kind of biopolitics, one that has become more pronounced in the decade that followed my fieldwork.

Returning to Thrace in the 2000s, domination and subjection continued to be the foci of my research. But this was now a more practice-oriented study on behalf of an international human rights organization, which looked at the abuses resulting from this governmentality. The subjects of research were no longer members of the minority (or not primarily, at least), but a much more rights-divested group: that of border crossers who enter the country without papers, and who can have no claims to assistance beyond their asylum requests. These 'subjects', whose subjectivity consists solely of 'bare life' in the Agambenian sense of the camp (the detention camp, in this case, or the border police station cell), are in fact not even always alive. The bodies washed up on the river banks, or accidentally fished out by local fishermen, testify to the loss of life that takes place along the border – a loss that is bodily in its most extreme and social in its widest spread.

The governmentality that is now shaping in Thrace mobilizes means and structures previously aimed at the minority. Materially, the large cover of militarized areas along the river banks that previously served to maintain the local balance of power (guarding against defection and enemy infiltration in its various guises) are now used to render opaque practices of pushing people back that contravene international standards. Practices of expulsion, refoulement, readmission and pushback have been documented by organizations such as Pro Asyl (2007), Amnesty International (2005; 2010), and Human Rights Watch (2008a; 2008b; 2009). Ideologically, the threat of infiltration that has kept repressive state mechanisms alert against 'internal' Muslims is now reconstituting around the conceptualization of 'illegal immigrants' as potential Islamic terrorists, who Turkey, it is said, is all too eager to see in Greece as agents of internal instability. A Greek coastguard commander on Lesvos has claimed that illegal immigrants crossing from Turkey constitute a military threat ('an Islamic invasion') not only to Greece but Europe as a whole, because they are 'all men between 15 and 35 years of age . . . very well trained, they swim very well! . . . They are all warriors!' (Pro Asyl 2007: 13).

'Illegal migration' had been a concern in Thrace since Andreades' time. In the final section of his book (Andreades 1956: 51–59) he dwells on the reasons that minority members seem to be fleeing to Turkey en masse, illegally (without using their Greek passports). The reasons for this flight that returnees, and in some cases individuals refouled from Turkey, provided in their sworn statements (*dhilósis*) of 1955 (the year in which Article 19 replaced older denationalization laws) include avoidance of army conscription, flight from the post-war economic recession, and – under no circumstances, the author emphasizes – 'oppression against the minority' (*enantíon tis mousoulmanikís mionótitos katapíesis*) (ibid.: 55). The similarity of the format of these statements to those that asylum-seekers are asked to present in order for their claims to refugee protection to be assessed is striking. And perhaps this is not only a similarity of format. Might some of the minority stateless of Greece today, like the old man in the MP's office, have been such illegal migrants in the 1950s?

The minority-migrant nexus of discrimination in Greece is yet to be addressed by academia and the state. Effie Voutira (2003) argued some time ago that the conceptualization of 'refugee' identity in Greece, tightly connected to the 1923 forced exchange of populations, has had a great impact on Greece's later refugee policy. The reception of non-Greek refugees, foreign asylum seekers, she found, is guided by the 'cultural assumption concerning the genuineness of the "refugee" label, which presumes that the only *true* refugees must be of Greek origin . . . [and hence is biased towards] Sudanese, Palestinian, Ethiopian, Iraqi or Afghani asylum seekers [who] are seen as "foreign refugees" and thus as essentially "others"' (ibid.: 74, emphasis in original). Through being spared from the 1923 forced population exchange, the minority is in terms of rights a 'privileged other', enjoying, as the phrase goes, Greek citizenship, political representation, access to separate educational and religious institutions, and so on – enjoying (or not), the kinds of rights that mark, for humanitarian discourse, the crossover from bare to political life. This accounts for why minority human rights issues rarely feature on the agenda of international fora, in comparison to migrants' rights (as well as in comparison to the rights of minority groups that are not recognized as such).

During a meeting of the UN Human Rights Committee examining Greece's initial report on civil and political rights, which I attended, one of the country's delegation members, when questioned on Greece's minority protection policies, retorted that apart from the Muslim minority in Thrace 'no other group fulfilled the objective and internationally recognized criteria for official recognition as ethnic or national minorities', and made specific reference to 'Macedonians' and Roma on the matter (UN-HRC 2005a: §35–37). Other officials in similar fora have repeated these claims (UN-CERD 2008: §24–27; ECRI 2004: 37–39). On the issue of migration, the head of the delegation explained to the Human Rights Committee that '[h]aving recently been transformed from a country of emigration to one of immigration, Greece was seeking to establish a functional system of law which protected immigrants['] rights' (UN-HRC 2005b, §33). In the 'intens[e]' and 'lively interaction' that followed (UN-HRC 2005c: §58, 64), migrant detention and minority identification were two of the issues discussed. A question on the first (UN-HRC 2005a: §13) elicited a response highlighting the efforts to build new facilities (ibid.: §26), while the second, included in the pre-circulated list of issues (UN-HRC 2004), elicited two long responses from the delegation, explaining the state's stance on the (non)exist-ence of Turkish and Macedonian minority groups and the stipulations of the Lausanne Peace Treaty in which the phrases 'national security', 'public safety', 'non-Greek agenda', 'special circumstances', 'political motivat[ion]', 'insecurity and tension', and 'particular sensitivity' were mentioned (UN-HRC 2005a: §32, 35–37).

Considering that all these phrases ultimately articulate an argument for exceptionalization, it seems that the claim being made through them is the sovereign's right to decide on the exception, à la Schmitt (1996) and Agamben (1995). It is important, in this frame, to note the lack of such a claim with respect to migrant detention, where on the contrary, what is being articulated is the apparently self-evident need to normalize the conditions of the camp by proliferating and 'modernizing' detention centres. To put it a different way, it is as though the exceptionalization of the minority question needs to be argued, whereas the exceptionalization of the migration question does not. Or, in slightly more controversial terms, it is as though the denial of minority rights is a question of the state skirting international law (but for good reason, it would argue, and in any case by adhering to the Lausanne Peace Treaty), whereas the denial of migrant detainee rights is a question of applying the law.

In the Greece of the 2010s recession, one of the apparatuses of neo-liberal governmentality has been the transfer of border control along the Greece–Turkey border to the European agency FRONTEX, which among other measures has reinforced the patrolling of the Thracian boundary. In February 2012, works to erect a razor-topped wire fence on the stretch of land where the state border stops following the flow of the river, pano-pticized with night-vision cameras connected to a control centre, were announced. Two months earlier, the EU had refused to fund the fence on the grounds of ineffectiveness. As the digital binary 'Greece-Turkey' is solidifying in the materiality of electric wire marking the 'inside' and 'outside' of Europe (while at the same time Greece's placement 'within' is being questioned), practices of expulsion, apprehension, arrest, detention and deportation dominate border lives in a much more total sense than was ever the case before, when the lives in question were not migrant, but minority ones. Thus, the complete divestment of rights taking place beyond the pale of bilateral priorities of protector states puts the very frame of liberalism and democracy, within which the 'minority condition' improved, seriously into question (the bilateral agreements now being applied concern readmission and more effective expulsion).

At the same time, the urgency of bare life on the border (the drowned or tortured bodies of undocumented crossers) demands that the atten-tion of international and national human rights activists is drawn to it and away from minority questions that still remain open (effective integration, political representation, the eradication of discrimination). By comparison to the bodily and mental scars that refugees and asylum seekers bring with them, the border lives that minority members live appear undoubtedly 'privileged'. And by comparison to the economic destitution gripping the rising number of the poor amongst the majority population, amongst whom a celebrated example has been the pensioners without access to pensions (and therefore with little to distinguish them from the old man in the MP's office), they may even appear 'normal'.

Such is the capricious life of 'otherness'.

REFERENCES

Αναπτυξιακή Ροδόπης Α.Ε. [Rhodoppe Development Company]. 1998. Στρατηγικό Σχέδιο Ανάπτυξης Ν. Ροδόπης: 1η Συνοπτική Έκθεση Προόδου [Strategic Development Plan for the Rhodoppe Prefecture: 1st Concise Progress Report].

Aarbakke, V. 2000. 'The Muslim Minority of Greek Thrace', Ph.D. Bergen: Department of History, University of Bergen.

ABTTF. 2008. 'Historical and Architectural Monuments', *Turkish Minority – Western Thrace – Greece*. Witten, Germany: Avrupa Batı Trakya Türk Federasyonu [Federation of Western Thrace Turks in Europe].

Agamben, G. 1998. *Homo Sacer: Sovereign Power and Bare Life*. Stanford: Stanford University Press.

_____. 2002. *Remnants of Auschwitz: The Witness and the Archive*. Cambridge, MA: Zone Books.

_____. 2004. *The Open: Man and Animal*. Stanford: Stanford University Press.

_____. 2005. *State of Exception*. Chicago: Chicago University Press.

Ahmad, N. 2009. 'A Critical Appraisal of "Triple Divorce" in Islamic Law', *International Journal of Law, Policy and the Family* 23(1): 53–61.

Akgönül, S. 1999. 'L'Emigration des Musulmans de Thrace occidentale', *Mésogeios* 3: 31–49.

_____ (ed.). 2008. *Reciprocity: Greek and Turkish Minorities: Law, Religion and Politics*. Istanbul: Bilgi University Press.

Aktar, A. 2003. 'Homogenising the Nation, Turkifying the Economy: The Turkish Experience of Population Exchange Reconsidered', in R. Hirschon (ed.), *Crossing the Aegean: An Appraisal of the 1923 Compulsory Population Exchange between Greece and Turkey*. Oxford: Berghahn, pp. 79–96

Alexandris, A. 1983. *The Greek Minority of Istanbul and Greek-Turkish Relations 1918–1974*. Athens: Centre for Asia Minor Studies.

Althusser, L. 1971. *Lenin and Philosophy and Other Essays*. New York: Monthly Review Press.

Amnesty International (AI). 2005. 'Greece: Out of the Spotlight: The Rights of Foreigners and Minorities are still a Grey Area' [AI Index: EUR 25/016/2005]. London: International Secretariat, Amnesty International.

_____. 2010. 'Greece: Irregular Migrants and Asylum-seekers routinely detained in Substandard Conditions' [EUR 25/002/2010]. London: International Secretariat, Amnesty International.

Anagnostou, D. 1997. 'Development, Discrimination and Reverse Discrimination: Effects of E.U. Integration and Regional Change on the Muslims of Southeast Europe', in A. al-Azmeh and E. Fokas (eds), *Islam in Europe: Diversity, Identity and Influence*. Cambridge: Cambridge University Press, pp. 149–182.

_____. 2001. 'Breaking the Cycle of Nationalism: The EU, Regional Policy and the Minority of Western Thrace, Greece', *South European Society & Politics* 6(1): 99–124.

Andreades, G.C. 1956. Η Μουσουλμανική Μειονότητα της Δυτικής Θράκης [The Muslim Minority of Western Thrace]. Thessaloniki: Society of Macedonian Studies.

Anonymous. 1999. Γεύση της Θράκης [A Taste of Thrace]. Komotini: Kentro Laikon Dromenon Komotinis [Komotini Public Events Centre].

Antoniou, D. 2011. 'The Mosque that wasn't there: an Ethnography of Political Imagination in contemporary Greece', D.Phil. Oxford: Faculty of Oriental Studies, University of Oxford.

Appadurai, A. 1998. 'Dead Certainty: Ethnic Violence in the Era of Globalization', *Public Culture* 10(2): 225–247.

Aretxaga, B. 1997. *Shattering Silence: Women, Nationalism and Political Subjectivity in Northern Ireland*. Princeton: Princeton University Press.

Bagavos, C. 2000. 'The Situation of Families in Greece', *General Monitoring Report*. Vienna: European Observatory on Family Matters.

Ballinger, P. 2003. *History in Exile: Memory and Identity at the Borders of the Balkans*. Princeton: Princeton University Press.

Barthes, R. 1973 [1964]. *Elements of Semiology*. New York: Hill and Wang.

Bastéa, E. 2000. *The Creation of Modern Athens: Planning the Myth*. Cambridge: Cambridge University Press.

Biehl, J.G. 2005. *Vita: Life in a Zone of Social Abandonment*. Berkeley: University of California Press.

_____. 2007. 'A Life: Between Psychiatric Drugs and Social Abandonment', in J.G. Biehl, B. Good and A. Kleinman (eds), *Subjectivity: Ethnographic Investigations*. Berkeley: University of California Press, pp. 397–422.

_____. B. Good, et al. 2007. *Subjectivity: Ethnographic Investigations*. Berkeley: University of California Press.

Boussiakou, I. 2008. 'Religious Freedom and Minority Rights in Greece: the Case of the Muslim Minority in Western Thrace', *GreeSE Paper No. 21, Hellenic Observatory Papers on Greece and Southeast Europe*. London: The Hellenic Observatory, The European Institute, London School of Economics and Political Science, pp. 1–48.

Bozos, S. 2004. 'National Symbols and Ordinary People's Response: London and Athens, 1850–1914', *National Identities* 6(1): 25–41.

Brown, K. 1998a. 'Whose Will be Done? Nation and Generation in a Macedonian Family', *Social Analysis* 42(1): 109–130.

_____. 1998b. 'Contests of Heritage and the Politics of Preservation on the Former Yugoslav Republic of Macedonia', in L. Meskell (ed.), *Archaeology Under Fire: Nationalism, Politics and Heritage in the Eastern Mediterranean and Middle East*. London: Routledge, pp. 68–86.

Brunnbauer, U. 1999. 'Diverging (Hi-)Stories: the Contested Identity of the Bulgarian Pomaks', *Ethologia Balkanica* 3: 35–50.

———. 2001. 'The Perception of Muslims in Bulgaria and Greece: Between the "Self" and the "Other"', *Journal of Muslim Minority Affairs* 21(1): 39–61.

Burchell, G., C. Gordon, et al. (eds). 1991. *The Foucault Effect: Studies in Governmentality: with two Lectures by and an Interview with Michel Foucault.* Chicago: University of Chicago Press.

Butler, J. 2008. 'Merely Cultural', in K. Olson (ed.), *Adding Insult to Injury: Nancy Fraser debates her Critics.* London: Verso, pp. 42–56.

Cadman, L. 2010. 'How (not) to be governed: Foucault, Critique, and the Political', *Environment and Planning D: Society and Space* 28(3): 539–556.

Campbell, J.K. 1964. *Honour Family and Patronage: A Study of Institutions and Moral Values in a Greek Mountain Village.* Oxford: Oxford University Press.

Castellan, G. 1996. Η Ιστορία των Βαλκανίων [The History of the Balkans]. Athens: Govosti Publications.

Çavusoglu, H. 1993. *Balkanlar'da Pomak Türkleri: Tarih ve Sosyo-kültürel Yapı.* Ankara: Kök Sosyal ve Stratejık Araştırmalar Vakfi Yayınları ['Root' Social and Strategic Studies Foundation Publications].

Clifford, J. and G.E. Marcus (eds). 1986. *Writing Culture: The Poetics and Politics of Ethnography.* Berkeley: University of California Press.

Cocco, E. 2006. 'Introduction: The Adriatic Space of Identity', *Croatian Journal of Ethnology and Folklore Research* 43(1): 7–14.

Cohn, B.S. 1984. 'The Census, Social Structure and Objectification in South Asia in Culture and History of India', *Folk* 26: 25–49.

———. 1996. *Colonialism and its Forms of Knowledge: The British in India.* Princeton: Princeton University Press.

———. 2000 [1971]. *India: The Social Anthropology of a Civilization.* Oxford: Oxford University Press.

Constantinou, C. 2006. 'On Homo-Diplomacy', *Space and Culture* 9(4): 351–364.

———. 2008. 'On the Cypriot States of Exception', *International Political Sociology* 2(2): 145–164.

Consultative Committee of the Turkish Minority of Western Thrace. 2009. Public Statement, 20 May 2009.

Corin, E. 1990. 'Facts and Meaning in Psychiatry. An Anthropological Approach to the Lifeworld of Schizophrenics', *Culture, Medicine, and Psychiatry* 14(2): 153–188.

———. 2007. 'The "Other" of Culture in Psychosis: The Ex-Centricity of the Subject', in J.G. Biehl, B. Good and A. Kleinman (eds), *Subjectivity: Ethnographic Investigations.* Berkeley: University of California Press.

Cornell, D. 1999. *At the Heart of Freedom: Feminism, Sex, and Equality.* Princeton: Princeton University Press.

Council of Europe (CoE). 2009. Report by Thomas Hammarberg, Commissioner for Human Rights of the Council of Europe, following his visit to Greece on 8–10 December 2008 – Issue reviewed: Human rights of minorities. Strasbourg: Council of Europe.

Cowan, J.K. 1996. 'Being a Feminist in Contemporary Greece: Similarity and Difference Reconsidered', in N. Charles and F. Hughes-Freeland (eds), *Practising Feminism: Identity, Difference, Power.* London: Routledge, pp. 61–85.

_____ (ed.). 2000. *Macedonia: The Politics of Identity and Difference*. London: Pluto Press.

_____. 2001. 'Ambiguities of an Emancipatory Discourse: The Making of a Macedonian Minority in Greece', in J.K. Cowan, M.-B. Dembour and R.A. Wilson (eds), *Culture and Rights: Anthropological Perspectives*. Cambridge: Cambridge University Press, pp. 152–176.

_____. 2007. 'The Success of Failure? Minority Supervision at the League of Nations', in M.-B. Dembour and T. Kelly (eds), *Paths to International Justice: Social and Legal Perspectives*. Cambridge: Cambridge University Press, pp. 29–56.

_____. 2009. 'Selective Scrutiny: Supranational Engagement with Minority Protection and Rights in Europe', in F. v. Benda-Beckmann, K. v. Benda-Beckmann and A.M.O. Griffiths (eds), *The Power of Law in a Transnational World*. Oxford: Berghahn, pp. 74–95.

_____, M.-B. Dembour, et al. (eds). 2001. *Culture and Rights: Anthropological Perspectives*. Cambridge: Cambridge University Press.

Crapanzano, V. 1980. *Tuhami: A Portrait of a Moroccan*. Chicago: University of Chicago Press.

Danforth, L.M. 1995. *The Macedonian Conflict: Ethnic Nationalism in a Transnational World*. Princeton: Princeton University Press.

Das, V. 1995. *Critical Events: An Anthropological Perspective on Contemporary India*. New Dehli: Oxford University Press.

_____. 2007. *Life and Words: Violence and the Descent into the Ordinary*. Berkeley: University of California Press.

_____, A. Kleinman, et al. (eds). 2000. *Violence and Subjectivity*. Berkeley: University of California Press.

_____ and D. Poole (eds). 2004. *Anthropology in the Margins of the State*. Oxford: James Currey.

Davis, E.A. 2012. *Bad Souls: Madness and Responsibility in Modern Greece*. Durham: Duke University Press.

Davison, A. 1998. *Secularism and Revivalism in Turkey: A Hermeneutic Reconsideration*. New Haven: Yale University Press.

Deleuze, G. and F. Guattari. 1987. *A Thousand Plateaus*. London: Continuum.

Demetriou, O. 2002. 'Divisive Visions: The Politicization of Minority Identities in Komotini, northern Greece', Ph.D. London: Social Anthropology Department, LSE.

_____. 2004a. 'The Turkish Oedipus: National Self and Stereotype in the Work of a 1960s Greek Cartoonist', *History and Anthropology* 15(1): 69–89.

_____. 2004b. 'The Cyclop's Cave: Local Appropriations of Thracian Antiquity', in D. Shankland (ed.), *Anthropology, Archaeology and Heritage in the Balkans and Anatolia*. Istanbul: Isis. pp. 407–428.

_____. 2004c. 'Prioritizing "Ethnicities": The Uncertainty of Pomak-ness in the Urban Greek Rhodoppe', *Ethnic and Racial Studies* 27(1): 95–119.

_____. 2006. 'Owing the Seed: The Discursive Economy of Sex Migration among Turkish-speaking Minority Urbanites in the Postsocialist Balkan Periphery', *Identities: Global Studies in Culture and Power* 13(2): 261–282.

Demirözü, D. 2008. 'The Greek-Turkish Rapprochement of 1930 and the Repercussions of the Ankara Convention in Turkey', *Journal of Islamic Studies* 19(3): 309–324.

Derrida, J. 1997. *Politics of Friendship*. London: Verso.

_____. 2000. *Of Hospitality*. Stanford: Stanford University Press.

Divani, L. 1999. Ελλάδα και Μειονότητες: Το Σύστημα Διεθνούς Προστασίας της Κοινωνίας των Εθνών (Greece and Minorities: The League of Nations' International Protection System). Athens: Kastaniotis.

Donnan, H. and T.M. Wilson 1999. *Borders: Frontiers of Identity, Nation and State*. Oxford: Berg.

Douglas, M. 1966. *Purity and Danger: An Analysis of the Concepts of Pollution and Taboo*. London: Ark.

ECRI. 2004. European Commission against Racism and Intolerance: Third Report on Greece. Strasbourg: Council of Europe.

Erdal Ilican, M. 2011. 'The Making of Sovereignty through Changing Property/Land Rights and the Contestation of Authority in Cyprus', D.Phil. Oxford: Department of Human Geography, University of Oxford.

Eriksen, T.H. 1993. *Ethnicity and Nationalism: Anthropological Perspectives*. London: Pluto Press.

Faroqhi, S., B. McGowan, et al. 1997. *An Economic and Social History of the Ottoman Empire 1600–1914*. Cambridge: Cambridge University Press.

Featherstone, K., D. Papadimitriou, et al. 2011. *The Last Ottomans: The Muslim Minority of Greece, 1940–1949*. Basingstoke: Palgrave Macmillan.

Fehlberg, B. and B. Smyth. 2002. 'Binding Pre-nuptial Agreements in Australia: The First Year', *International Journal of Law, Policy and the Family* 16(1): 127–140.

Fessopoulos, G. 1957. Φωνή από την Ακριτικήν Περιοχήν, Γυμνήν την Αλήθεια – Το Κράτος: Η Μαρτυρική Ζωή του Αγρότου – Σοβαροί Εθνικοί Κίνδυνοι [Cry from the Border Region, The Naked Truth – The State: The Tortuous Life of the Peasant – Serious National Threats]. Athens: Author's publication.

Finkel, C. 2005. *Osman's Dream: The Story of the Ottoman Empire 1300–1923*. London: John Murray.

Foteas, P. 1977. Οι Πομάκοι και το Βυζάντιο [The Pomaks and Byzantium]. Komotini: Morfotikos Syllogos Komotinis.

Foucault, M. 2000 [1974]. *The Order of Things: An Archeology of the Human Sciences*. London: Routledge.

_____. 2001 [1961]. *Madness and Civilization: A History of Insanity in the Age of Reason*. London: Routledge.

_____. 2003. *'Society Must Be Defended': Lectures at the Collège de France, 1975–1976*. London: Penguin.

_____. 2004 [1969]. *The Archaeology of Knowledge*. London: Routledge.

_____. 2006. *Psychiatric Power: Lectures at the Collège de France*. New York: Picador.

_____. 2007. *Security, Territory, Population: Lectures at the Collège de France 1977–1978*. Basingstoke: Palgrave Macmillan.

_____. 2008. *The Birth of Biopolitics: Lectures at the Collège de France 1978–1979*. Basingstoke: Palgrave Macmillan.

Fraser, N. 2009. 'Feminism, Capitalism, and the Cunning of History', *New Left Review* 56(1): 97–117.

_____. 2008. 'From Redistribution to Recognition? Dilemmas of Justice in a "Postsocialist" Age', in K. Olson (ed.), *Adding Insult to Injury: Nancy Fraer debates her Critics*. London: Verso, pp. 9–41.

Geromylatos, A. 2002. *The Balkan Wars: Conquest, Revolution, and Retribution from the Ottoman Era to the Twentieth Century and Beyond*. New York: Basic Books.

GHM and MRG-G. 2002. 'Religious Freedom in Greece'. Athens: Greek Helsinki Monitor and Minority Rights Group-Greece: 1–98.

_____. 2005. 'Contribution on the Point in the Agenda: Tolerance and Non-discrimination: Gender Equality. Warsaw: OSCE Human Dimension Implementation Meeting.

Gilbert, G. 1996. 'The Council of Europe and Minority Rights', *Human Rights Quarterly* 18(1): 160–189.

Glenny, M. 2000. *The Balkans: Nationalism, War, and the Great Powers, 1804–1999*. London: Granta Books.

Gourgouris, S. 1996. *Dream Nation: Enlightenment, Colonization and the Institution of Modern Greece*. Stanford: Stanford University Press.

Green, S. 2005. *Notes from the Balkans: Locating Marginality and Ambiguity on the Greek-Albanian Border*. Princeton: Princeton University Press.

_____. 2009. 'Lines, Traces and Tidemarks: Reflections on Forms of Borderli-ness', *EastBordNet Working Papers*, 1–19.

_____. 2010a. 'Performing Border in the Aegean: On Relocating Political, Economic and Social Relations', *Journal of Cultural Economy* 3(2): 261–278.

_____. 2010b. 'Of Gold and Euros: Locating Value on the Greek-Turkish Border. *EastBordNet/COST Action IS0803 Working Papers Series*. http://www.eastbord net.org/working_papers/open/: 1–23.

_____ and G. King. 2001. 'Seeing What You Know: Changing Constructions and Perceptions of Landscape in Epirus, northwestern Greece, 1945 and 1990', *History and Anthropology* 12(3): 255–288.

Gupta, A. and J. Ferguson. 1996. 'Culture, Power, Place: Ethnography at the End of an Era', in A. Gupta, J. Ferguson (eds), *Culture, Power, Place: Explorations in Critical Anthropology*. Boston: Duke University Press. pp. 1–32.

Güven, D. 2006. Εθνικισμός, κοινωνικές μεταβολές και μειονότητες: Τα επεισόδια εναντίον των μη Μουσουλμάνων της Τουρκίας 6/7 Σεπτεμβρίου 1955 [Nationalism, social changes and minorities: The 6–7 September 1955 incidents against Turkey's non-Muslims]. Athens: Estia.

Halkias, A. 2004. *The Empty Cradle of Democracy: Sex, Abortion, and Nationalism in Modern Greece*. Durham: Duke University Press.

Hall, R.C. 2000. *The Balkan Wars 1912–1913: Prelude to the First World War*. London: Routledge.

Harvey, D. 2003. *The New Imperialism*. Oxford: Oxford University Press.

Hayden, R.M. 1996. 'Imagined Communities and Real Victims: Self Determination and Ethnic Cleansing in Yugoslavia', *American Ethnologist* 23(4): 783–801.

Hellenic Parliament. 2010. Πόρισμα της Εξεταστικής Επιτροπής για την Ολοκλήρωση της Διερεύνησης του Συνόλου του Σκανδάλου της Μονής Βατοπεδίου [Report of the Investigation Commitee on the Conclusion of the Holistic Examination of the Vatopedion Monastery Scandal].

Helsinki Watch. 1990. Destroying Ethnic Identity: The Turks of Greece. New York: International Helsinki Federation for Human Rights: 1–58.

Herzfeld, M. 1997. *Cultural Intimacy: Social Poetics in the Nation-State*. London: Routledge.

_____. 2002. 'The Absent Presence: Discourses of Crypto-Colonialism', *South Atlantic Quarterly* 101(4): 899–926.

Hirschon, R. (ed.). 2003. *Crossing the Aegean: An Appraisal of the 1923 Compulsory Population Exchange Between Greece and Turkey.* Oxford: Berghahn Books.

Howard, R.E. 1995. 'Occidentalism, Human Rights, and the Obligations of Western Scholars', *Canadian Journal of African Studies* 29(1): 110–126.

Human Rights Watch (HRW). 1999. 'Greece: The Turks of Western Thrace'. *Human Rights Watch Report.* New York: Human Rights Watch.

_____. 2008a. 'Left to Survive: Systematic Failure to Protect Unaccompanied Migrant Children in Greece', *Human Rights Watch Report.* New York: Human Rights Watch.

_____. 2008b. 'No Refuge: Migrants in Greece'. *Human Rights Watch Report.* New York: Human Rights Watch.

_____. 2009. 'Greece – The EU's Dirty Hands: Frontex Involvement in Ill-Treatment of Migrant Detainees in Greece'. *Human Rights Watch Report.* New York: Human Rights Watch.

Hüseyinoğlu, O. 1972. 'Batı Trakya ve Pomak Türklerinin Durumu' [Western Thrace and the Situation of the Pomak Turks], *Batı Trakya* 6: 7–9.

Iliadis, C. 2004. 'Η Εθνική Ταυτότητα της Μουσουλμανικής Μειονότητας και η Εκπαιδευτική Πολιτική: Μελέτη Αρχειακών Πηγών, 1945–1967' [The Ethnic Identity of the Muslim Minority and Educational Policy: A Study of Archival Sources, 1945–1967], M.Sc. Athens: Kapodistrian University.

_____. 2006. Ένα "απωθημένο αρχείο": Το Συντονιστικό Συμβούλιο Μειονοτικής Πολιτικής Θράκης' [A 'Secret Archive': The Coordination Council of Minority Policy in Thrace], in A. Rigos, S. Seferiadis and E. Hatzivassiliou (eds), Η 'Σύντομη' Δεκαετία του '60: Θεσμικό Πλαίσιο, Κομματικές Στρατηγικές, Κοινωνικές Συγκρούσεις, Πολιτισμικές Διεργασίες [The 'Short' Decade of the 1960s: Institutional Frame, Party Strategies, Social Conflicts, Cultural Processes]. Athens: Kastaniotis, pp. 344–360.

Imam, M. and O. Tsakiride. 2003. Μουσουλμάνοι και Κοινωνικός Αποκλεισμός [Muslims and Social Exclusion]. Athens: A.A. Livani.

İnalcik, H. 1997. *An Economic and Social History of the Ottoman Empire 1300–1600.* Cambridge: Cambridge University Press.

Ios. 2005. 'Επιδότηση Ελληνοχριστιανικών Γεννήσεων στη Θράκη: Η Συνταγή της Χούντας' [Funding Greek-Christian Births in Thrace: The Junta Recipe], *Ios tis Eleftherotypias* (17 April 2005).

Ios. 2006. 'Τα "Δάνεια Εθνικής Σκοπιμότητος" στη Θράκη: Εθνικοφροσύνη με το Στρέμμα' [The 'National Expediency Loans' in Thrace: National Loyalty by the Acre], *Ios Press* (19 February 2006).

Jansen, S. 2010. 'Sovereignty and Practical Geography on a very Material Immaterial Border'. *COST Action IS0803 Network on Remaking Eastern Borders Working Papers.*

Kantzilaris, G. (ed.). 2001. *Treaty of Peace with Turkey and Other Instruments: Signed at Lausanne , July 24th, 1923 – Treaty Series No 16 (1923), London: HM Stationery Office.* Nicosia: Kantzilaris Ltd.

Karakasidou, A.N. 1997. *Fields of Wheat, Hills of Blood: Passages to Nationhood in Greek Macedonia, 1870–1990.* Chicago: University of Chicago Press.

Kenna, M.E. 2001. *Greek Island Life: Fieldwork on Anafi.* London: Routledge.

Kiel, M. 1983. 'The Oldest Monuments of Ottoman-Turkish Architecture in the Balkans, the Imaret and Mosque of ghazi Evrenos in Gümülcine/Komotini, and the Khan of Evrenos Bey in Ilica/Loutra in Greek Thrace, 1370–1390', *Sanat Tarihi Yıllığı – Kunsthistorische Forschungen XII*: 117–144.

Kipouros, C. 1984. Δεν Θέλουμε η Θράκη να γίνει νέα Κύπρος: Μορφωτική Κρίση και Πτώχευση της Ελληνικής Κουλτούρας [We Don't Want Thrace to become a new Cyprus: Educational Crisis and the Impoverishment of Greek Culture]. Athens: Pentadaktylos.

Kleinman, A. 1995. *Writing at the Margin: Discourse between Anthropology and Medicine*. Berkeley: University of California Press.

_____. 1999. 'Moral Experience and Ethical Reflection: Can Ethnography Reconcile Them? A Quandary for "The New Bioethics"', *Daedalus* 128(4): 69–97.

Klik magazine. 1999. 'Interview with Minister of Foreign Affairs George Papandreou', *Klik* (24 July 1999).

Kotzabassi, A. 2001. 'Οικογενειακές έννομες σχέσεις Ελλήνων Μουσουλμάνων' [Family Relations in Law amongst Greek Muslims]. Thessaloniki: Kentro Erevnon gia Themata Isotitas (Kethi) [The Research Centre for Gender Equality].

Ktistakis, Y. 2006. Ιερός Νόμος του Ισλάμ και Μουσουλμάνοι Έλληνες πολίτες: Μεταξύ κοινοτισμού και φιλελευθερισμού [Islamic Holy Law and Muslim Greek Citizens: Between Communalism and Liberalism]. Athens: Sakkoula.

Kymlicka, W. 1996. 'Justice and Minority Rights', *Multicultural Citizenship* 1(9): 107–131.

Kyriakides, S. 1966. 'Η Ιστορία της Κομοτηνής' [The History of Komotini], Θρακικά Χρονικά [Thracian Chronicles] 22: 64–71.

_____. 1993 [1960]. Περί της Ιστορίας της Θράκης: Ο Ελληνισμός των Σύγχρονων Θρακών – Αι Πόλεις Ξάνθη και Κομοτηνή [Concerning the History of Thrace: The Hellenism of Modern Thracians – The Towns of Xanthi and Komotini]. Thessaloniki: IMXA.

Kyriakidou-Nestoros, A. 1986. Η Θεωρεία της Ελληνικής Λαογραφίας [The Theory of Greek Folklore]. Athens: Εταιρεία Σπουδών Νεοελληνικού Πολιτισμού και Γενικής Παιδείας [Modern Greek Culture and General Education Research Corporation].

Labrianidis, L. 1997. 'Τοπική Ανάπτυξη και Περιοριστικές Ρυθμίσεις: Η Περίπτωση της Επιτηρούμενης Ζώνης στα Χωριά των Πομάκων της Ξάνθης' [Local Development and Restrictive Regulations: The Case of the Surveillance Zone in the Villages of the Xanthi Pomaks], *Topos* 13: 17–46.

_____. 1999. 'The Impact of the Greek Military Surveillance Zone on the Greek Side of the Bulgarian-Greek Borderlands', *Boundary and Security Bulletin* 7(2): 82–93.

Lambropoulos, V. 1988. *Literature as National Institution: Studies in the Politics of Modern Greek Criticism*. Princeton: Princeton University Press.

Legg, S. 2005. 'Foucault's Population Geographies: Classifications, Biopolitics and Governmental Spaces', *Population, Space and Place* 11(1): 137–156.

Lemke, T. 2001. '"The Birth of Bio-Politics" – Michel Foucault's Lecture at the Collège de France on Neo-Liberal Governmentality', *Economy and Society* 30(2): 190–207.

_____. 2011. *Biopolitics: An Advanced Introduction*. New York: New York University Press.

Levinas, E. 2002 [1981]. *Otherwise than Being or Beyond Essence*. Pittsburgh: Duquesne University Press.

Llewellyn-Smith, M. 1998. *Ionian Vision: Greece in Asia Minor 1919–1922*. London: Hurst and Company.

Loupis, D. 2001. The Postin Puş Baba Zaviye in Gümülcine (Komotini). An Epigraphical Study. Conference presentation. *Archaeology, Anthropology and Heritage in the Balkans and Anatolia: The Life and Times of F. W. Hasluck, 1878–1920*. Gregynog, University of Wales.

Mackay, A. 2012. 'Who gets a Better Deal? Women and Prenuptial Agreements in Australia and the USA', *University of Western Sydney Law Review* 7(1): 109–133.

Macmillan, M. 2001. *Peacemakers: Six Months that Changed the World*. London: John Murray.

Malkki, L.H. 1995. *Purity and Exile: Violence, Memory, and National Cosmology among Hutu Refugees in Tanzania*. Chicago: University of Chicago Press.

Manji, I. 2003. *The Trouble with Islam: A Wake-up Call for Honesty and Change*. Toronto: Random House Canada.

Mashhour, A. 2005. 'Islamic Law and Gender Equality: Could there be a Common Ground? A Study of Divorce and Polygamy in Sharia Law and Contemporary Legislation in Tunisia and Egypt', *Human Rights Quarterly* 27(2): 562–596.

Massey, D. 2005. *For Space*. London: Sage.

May, S., T. Modood, et al. 2004. *Ethnicity, Nationalism, and Minority Rights*. Cambridge: Cambridge University Press.

Mazower, M. 2002. *The Balkans: A Short History*. London: Weidenfeld and Nicolson.

Meindersma, C. 1997. 'Population Exchanges: International Law and State Practice', *International Journal of Refugee Law* 9(3): 335–364.

Memisoğlu, H. 1991. *Balkanlar'da Pomak Türkleri*. Ankara: Türk Dünyası Araştırmaları Vakfı.

Michailidis, I.D. 1998. 'The War of Statistics: Traditional Recipes for the Preparation of the Macedonian Salad', *East European Quarterly* 32(1): 9–21.

Mignolo, W. 2002. 'The Many Faces of Cosmo-polis: Border Thinking and Critical Cosmopolitanism', in C. Breckenridge, S. Pollock, H.Bhabha and D.Chakrabarty (eds), *Cosmopolitanism*. Durham: Duke University Press, pp. 157–188.

_____. 2009. 'Epistemic Disobedience, Independent Thought and De-Colonial Freedom', *Theory, Culture and Society* 26(7–8): 1–23.

Miller, M.L. 1975. *Bulgaria During the Second World War*. Stanford: Stanford University Press.

Mitchell, S. 2007. *A History of the Later Roman Empire, AD 284 – AD 641: The Transformation of the Ancient World*. Oxford: Blackwell.

Mitchell, T. 1991. *Colonising Egypt*. Berkeley: University of California Press.

_____. 2002. *Rule of Experts: Egypt, Techno-politics, Modernity*. Berkeley: University of California Press.

Mouffe, C. 2000. *The Democratic Paradox*. London: Verso.

_____. 2005 [1993]. *The Return of the Political*. London: Verso.

Mounin, G. 1980. 'The Semiology of Orientation in Urban Space', *Current Anthropology* 21(4): 491–501.

Mylonas, P. 1990. Οι Πομάκοι της Θράκης [The Pomaks of Thrace]. Athens: Nea Sinora.

Myrivili, L. 2004. 'The Liquid Border: Subjectivity at the Limits of the Nation-state in Southeast Europe (2004)', Ph.D. New York: Anthropology Department, Columbia University.

Nancy, J.-L. 1991. *The Inoperative Community*. Minneapolis: University of Minnesota Press.

_____. 2000. *Being Singular Plural*. Stanford: Stanford University Press.

Narayan, K. 1993. 'How Native is a "Native" Anthropologist?', *American Anthropologist* 95(3): 671–686.

Navaro-Yashin, Y. 2002. *Faces of the State: Secularism and Public Life in Turkey.* Princeton: Princeton University Press.

_____. 2007. 'Make-Believe Papers, Legal Forms, and the Counterfeit: Affective Interactions Between Documents and People in Britain and Cyprus', *Anthropological Theory* 7(1): 79–96.

_____. 2010. 'The Materiality of Sovereignty: Geographical Expertise and Changing Place Names in Northern Cyprus', in N.P. Diamantouros, T. Dragonas and Ç. Keyder (eds), *Spatial Conceptions of the Nation: Modernizing Geographies in Greece and Turkey.* London: I.B. Tauris. pp. 127–143.

_____. 2012. *The Make-Believe Space: Affective Geography in a Postwar Polity.* Durham: Duke University Press.

Odysseos, L. 2011. 'Governing Dissent in the Central Kalahari Game Reserve: "Development", Governmentality, and Subjectification amongst Botswana's Bushmen', *Globalizations* 8(4): 439–455.

OED. 1993. 'The New Shorter Oxford English Dictionary', in L. Brown (ed.), *Oxford English Dictionary.* Oxford: Oxford University Press.

Oğuz, Z. 2006. 'Multi-functional Buildings of the T-type in Ottoman Context: A Network of Identity and Territorialization', MA. Ankara: Middle East Technical University.

Öktem, K. 2004. 'Incorporating the Time and Space of the Ethnic "Other": Nationalism and Space in Southeast Turkey in the Nineteenth and Twentieth Centuries', *Nations and Nationalism* 10(4): 559–578.

_____. 2011. *Angry Nation: Turkey since 1989.* London: Zed Books.

Oran, B. 1984. 'The Inhanli Land Dispute and the Status of the Turks in Western Thrace', *Journal of Muslim Minority Affairs* 5(2): 360–370.

_____. 1991. *Türk-Yunan İlişkilerinde Batı Trakya Sorunu.* Ankara: Bilgi Yayınevi.

_____. 2003. 'The Story of Those Who Stayed: Lessons from Articles 1 and 2 of the 1923 Convention', in R. Hirschon (ed.), *Crossing the Aegean: An Appraisal of the 1923 Compulsory Population Exchange Between Greece and Turkey.* Oxford: Berghahn. pp. 97–116.

OSCE. 2006. 'Statement on "the continuous Greek violation of the right of freedom of association of the Turkish minority of Western Thrace" – Organization for Security and Cooperation in Europe'. Warsaw.

Özoğlu, H. 2011. *From Caliphate to Secular State: Power Struggle in the Early Turkish Republic.* Santa Barbara: Praeger.

Panourgiá, N. 1995. *Fragments of Death, Fables of Identity: An Athenian Anthropography.* Madison: University of Wisconsin Press.

_____. 2009. *Dangerous Citizens: The Greek Left and the Terror of the State.* New York: Fordham University Press.

Pantziara, N. 2003. 'From Ancient to Modern: Greek Women's Struggle for Equality', *Social Education* 67(1): 28–32.

Pavlowitch, S. 1999. *A History of the Balkans 1804 – 1945.* London: Longman.

Popke, J.E. 2003. 'Poststructuralist Ethics: Subjectivity, Responsibility and the Space of Community', *Progress in Human Geography* 27(3): 298–316.

Poulton, H. 2000. 'The Muslim Experience in the Balkan States, 1919–1991', *Nationalities Papers: The Journal of Nationalism and Ethnicity* 28(1): 45–66.

Pratt, G. and V. Rosner 2006. 'Introduction: The Global & the Intimate', *Women's Studies Quarterly* 34: 13–24.

Pro Asyl. 2007. 'The Truth may be Bitter, but it must be told: The Situation of Refugees in the Aegean and the Practices of the Greek Coast Guard. Frankfurt/Main: Pro Asyl Foundation.

Psomiades, H.J. 1968. *The Eastern Question: The Last Phase*. Thessaloniki: Institute for Balkan Studies.

Quingley, J.B. 2010. *The Statehood of Palestine: International Law in the Middle East Conflict*. Cambridge: Cambridge University Press.

Rabinow, P. 2007. *Reflections on Fieldwork in Morocco*. Berkeley: University of California Press.

Ramaga, P.V. 1992. 'Relativity of the Minority Concept', *Human Rights Quarterly* 14(1): 104–119.

Rose-Redwood, R., D. Alderman, et al. 2010. 'Geographies of Toponymic Inscription: New Directions in Critical Place-name Studies', *Progress in Human Geography* 34(4): 453–470.

Saldívar, J.D. 2006. 'Border Thinking, Minoritized Studies, and Realist Interpellations: The Coloniality of Power from Gloria Azaldúa to Arundhati Roy', in L.M. Alcoff, M. Hames-García, S.P. Mohanty and P.M.L. Moya (eds), *Identity Politics Reconsidered*. Basingstoke: Palgrave Macmillan. pp. 152–170.

Scheper-Hughes, N. 2000. 'The Global Traffic in Human Organs', *Current Anthropology* 41(2): 191–224.

_____. 2004. 'Parts Unknown: Undercover Ethnography of the Organs-trafficking Underworld', *Ethnography* 5(1): 29–73.

_____. 2007. 'Violence and the Politics of Remorse: Lessons from South Africa', in J. Biehl, B. Good and A. Kleinman (eds), *Subjectivity: Ethnographic Investigations*. Berkeley: University of California Press. pp. 179–233.

Schmitt, C. 1996 [1932]. *The Concept of the Political*. Chicago: The University of Chicago Press.

Scott, J.C. 1987. *Weapons of the Weak: Everyday Forms of Peasant Resistance*. New Haven: Yale University Press.

Secomb, L. 2006. 'Amorous Politics: Between Derrida and Nancy', *Social Semiotics* 16(3): 449–460.

Shaheed, F. 1986. 'The Cultural Articulation of Patriarchy: Legal Systems, Islam and Women', *Comparative Studies of South Asia, Africa and the Middle East* 6(1): 38–44.

Sitaropoulos, N. 2006. 'Discriminatory Denationalisations Based on Ethnic Origin: The Dark Legacy of Ex Art 19 of the Greek Nationality Code', in P. Shah and W.F. Menski (eds), *Migration, Diasporas and Legal Systems in Europe*. London: Routledge, pp. 107–125.

Somel, S.A. 2003. *Historical Dictionary of the Ottoman Empire*. London: Rowman and Littlefield.

Spencer, K. 2011. '*Mahr* as Contract: Internal Pluralism and External Perspectives', *Onati Socio-Legal Series* 1(2): 1–20.

Stavros, S. 1995. 'The Legal Status of Minorities in Greece Today: The Adequacy of their Protection in the Light of Current Human Rights Perceptions', *Journal of Modern Greek Studies* 13(1): 1–32.

Stoler, A.L. 1995. *Race and the Education of Desire: Foucault's History of Sexuality and the Colonial Order of Things*. Durham: Duke University Press.

_____. 2008. 'Imperial Debris: Reflections on Ruins and Ruination', *Cultural Anthropology* 23(2): 191–219.

_____. 2009. *Along the Archival Grain: Epistemic Anxieties and Colonial Common Sense*. Princeton: Princeton University Press.

_____. 2010 [2002]. *Carnal Knowledge and Imperial Power: Race and the Intimate in Colonial Rule*. Berkeley: University of California Press.

Symeonidou, H. 2009. 'Low Divorce Incidence in Greece: Facts and Figures', in H.-J. Andress and D. Hummelsheim (eds), *When Marriage ends: Economic and Social Consequences of Partnership Dissolution*. Cheltenham: Edward Elgar Publishing, pp. 211–229.

Tarlo, E. 2003. *Unsettling Memories: Narratives of the Emergency in Delhi*. Berkeley: University of California Press.

Todorova, M.N. 1997. *Imagining the Balkans*. Oxford: Oxford University Press.

_____. 1998. 'Identity (Trans)formation among Bulgarian Muslims', in B. Crawford and R.D. Lipschutz (eds), *The Myth of 'Ethnic Conflict'*. Berkeley: University of California. International and Area Studies Research Series/Number 98: 301–329.

Toynbee, A. and F.L. Israel (eds.). 1967. *Major Peace Treaties of Modern History 1648–1967*. London: McGraw-Hill Book Co.

Troubeta, S. 2001. Κατασκευάζοντας Ταυτότητες για τους Μουσουλμάνους της Θράκης: Το Παράδειγμα των Πομάκων και των Τσιγγάνων [Constructing identities for the Muslims of Thrace: The Examples of the Pomaks and the Gypsies]. Athens: Kritiki and KEMO.

Tsaoussis, A. 2003. *The Greek Divorce Law Reform of 1983 and its Impact on Homemakers: A Social and Economic Analysis*. Athens-Komotini: Ant. N. Sakkoulas Publishers.

Tsibiridou, F. 1994. 'Χώρος: Δομές και Αναπαραστάσεις – Ανθρωπολογική Πρόταση Ανάγνωσης του Χώρου στα Πομακοχώρια του Νομού Ροδόπης' [Space: Structures and Representations – An Anthropological Suggestion for Reading Space in the Pomak Villages of the Rhodoppe Prefecture], *Ethnologia* 3: 5–31.

_____. 2006. 'How can one be a "Pomak" in Greece Today: Reflections on Hegemonic Policies in Marginal Populations', in E. Papataxiarchis (ed.), *Adventures of Alterity: The Production of Cultural Difference in Today's Greece*. Athens: Alexandria, pp. 209–238.

_____. 2007. 'Writing about Turks and Powerful Others: Journalistic Heteroglossia in Western Thrace', in D. Theodossopoulos (ed.), *When Greeks Think About Turks: The View from Anthropology*. London: Routledge, pp. 129–144.

Tsitselikis, K. 2004a. 'The Legal Status of Islam in Greece', *Die Welt des Islams* 44(3): 402–431.

_____. 2004b. 'Personal Status of Greece's Muslims: A Legal Anachronism or an Example of Applied Multiculturalism?', in B.-P. Aluffi and G. Zincone (eds), *The Legal Treatment of Islamic Minorities in Europe*. Oakville, Connecticut: David Brown Book Co. pp. 109–132.

_____. 2006. 'The Shariatic Courts of Greek Thrace and the "Principle of Reciprocity" regarding Minorities in Turkey and Greece', in F. Aksu (ed) *Proceedings of the International Conference on Turkish-Greek Relations: Issues, Solutions, Prospects. March 9th 2006*. Istanbul: Foundation for Middle East and Balkan Studies. pp. 75–81.

Tucker, J. 1998. *In the House of Law: Gender and Islamic Law in Ottoman Syria and Palestine*. Berkeley: University of California Press.

Tziovas, D. 1986. *The Nationalism of the Demoticists and Its Impact on Their Literary Theory (1888–1930): An Analysis Based on Their Literary Criticism and Essays*. Amsterdam: Hakkert.

UN-CERD. 2008. 'Reports Submitted by States Parties under Article 9 of the International Convention on the Elimination of all Forms of Racial Discrimination: Nineteenth periodic reports of States parties due in 2007 – Greece'. New York: United Nations.

UN-HRC. 2004. 'Human Rights Committee – 82nd Session, International Covenant on Civil and Political Rights – List of Issues to be Taken Up in Connection with the Consideration of the Initial Report of Greece (CCPR/C/GRC/2004/1). New York: United Nations.

_____. 2005a. 'Summary record of the 2268th meeting: Consideration of Reports – Greece'. New York: United Nations – Human Rights Committee.

_____. 2005b. 'Summary record of the 2267th meeting: Consideration of Reports – Greece'. New York: United Nations – Human Rights Committee.

_____. 2005c. 'Summary record of the 2269th meeting: Consideration of Reports – Greece'. New York: United Nations – Human Rights Committee.

Valentine, G. 2007. 'Theorizing and Researching Intersectionality: A Challenge for Feminist Geography', *The Professional Geographer* 59(1): 10–21.

Vereni, P. 2000. 'O Ellin Makedonas: Autobiography, Memory and National Identity in Western Greek Macedonia', in J. Cowan (ed.), *Macedonia: the Politics of Identity and Difference*. London: Pluto Press, pp. 47–67.

Voutira, E. 2003. 'When Greeks Meet Other Greeks: Settlement Policy Issues in the Contemporary Greek Context', in R. Hirschon (ed.), *Crossing the Aegean: An Appraisal of the 1923 Compulsory Population Exchange Between Greece and Turkey*. Oxford: Berghahn Books, pp. 145–162.

Wace, A.J.B. and M.S. Thompson. 1914. *The Nomads of the Balkans: an Account of Life and Customs among the Vlachs of Northern Pindus*. London: Methuen & co., ltd.

Wegner, J.R. 1982. 'The Status of Women in Jewish and Islamic Marriage and Divorce Law', *Harvard Women's Law Journal* 5: 1–34.

Wright, M.W. 2009. 'Justice and the Geographies of Moral Protest: Reflections from Mexico', *Environment and Planning D: Society and Space* 27(2): 216–233.

Xirotiris, N.I. 1971. Ίδιαι παρατηρήσεις επί της κατανομής των συχνοτήτων των ομάδων αίματος εις τους Πομάκους' [Findings on the Classification of the Frequency of Blood Groups Among Pomaks], PhD. Thessaloniki: Aristotle University of Salonica.

Yaz, N. 1986. *Ağlayan Batı Trakya* [Weeping Western Thrace]. Istanbul: Yeni Batı Trakya Dergisi Yayınları.

Yiakoumaki, V. 2006a. 'Ethnic Turks and "Muslims", and the Performance of Multiculturalism: The Case of the Drómeno of Thrace', *South European Society and Politics* 11(1): 145–161.

_____. 2006b. '"Local", "Ethnic", and "Rural" Food: On the Emergence of "Cultural Diversity" in Greece since its Integration in the European Union', *Journal of Modern Greek Studies* 24(2): 415–445.

Young, I.M. 1990. *Justice and the Politics of Difference*. Princeton: Princeton University Press.

Zakaria, R. 2011. 'Sharia, Justice, and the Politics of Intimacy', *Asia Network Exchange: A Journal for Asian Studies in the Liberal Arts* 19(1): 7–16.

Zenginis, E. 2001. Ο Μπεκτασιμός στη Δυτική Θράκη: Συμβολή στην Ιστορία της Διαδόσεως του Μουσουλμανισμού στον Ελλαδικό Χώρο *[Bektashism in Western Thrace: A Contribution to the History of the Spread of Islam in Greece]*. Thessaloniki: Pournaras Books.

Žižek, S. 2000. *The Ticklish Subject: The Absent Centre of Political Ontology*. London: Verso.

INDEX

Lightning Source UK Ltd.
Milton Keynes UK
UKOW05n1532100517
300907UK00005B/30/P